TRANSLATING POETRY

Translating Poetry

The Double Labyrinth

Edited by
DANIEL WEISSBORT

University of Iowa Press, Iowa City

Copyright © 1989 by Daniel Weissbort

All rights reserved

Printed in the People's Republic of China

First edition, 1989

University of Iowa Press, Iowa City 52242

International Standard Book Number 0-87745-225-3
Library of Congress Catalog Card Number 88-50870

No part of this book may be reproduced or utilised in any form or by any means, electronic or mechanical, including photocopying and recording, without permission in writing from the publisher.

dedicated to the memory of

JAMES S HOLMES
(1924–1986)

Contents

Preface ix

Acknowledgements xv

Notes on the Contributors xix

James S Holmes (1924–86) xxvi

Translating La Ceppède 1
Keith Bosley

János Pilinszky's 'Desert of Love': A Note 9
János Csokits

Postscript to János Csokits' Note 16
Ted Hughes

Kafka and the Golem: Translating Paul Celan 35
John Felstiner

Brief Afterthoughts on Versions of a Poem by Hölderlin 51
Michael Hamburger

Translating Martial and Vergil: Jacob Lowland among the Classics 57
James S Holmes

Translating Nerval: A Reply to a Letter by Richard Holmes 73
Peter Jay

Translating Penna and Cernuda: Working Papers 83
James Kirkup

Contents

Revising Brodsky   95
George L. Kline

Translating Anna Akhmatova   107
Stanley Kunitz

Voice; Landscape; Violence: Sonnevi into English in Helsinki   125
Rika Lesser

Translating Juarroz and Noren: Working Papers   138
W.S. Merwin

Playing Scrabble without a Board: On Formal Translation from the Swedish   144
Judith Moffett

'The Voice Inside': Translating the Poetry of T. Carmi   161
Grace Schulman

Working at Someone Else's Poem   178
Jon Silkin

Translating Horace: Working Papers   185
C.H. Sisson

Finding the Proper Equivalent: Translating the Poetry of Andrei Voznesensky   201
William Jay Smith

Translating Brodsky: A Postscript   221
Daniel Weissbort

Le Pont Mirabeau   228
Richard Wilbur and Paul Auster

Preface

The contributions to this volume all have to do with the 'poetic' translation of poetry. My brief comments in this Preface, therefore, also revolve around that most problematical and challenging mode of translation. The collection originated in a series of articles, under the general title of 'Approaches to Translation', which was published in the magazine *Modern Poetry in Translation*. The intention was to provide a platform for translators to convey more specific information about their craft than they are generally encouraged to do, to communicate more directly with their readers (in the pious hope that this collection of papers would be the first in a series) and thus to help to raise the general and even professional level of literary consciousness, which as reviews of translations for the most part demonstrate is exceedingly limited.

What is presented here, then, is a number of engagements with the translation of poetry, focusing, as it were, on the pragmatics. There is of course a huge and diverse literature on and about translation, but there are relatively few narrations which attempt to render an account of the actual process, what happens while the translator is about his or her business. And yet it is precisely such first-hand evidence (as George Steiner remarks in *After Babel*) that is needed. Theory proliferates, whereas the data remain more or less undisclosed.

One effect of this is that translation theorists increasingly address each other rather than a wider public, which might benefit from some of these discussions, insofar as they bear on the *quiddity* of the translation product. And within the 'discipline' itself the distance between critics and practitioners seems, if anything, to be growing. The exclusiveness of some of the jargon invented by translation critics (ironically, since translation has to do with transcending barriers) springs partly, no doubt, from a justifiable exasperation with the vagueness of most writing by translators on translation. The belletristic nature of much of this writing – usually in the form of introductions to books or that of papers presented at translation conferences – does not finally advance our understanding of the process very much, tending to be repetitious and clichéd, however stylishly cobbled together, though some wonderfully insightful and illuminating pieces have of course been published from time to time. But while it is thus possible to sympathise with contemporary theorists (and even with the perpetrators of what André Lefevere has called 'semantic terrorism'), one can also find excuses for the translators, whose publishers have led them to believe that readers want to be lulled rather than informed, and that nobody is interested in what happens privately – both assumed to be consenting – between translator and translated.

After all, it was once not unusual to omit the translator's name from published works, the assumption perhaps being that his contribution, as a slightly more glorified copier or transcriber, was not really worth mentioning, since the original text virtually dictated its own rendering in another language. Yet even if, from a certain point of view and in certain cases, this may appear to be so, the most rudimentary understanding of the ways in which languages function would seem to require a more serious estimation of the intermediary's role. The point is that in recent times translators, feeling themselves undervalued, have tended to take refuge either in silence or in a great deal of sound and fury signifying very little. Thus the confidence, or at least the assertiveness and querulousness, of the sixteenth- or seventeenth-century translators in their prefaces has been replaced by diffidence, defensiveness or (at best) irony.

But zestful as many of the Tudor and Jacobean prefaces indeed are, they too provide us with comparatively little specific information about the actual work of translation, the purpose of the preface being simply to deter or placate potential opponents or rivals, to trounce former denigrators, to propitiate patrons and so forth. Yet, as Ezra Pound remarked, translation is also a form of criticism, the highest in his view, since it represents a fusion of the creative and the critical. Who has lived more closely with a text than its translator, arguably closer even than the original author, since the latter – after bringing as much verbal order to non-verbal or pre-verbal chaos as he can – must abandon his project, whereas the former is, for the duration, wedded to it? Having penetrated, he hopes, to the heart of a work, he has, then, to find his way out again – the double-labyrinthine process referred to in the subtitle of this volume. At the same time every translator knows that compromise is implicit – a tissue of compromises, in fact, even if this can itself be the source of much fresh creativity. And how can it be otherwise, if the translation is to remain in contact with an irreducible original, if in other words it is to remain a translation? Since the translator is writing something which must also 'stand on its own' as an artifact, to a large extent unsupported by glosses or commentary, either in the form of footnotes or embodied in the text, it is inevitable that many of the hard-earned insights and perceptions will, for all practical purposes, go unrepresented in the 'final' version.

Judging from the response of many translators to requests for materials for the present collection, there is, however, a strong feeling that whatever remains unsaid in a translation is best left unsaid. In any case, translators themselves are generally more interested in getting on with the next task than in rehearsing an old one. Nevertheless, in view of the still widespread failure to appreciate the complexities of translation, it seemed worth persevering with the effort to persuade practitioners to allow us into their workshop. Translation, as a specialised branch of practical criticism, of concentrated reading, is well worth exploring. And while detailed commentaries or monographs by translators, such as John Felstiner's recent book *Translating Neruda: The Way to Macchu Picchu* (Stanford University Press, 1980), may well be on the way to becoming an accepted critical genre, there is a continuing need for further sharing by a variety of translators of the kinds of insights that are not necessarily accommodated in the final text.

We therefore asked translators if they would eavesdrop, as it were, on themselves, jot down thoughts and preserve drafts as they translated, or failing that try to reconstruct after the event, though as undefensively as possible, what had happened. The first is clearly preferable, as there is less likelihood of self-censorship. On the other hand few can be so detached that they are able to function creatively and to observe and comment on themselves at the same time. Still – perhaps as an exercise in self-awareness – our project did commend itself to a number of translators, though it must be admitted that it deterred rather more of them, some evidently finding unpalatable what they took to be a mechanistic approach. For what it is worth, British translators reacted more negatively than Americans, which may or may not say something about our respective national characteristics!

This seems a convenient point to interject that there are those who regard the whole enterprise treated in this volume as dubious. Most of the contributors here would probably agree with the present writer that, from an absolutist standpoint, the poetic translation of poetry is an impossible task. Nonetheless they clearly think it worth attempting, even if crises of faith are quite frequent. Robert Frost's assertion, quoted gleefully by some and defensively by others, that in the translation of poetry it is the poetry that gets left out cannot satisfactorily be answered, since it is both true and false. Nor is it my purpose here to meditate upon it.

I feel, though, that I should at least mention another approach to the translation of poetry, an approach well exemplified in the work of Stanley Burnshaw in his two anthologies, *The Poem Itself* (New York: Holt, Rinehart & Winston, 1960) and *The Hebrew Poem Itself* (New York: Schocken Books, 1966). In the preface to the former it is claimed that, since poetry cannot be poetically translated, the most satisfactory procedure is to provide the non-linguist reader with a lexical and contextual commentary and an *ad verbum*, non-literary translation alongside the original, thereby enabling him to experience the source text for himself. In any case, whatever distance he is able to travel, it will at least be in the right direction. There will have been substantive gain. Nabokov too, in the introduction to his translation of *Evgeny Onegin* (and elsewhere), subscribes to a similar view, eloquently insisting on an exhaustive commentary and a rigorous word-for-word translation, though how far his own practice substantiates this theory is problematical. Not surprisingly, this view of things translational is reflected, or implied, in some of the remarks made by contributors to the present volume too. Of particular interest in this respect are Ted Hughes' observations about his work with János Csokits, whose 'literal renderings, very often, are all one could desire in a final version'. Again, he attests to the substantive gain, the contact with something real, distinct, that a literal translation seems sometimes able to establish, when made by the right person, of course: 'I am certain I would never have become as interested in Pilinszky as I eventually did, if my curiosity had not been caught in the first place by Csokits' swift word-for-word translations from the page.'

Given the relative novelty of the present venture it was probably inevitable that most of our contributions would, in fact, be reconstructions some time after the event. In any case it is clear that the complexity of the process permits only a fraction of the conscious material to be got down, not to speak of the unconscious material that might be recovered through analysis. In fairness to the translators it must be emphasised that the whole business is far more arduous and intensive than most of these papers suggest. This will of course come as no surprise to anyone who has taught or attended a translation workshop, where typically an entire session will be devoted to, say, two or three short poems.

While, therefore, it was usually hard to persuade translators to comment on work in hand, since quite understandably they preferred to carry on with it undisturbed, there was not always so much resistance to the alternative suggestion that they present, with at most a few brief introductory remarks, several drafts of a translation, together with the original and the version finally printed (or until now unprinted, as in the case of those by James Kirkup and one by C.H. Sisson).

The emphasis, then, is on translation practice. The texts in this collection do not constitute a handbook on translating, since there are as many approaches as there are translators, and as W.S. Merwin points out, 'there is no perfect way to do it, and much of it must be found for each particular poem, as we go'. Nor are they intended to serve as exemplary texts for beginners. But of course certain tendencies – not to say principles or norms – do emerge. Rather than comment redundantly on these texts in the preface it seemed better to let individual users of this book form their own conclusions. Nevertheless it would be churlish of me not to pay tribute to the particular dedication of translators to their originals. If we learn anything from observing them at work, it is about reading. In comparison with them, so many only *seem* to read. At the same time, the translator-reader, who necessarily makes a critical estimate of the text, is not in the nature of things as detached as the literary critic, so that the latter, however perceptive, need not be an effective translator. Similarly the practising poet, as has been frequently observed, will not always be the best translator of verse, though there are a number of fine poets who are also major translators (viz. the poet-translators represented in the present volume). The balance of meticulous observation, linguistic skill and critical acumen, of rapt attention and boldness in expression, is unique to translation. Translators do many things and here we see them at some of these.

The short answer to the question 'Why do you do it?' – a question which we did not ask our contributors, but on which a number of them comment wryly – is 'Because it is there to be done!' To be truly enjoyed, the world of literature has to be shared. The translator, however guarded, is in essence a sharer, an enthusiast . . . But let us leave it at that before we are drawn still further down historical, sociological and psychological byways.

It remains only for me to thank the contributors to this volume, who indulged me, responding to my importunate requests for material; my two research assistants at the University of Iowa, Margitt Lehbert and Elizabeth Floyd, talented young translators of poetry themselves; Scott Rollins of Bridges Books, Amsterdam, whose enthusiasm for this project never flagged; all my students, over more than a decade of enjoyable and stimulating interaction, in the University of Iowa Translation Workshop; and last, but also principally, Jim Holmes, of whom more below.

Daniel Weissbort
London and Iowa City

Acknowledgements

The editor, contributors and publishers gratefully acknowledge the permission of the copyright holders to reproduce the following works in whole or in part.

Translating La Ceppède

'To conquering monarchs the red coat of arms' from *The Theorems of Master Jean de la Ceppède: LXX Sonnets*, translated by Keith Bosley (MidNAG and Carcanet New Press, 1983).

János Pilinszky's 'Desert of Love': A Note and Postscript

'The Desert of Love' from János Pilinszky, *Selected Poems*, translated by Ted Hughes and János Csokits (Carcanet New Press, 1976).
'Egy KZ-Láger Falára' from *Harmadnapon* (Szépirodalmi Könyvkiadó, Budapest, 1959), reprinted by permission of Artisjus, Budapest.
'On the Wall of a KZ-Lager' from János Pilinszky, *Selected Poems* (Carcanet New Press, 1976).
'Van Gogh Imája' from *Szálkák* (Szépirodalmi Könyvkiadó, Budapest, 1972), reprinted by permission of Artisjus, Budapest.

Kafka and the Golem

This essay is reprinted from *Prooftexts*, May 1986, Volume 6, Number 12 (Johns Hopkins University Press, Baltimore). All quotations are acknowledged in the notes to the essay.
A poem by Paul Celan, 'Einem, der vor der Tür stand', from *Die Niemandsrose*, © S. Fischer Verlag, Frankfurt am Main, 1963, is reprinted by permission.

Brief Afterthoughts on Versions of a Poem by Hölderlin

This essay is reprinted from *Modern Poetry in Translation* Nos 41–2, edited by Daniel Weissbort (London, March 1981).
'The Middle of Life', translated by Michael Hamburger, from

Friedrich Hölderlin, *Poems and Fragments* (Cambridge University Press, 1980).
'Hälfte des Lebens' from Hölderlin, *Sämtliche Werke* (Stuttgart, 1951).

Translating Nerval

This is reprinted from *Gérard de Nerval, The Chimeras*, translated by Peter Jay, with an essay by Richard Holmes (Anvil Press Poetry, London, 1984).

Translating Penna and Cernuda

'Sera nel giardino', 'Il mio amore e furtivo', 'Quando tornai al mare di una volta', 'Ma se ognuno dormiva il treno e io' from Sandro Penna, *Tutte le poesie* (Garzanti, 1970).
'Adónde Fueron Despeñadas' from *La realidad y el deseo* (Fondo de Cultura Económica, Mexico, 1970).

Revising Brodsky

This is reprinted from *Modern Poetry in Translation: 1983*, edited by Daniel Weissbort (Carcanet Press UK, Persea Books USA, 1983).
'Vtoroye Rozhdestvo na beregu' from *Konets Prekrasnoi Epokhi* (Ardis, Ann Arbor, 1977).
'Nature Morte' and 'Pisma Russkomu drugu' from *Chast' Rechi* (Ardis, 1977).
'Razvivaya Platona' from *Urania* (Ardis, 1987).

Translating Anna Akhmatova

This is reprinted from *Modern Poetry in Translation: 1983*, edited by Daniel Weissbort (Carcanet Press UK, Persea Books USA, 1983).
'We're all drunkards' and 'Boris Pasternak', translated by Stanley Kunitz and Max Hayward, from *The Poems of Anna Akhmatova* (Atlantic Monthly Press, 1973).

Voice; Landscape; Violence

'Sommaren har nu vänt' from *Dikter utan ordning* (Bonniers, Stockholm, 1983).

Translating Juarroz and Noren

'Los rostros que has ido abandonando' by Roberto Juarroz from *Vertical Poetry*.
'Idag är allting' by Lars Noren, quoted from 'W.S. Merwin, Translator Poet' by Michael Gormon, *Translation Review*, No. 9 (Dallas, 1982).

Playing Scrabble without a Board

'Kannick' by Esaias Tegnér, from *Samlade Skrifter* (P.A. Norstedt, Stockholm, 1923).

'The Voice Inside'

'At the Stone of Losses', 'Song of Thanks', 'I say "love"', 'My Beloved is Mine and I am His', 'In a Flash', 'Eve Knew' from T. Carmi, *At the Stone of Losses*, translated by Grace Schulman (Jewish Publications Society of America, Philadelphia, 1983).

Working at Someone Else's Poem

Part of this is reprinted from *Modern Poetry in Translation* Nos 41–2, edited by Daniel Weissbort (London, March 1981).
Hebrew text and transliteration and prose translation of 'Joshua's Face / Pney Yehusua' from *The Modern Hebrew Poem Itself*, edited by Stanley Burnshaw, T. Carmi, Ezra Spicehardler (Schocken Books, New York, 1966).

Translating Horace

Horace I, ii, translated by C.H. Sisson, from *In the Trojan Ditch*, by C.H. Sisson (Carcanet Press, 1974).
Horace I, ii and IV, vii and prose versions of these poems from Horace, *The Odes and Epodes*, edited by C.E. Bennett (Heinemann, 1914).

Finding the Proper Equivalent

'Lodka na beregu' from *Ten' zvuka* (Moscow, 1970).
'Oza', original and translation, from *Anti Worlds and the Fifth Ace* by

Andrei Voznesensky, edited by Patricia Blake and Max Hayward (Basic Books, New York, 1966).

'Saga' from *Nostalgia for the Present*, edited by Vera Dunham and Max Hayward (Doubleday, New York, 1978).

'Derzhavin' from *Metropol* (Moscow, 1979).

Translating Brodsky

'Shorokh Akatsii' from *Urania* (Ardis, Ann Arbor, 1987).

'The Rustle of Acacias' from *The Iowa Review*, Vol. 9, No. 4 (Iowa City, Fall 1978).

Notes on the Contributors

Keith Bosley was born in Thames Valley, England, in 1937. Educated at the universities of Reading, Paris and Caen, he has had various jobs at the BBC External Services since 1961. Since 1980 he has been a Corresponding Member of the Finnish Literature Society. He has published five collections of his own poetry, most recently *A Chiltern Hundred* (1987), and very many translations of poetry from Russian, French, Vietnamese, Finnish, Polish and other languages, including *Mallarmé: The Poems* (1977) and *Finnish Folk Poetry: Epic* (1977), for which he was awarded the Finnish State Prize. He is now translating the *Kalevala*. *From the Theorems of Master Jean de la Ceppède* appeared in 1983.

János Csokits was born in Budapest in 1928. In 1944 he took part in the resistance movement against the German occupation and the Hungarian Nazi government. After the siege of Budapest he joined the New Democratic Army against the Nazis. He read law at the Pazmány Péter University, Budapest (1946–9). He was a member of the short-lived Freedom Party and fled to the West as a political refugee in May 1949. Since then he has lived mainly in Paris, Munich and London, and most recently in Andorra. He is now a British subject. His poems, essays and radio plays have appeared in Hungarian literary magazines in the West. His *Selected Poems* is to be published in the near future. *Selected Poems of János Pilinszky*, translated by Ted Hughes and János Csokits, was published in 1977.

John Felstiner is Professor of English at Stanford University. His books include *The Lies of Art: Max Beerbohm's Parody and Caricature* and *Translating Neruda: The Way to Macchu Picchu* (1980). He is writing a book on Paul Celan.

Michael Hamburger was born in Berlin in 1924, emigrating with his family to England in 1933. He spent four years in military service during the second world war, after the war attending Oxford University. He was Lecturer and Reader in German at University College, London, and the University of Reading, where he taught until 1964. He has also been a visiting professor at many universities in the USA. Fourteen volumes of his own poems have appeared, including the recent *Collected Poems* (1984). He has published a number of critical studies and collections of critical essays. As a translator he has concentrated on German poetry, notably the work of Friedrich Hölderlin: *Hölderlin: Poems and Fragments* (1980). He has also edited and largely translated a number of important anthologies, including *German Poetry 1910–1975* (1977).

James S Holmes was born in 1924 and raised on a farm in central Iowa. He was educated at William Penn College, Haverford, and Brown University. In 1949 he went to the Netherlands as a Fulbright exchange teacher and stayed on, working as a freelance editor and translator, and in 1964 becoming Lecturer in Translation Studies at the University of Amsterdam. He retired, in 1985, as Senior Lecturer. He was a founding editor of *Delta*, a literary-cum-cultural review of Dutch life published in English from 1958 to 1974, and has received major awards for his translations of Dutch poetry, including *Dutch Interior: Postwar Poetry of the Netherlands and Flanders* (co-edited with William Jay Smith, 1984). He has also edited a number of important collections of essays, among them *The Nature of Translation* (1970) and *Literature and Translation* (1978). Jim Holmes, who was involved in the planning of the present volume, died in Amsterdam in 1986. His volume of collected essays, *Translated! Essays and Papers on Translation and Translation Studies*, was recently published by Rodopi (Amsterdam).

Ted Hughes was born in the West Riding of Yorkshire in 1930. He has published many collections of poetry. He has also published widely for children and has written radio plays. Besides translating the poetry of János Pilinszky, with János Csokits, he has co-translated poetry by the Israeli poet Yehuda Amichai. He co-founded the magazine *Modern Poetry in Translation* in 1965 with Daniel Weissbort. In 1985 Ted Hughes succeeded John Betjeman as Poet Laureate.

Peter Jay was born in Chester, England, in 1945 and educated at Oxford University. He is founder-director of the Anvil Press and is well known for his many translations from Greek, Latin, French, Hungarian and Romanian. He edited *The Greek Anthology* (Penguin

Classics, 1981) and has published translations of Gérard de Nerval's *The Chimeras* (1985). His translation of János Pilinszky's *Crater* was published in 1978 and he is currently working on a larger selection from Pilinszky. His own poetry has appeared with Carcanet.

James Kirkup was born in South Shields, England, in 1923. He has taught in Hawaii and since 1976 has been teaching Comparative Literature at Kyoto University of Foreign Studies. He has published many collections of his own poetry, as well as much prose. He has translated poetry and prose from French, German, Spanish, Italian, Catalan, Japanese, Malay and Chinese, and has published many volumes of translations, including, most recently, *Ecce Homo: My Pasolini – Poems and Translations* and *Cold Mountain Poems: Interpretations of the Poems of Han Shan* (produced by his own press, Kyoto Editions) and *Modern Japanese Poetry*.

George L. Kline is Milton C. Nahm Professor of Philosophy at Bryn Mawr College, where he regularly offers graduate seminars (in the Russian Department) on 'The Theory and Practice of Literary Translation'. He is the author of *Religious and Anti-Religious Thought in Russia* (1968), translator of V.V. Zenkovsky's *A History of Russian Philosophy* (1953), *Boris Pasternak: Seven Poems* (1969) and *Joseph Brodsky: Selected Poems* (1973), and co-translator of Brodsky's *A Part of Speech* (1980) and *To Urania* (1988).

Stanley Kunitz was born in Worcester, Massachusetts, in 1905. He studied at Harvard. He has taught widely and published collections of critical essays, as well as many collections of his own poetry. Mr Kunitz received the Senior Fellowship Award of the National Endowment of the Arts in 1984. His publications include *Selected Poems 1928–1958*, for which he was awarded the Pulitzer Prize in 1959; *Poems of Akhmatova* (with Max Hayward, 1973); *A Kind of Order, A Kind of Folly: Essays and Conversations* (1975); *The Poems of Stanley Kunitz (1928–1978)* (1979); and *The Wellfleet Whale and Companion Poems* (1983).

Rika Lesser was born in Brooklyn, New York, in 1953. She was educated at Yale College and Columbia University. She has taught translation workshops at Yale and poetry workshops in New York.

For both her own poetry and her translations she has been the recipient of several grants and awards, among them the Amy Lowell Poetry Travelling Scholarship and an Ingram Merrill Foundation grant. Her translation of Gunnar Ekelöf's *Guide to the Underworld* (1980) received the Harold Morton Landon Poetry Translation Prize of the Academy of American Poets in 1982. She has in addition published collections of Rilke and Hermann Hesse and is currently learning Finnish and translating the contemporary Finnish poet Göran Sonnevi. *Etruscan Things*, a collection of her own poetry, appeared in 1983.

W.S. Merwin was born in New York City in 1927. He lived and worked as a tutor in France, Portugal and Majorca from 1949 to 1951, after which, for several years, he earned the greater part of his living by translating from French, Spanish, Latin and Portuguese. He has also lived in England and the United States. Mr Merwin is both a prolific poet and translator. His first collection of poetry appeared in 1952. In 1970 he was awarded the Pulitzer Prize for *The Carrier of Ladders*. He received the PEN Translation Prize in 1968 for his *Selected translations 1948–1968*, and in 1974 he was awarded the Fellowship of the Academy of American Poets. Atheneum has reprinted *Four French Plays* (1985) and *From the Spanish Morning* (1985), while North Point has reprinted *Products of the Perfected Civilization: Selected Writings of Chamfort* (1984).

Judith Moffett was born in Louisville, North Kentucky, in 1942. She teaches English at the University of Pennsylvania, having previously taught at the University of Iowa Writers' Workshop. Besides two volumes of original poetry she has published a critical study of the poet James Merrill. She went to Sweden, to the University of Lund, as a Fulbright Lecturer in 1967 and again on a Fulbright grant in 1973, when she undertook a translation project which was ultimately published as *Gentleman, Single, Refined and Selected Poems 1937–1959* by Hjalmar Gullberg (1979). This book was awarded the Translation Prize of the Swedish Academy for 1982. She is currently working on an anthology of poems by seven nineteenth-century Swedish poets.

Grace Schulman was Poetry Editor of *The Nation* for many years, and Director of the Poetry Center, 92nd Street, YM-YWHA (1974–84). A former Vice-President of PEN, she is a professor at

Baruch College, CUNY, and holds a PhD from New York University. Her poems, essays and translations have appeared in many publications and she has taught at Princeton, Columbia and Wesleyan, as well as at the YM-YWHA Poetry Center. She was awarded a Witter Bynner Grant-in-Aid for her translation of T. Carmi's *At the Stone of Losses* (1983). Her publications also include *Songs of Cifar and the Sweet Sea*, by Pablo Antonio Cuadra (1979), as well as two critical works and three collections of her own poetry.

Jon Silkin was born in London in 1930 and was educated at Wycliffe and Dulwich College. After a period of national service he worked as a manual labourer in London and as a teacher of English to foreign students. He held a Gregory Fellowship in Poetry at the University of Leeds (1958–60) and in 1965 moved to Newcastle, where he co-edits the literary magazine *Stand*, which he founded in 1952. He has taught at several American universities, including the University of Iowa Writers' Workshop. He has published numerous collections of poetry, anthologies and many critical articles, including *The Principle of Water* (1974), which was awarded the Geoffrey Faber Memorial Prize, *Selected Poems* (1980), *The Penguin Book of First World War Poetry* (1979) and *Out of Battle*, a critical study of the poetry of the first world war.

C.H. Sisson was born in Bristol in 1914. Educated at Bristol University and in France and Germany, he started work in Whitehall in 1936. Army service (1942–5) was spent mainly in India, and after the war he served in the Ministry of Labour/Department of Employment until 1973, rising to the position of Undersecretary. He now lives in Somerset. His publications, other than translations, include *The Avoidance of Literature* (collected essays, 1978) and *Collected Poems* (1984). Translations comprise *Versions & Perversions of Heine* (1955); *The Poetry of Catullus* (1966); *The Poetic Art of Horace* (1975); *Lucretius, the Poem on Nature* (1976); *Some Tales of La Fontaine* (1979); *The Divine Comedy of Dante* (1980); *The Song of Roland* (1983); *The Regrets of Joachim du Bellay* (1983). At present he is translating the Aeneid.

William Jay Smith has translated poetry by Valéry Larbaud and Jules Laforgue, plays by Charles Bertin and work by Kornei Chukovsky, Artur Lundkvist, Lennart Hellsing and Thorkild Bjornvig. He has edited, with Emanuel Brasil, *Brazilian Poetry 1950–1980*

(1984) and, with James S Holmes, *Dutch Interior: Postwar Poetry of the Netherlands and Flanders* (1984). He was also a major contributor to *Modern Hungarian Poetry*, edited by Miklós Vajda (1978), and to *Nostalgia for the Present*, by Andrei Voznesensky, edited by Max Hayward and Vera Dunham in 1975. Mr Smith was awarded the Gold Medal of Labour by the Hungarian government for his translations of Hungarian poetry. He is a member of the board of the Translation Center, Columbia University, and an editor of *Translation*, the journal published by the Center. Eight volumes of his own poetry have been published.

Daniel Weissbort was born in London in 1935. He was educated at Cambridge University and the LSE, where he worked under Professor Leonard Schapiro. In 1965 he co-founded, with Ted Hughes, the magazine *Modern Poetry in Translation*, which appeared irregularly between 1965 and 1983, the present collection of texts originating as an MPT project. Since 1986 the magazine has been published under a new name, *Poetry World*, by Anvil Press. Daniel Weissbort has translated mostly from Russian and French. His translations of poetry are included in *Post-War Russian Poetry* (Penguin, 1974), which he edited, and *Russian Poetry: The Modern Period* (1978), which he edited with John Glad. He has also published individual collections of Yevgeny Vinokurov, Yevgeny Yevtushenko and Natalya Gorbanevskaya, and has contributed translations to numerous other anthologies. His anthology, *The Poetry of Survival: Poetry from Central Europe*, is due from Anvil Press shortly. He is Professor of English and Comparative Literature at the University of Iowa, where he directs the Translation Workshop. Three collections of his own poetry have been published by Carcanet.

Richard Wilbur was born in New York City in 1921. He studied at Amherst and Harvard. He served in the army in Italy and France (1943–5) and has taught at Harvard, Wellesely and Wesleyan, and since 1977 at Smith. Besides many volumes of his own poetry, he has published translations of four plays by Molière, as well as Racine's *Andromaque* and most recently *Phèdre*. *The Whale* (uncollected translations) appeared in 1982. He has received numerous awards, including a Guggenheim Fellowship, the Prix de Rome Fellowship, the National Book Award, the Pulitzer Prize, a Ford

Foundation Fellowship, the Bollingen Prize, the PEN Translation Prize and others.

Paul Auster was born in Newark, New Jersey, in 1947 and studied at Columbia University. From 1971–4 he lived in Paris, and since returning to New York he has published five books of poetry, numerous articles and translations, as well as several works of fiction including *City of Glass*, volume one of *The New York Trilogy*, to be followed shortly by volume two, *Ghosts*. Mr Auster has edited *The Random House Book of 20th-Century French Poetry* (1986).

James S Holmes (1924–86)

The 'we' used in my preface is not the royal 'we'! My close collaborator on this book, James S Holmes, Jim Holmes, died in late 1986 after a year of failing health, a major loss to the world of translation and a grievous personal loss.

Jim had expressed interest in the project for this collection from the moment I mentioned it to him. He remained thoroughly committed to it over the years and we discussed it in detail during our regular, if somewhat widely spaced, meetings, in Iowa City, London and Amsterdam. Geography in fact conspired to help bring us together, in spite of our living on different continents, since Jim, a native Iowan, visited family in the Midwest at Christmas, while I taught (primarily translation) in the Comparative Literature Program at the University of Iowa, but also spent summers in London, my home town, from where it was my habit to travel to Rotterdam for the annual International Poetry Festival. Jim would stay with me and my wife in Iowa City, during which time he would also talk to the Translation Workshop, which I direct, while I would correspondingly enjoy his and Hans van Marle's hospitality in Amsterdam, a short train ride from Rotterdam. The last time I saw Jim, when he came to London especially to discuss the book with me and to finalise plans for publication (a different publisher at that time), I drafted the Preface, which I gave him, in the hope that he would supplement my remarks with what he himself wished to say on the subject; we would sign it jointly and then proceed to the joint final editing of the book. Unfortunately his illness intervened, even though he did somehow find the energy to begin to prepare the manuscript for printing.

It is impossible, in a brief tribute, to do justice to Jim's achievement as a translator and as one of the creators or originators of the discipline of Translation Studies from his base at the University of Amsterdam, where for twenty years, until shortly before he died, he was Senior Lecturer in General Literary Studies, most of that time with emphasis on Translation Studies. It should be said, however, that this achievement was as substantial, as crucial, in the field of theory as in that of practice, even if he never wrote the

James S Holmes (1924–86)

book on literary translation (I was going to say the 'definitive' book, but Jim would not have approved of that) of which many who knew his work believed him capable. Fortunately his several elegant, and often landmark, essays have been collected and are now available from by Rodopi (Amsterdam) under the title *Translated! Essays and Papers on Translation and Translation Studies*, in the Approaches to Translation Studies Series, which Jim himself founded and of which he was general editor.

Jim's achievement as a translator is, of course, more readily quantifiable, since he quite simply put modern Dutch poetry on the world literary map, thus repaying the Netherlands for the hospitality afforded him when he settled there shortly after the second world war as a kind of refugee from provincial America. The Netherlands was dear to him, as was the Dutch language, and he made no secret of his pen name: Jacob Lowland! He was a founding editor – the principal editor and then poetry editor for many years – of *Delta: A Review of Arts, Life, and Thought in the Netherlands*, the superb showcase magazine, published in English. As early as 1956 he became the first non-native speaker to be awarded the Martinus Nijhoff Prize, the leading Dutch award for literary translation, and again in 1984 he was the first foreign recipient of the Vlaamse Gemeenschap Vertaalprijs. His monumental *Dutch Interior: Postwar Poetry of the Netherlands and Flanders* (co-edited with William Jay Smith, 1984) is the culmination, perhaps, of his work in this area, but in recent years he had also been experimenting with a much freer form of translation, under his pen name, of Classical Latin poetry, especially Martial and Catullus. In fact his own contribution to the present volume was to have been a presentation of his translations of Catullus' homo-erotic verse, entitled 'Some Catullus for Today'. How I wish that, instead of futilely pestering him over the years with letters to write this piece, I had instead taken advantage of one of our meetings in Iowa to lock him in overnight with a twelve-pack of Bud and challenge him to turn it out by morning! In the event, rather than reprint one of Jim's articles in the present volume, I have included an abbreviated transcription of a talk-cum-reading that he gave to the University of Iowa Translation Workshop, in which he at least touches on some of the issues that he had intended to discuss more comprehensively in his article.

I should add, even if this is not the place for a proper appreciation, that he was also (also?) a poet of exquisite sensibility and, in his later years, of the frankest self-exposure. Here too Jim Holmes was the consummate translator.

DW

Translating La Ceppède
Keith Bosley

Jean de La Ceppède (c. 1548–1623) is a modern rediscovery. Highly regarded in his day (and praised by St Francis de Sales for his 'learned piety') he was forgotten as his friend Malherbe laid the foundations of a classical style befitting Louis XIV's Golden Age. Several good poets suffered eclipse by *le Roi Soleil*: too serious to be classified as *précieux*, their work was judged offensive to good taste, reflecting as it did the troubled world of the Wars of Religion. Later in the seventeenth century the English Metaphysicals were to suffer a similar fate, and it is only in the twentieth century that Baroque poetry has been rescued from either oblivion or Curiosity Corner, to be seen as a development rather than a degeneration of the Renaissance.

La Ceppède's principal work, which occupied him for most of his life, is *Les Théorèmes*, a sequence of 520 sonnets on the Christian Redemption. Published in two parts, in 1613 and 1622 (and reissued in full only in 1966), the work meditates on events from the arrest of Jesus to the gift of tongues at Pentecost. Each sonnet is followed by a commentary ranging from little more than a footnote to a treatise of 27 pages. As the title indicates, the *Theorems* are 'demonstrations' of the Christian faith by a devout Catholic: instead of Protestant soul-searching we find celebrations of truths not self-evident. Since the truths are universal, the poet draws on many disciplines for his 'proofs': classical mythology (Christ as Orpheus), the Hebrew Bible, colour symbolism, medicine, astrology, even physics in a magnificent sonnet which presents divine love in terms of the force of gravity. In the best sonnets the learning is leavened by a quite journalistic vividness reminiscent of Spanish spirituality: the poet came of a Spanish family long settled in Provence (where he was born and lived most of his life) and may have been related to St Teresa of Avila, who was born a Cepeda. Jesus arrives at Golgotha (Part 1, Book 3, Sonnet 10): *Debout, parmi l'horreur des charognes relantes / En cette orde voirie* ('Amid the horror of stale meat he stands / In this foul shambles'); he is nailed to the Cross (1:3:15):

Soudain que sur le trou cette main fut tenduë,
Dans sa paume on enfonce à grans coups de marteau
Vn clou gros & quarré, iusqu'au dos du posteau:
Sans qu'on ait de sa bouche vne plainte entenduë.

Immediately this hand is stretched out, hard
Into the palm with juddering blows they whack
A fat square nail that goes straight through the stake:
Yet not a murmur from his lips is heard.

  I first came upon La Ceppède in 1967, when I was reading French Baroque poetry for the first time; a degree course that had ended seven years before had somehow failed to mention it. One memorable weekend I translated nine sonnets, seven of which were used in 1971 for a week's God Spots on the BBC World Service. In 1979 I submitted them for an EEC translation competition; they won second prize, and the organisers, the Mid-Northumberland Arts Group (MidNAG) and Carcanet New Press, offered to publish a book of similar translations. In 1983 they published *From the Theorems of Master Jean de La Ceppède: LXX Sonnets*; meanwhile the sonnet to be discussed below was used in 1981 in my World Service series *The Poetry of Europe*. I mention all this because, with so much translation going on, I just do not have house room for successive drafts; but because they were broadcast I have kept my earlier versions, one of which I propose to compare with the final published version.
  Part 1, Book 2, Sonnet 63 is a meditation on the colour red:

Aux Monarques vaincueurs la rouge cotte-d'armes
Appartient iustement. Ce Roy victorieux
Est iustement vestu par ces mocqueurs gens-d'armes
D'vn manteau, qui le marque & Prince, & glorieux.

O pourpre emplis mon test de ton ius precieux
Et luy fay distiller mille pourprines larmes,
A tant que meditant ton sens mysterieux,
Du sang trait de mes yeux i'ensanglante ces Carmes.

Ta sanglante couleur figure nos pechez
Au dos de cet Agneau par le Pere attachez:
Et ce Christ t'endossant se charge de nos crimes.

Translating La Ceppède

O Christ, ô sainct Agneau, daigne toy de cacher
Tous mes rouges pechez (brindelles des abysmes)
Dans les sanglans replis du manteau de ta chair.

Here is my translation of 1967:

> To conquering monarchs the red coat of arms
> Justly belongs. This King, victorious
> Is justly clothed by mocking men-at-arms
> In robes that dub him prince and glorious.
>
> O purple, fill my head with your dear juice
> Distil it into weeping crimson wine
> Till thinking on that mystery this puce
> Milk of my eyes these songs incarnadine.
>
> Your bloodstained colour figures forth our sin
> Bound by the Father to this Lamb's fair skin
> And this Christ wearing you bears our foul globe.
>
> O Christ, O holy Lamb, deign to conceal
> All my red sins, these kindling-twigs of hell
> Under the stained folds of your body's robe.

First, the assumptions. Culturally speaking, French alexandrines correspond to English iambic pentameters. In terms of specific gravity (or, if you are a radio buff, the signal-to-noise ratio) this is largely true, as long as you realise that the alexandrine is symmetrical, whereas the iambic pentameter is not: compare La Ceppède's line (1:3:20) *Son amour est si grand, son amour est si fort* with my translation 'So great his love, his great love is so mighty'. And a sonnet is a sonnet, whatever the language: eight lines plus six, whatever the rhyme scheme. For La Ceppède I used a Baudelairean version of Petrarch, introducing new rhymes for the second quatrain – though in this sonnet I softened the impact of the second quatrain with the half-rhyme 'glorious / juice'.

Here is the final version – final only in the sense that I was called away:

> To conquering monarchs the red coat of arms
> Justly belongs. This King, victorious

Is justly clothed by mocking men-at-arms
In robes that dub him prince and glorious.

O purple, fill my head with your dear juice
And make it drip a thousand crimson tears
That as I think on your mysterious
Meaning my eyes' drawn blood may stain these airs.

Your bloody colour figures forth our sin
Bound by the Father to this Lamb's fair skin
And this Christ wearing you bears all our ill.

O Christ, O holy Lamb, I beg you, hold
All my red sins, these kindling-twigs of hell
Hid in your flesh's robe's each bloody fold.

The first quatrain is unchanged. French rhyme is less demanding than English, but I could not here resist rhyming on words our languages share; to do otherwise would have meant making La Ceppède sound more Baroque than he is already. In rhyme it is often better to take the path of least resistance – that way your rhythms survive because you have felt them. La Ceppède may be a 'learned' poet, but he is also a passionate one: Eliot's remark (*The Metaphysical Poets*, 1921) that 'a thought to Donne was an experience' can be applied equally to his French contemporary, for both lived at a time when thought and feeling could pull in the same direction – Renaissance man was still in one piece.

It must be admitted that our poet does not always bring it off. One of the Pentecost sonnets of his old age, about the 'rushing mighty wind' (2:4:6), opens with what is only too obviously a versified thought:

> Nous aprenons aussi de céte vehemence
> La presence de Dieu, qui coustumierement
> Nous marque les efforts de sa grandeur immense
> Par des signes bruyants mysterieusement.

Here I did not follow my poet down his primrose path ('vehemence / customarily' etc.); nor indeed did I abandon him. I tried instead to make the opening as good as the poet in his prime would have made it:

Vehemence teaches us the work of God:
We learn from it his presence, for his way
To make his mighty power known abroad
Is with great noises that attest his sway.

Is this an example of *traduttore = traditore*?

The second quatrain of the sonnet under discussion hinges, for the translator, on two words: *distiller* and *trait*. (*Test*, by the way, is *le têt*, a defunct equivalent of *la tête*.) *Distiller* does not have its English counterpart's later obsession with hard liquor (so in the 1967 version 'wine' is doubly wrong) for in French even the dew does it – hence 'drip'; this is a lesson for 'tourist' translators. *Trait* is the past participle of the verb *traire*, which in modern French means only 'to milk' – hence my misunderstanding. I thought the poet was using the conventional contrast of red and white: lip and cheek in love poetry, blood and flesh in sacred; but in Renaissance French, anxious to emulate classical Latin, *traire* was above all *trahere*, 'to draw', so *trait* was no more than 'drawn' – as in modern Anglo-French usage, where a *trait* is a '(drawn) feature'. This latter had to win the day – though I regret the passing of the expressive 'puce'. My Shakespearean 'incarnadine' (with its ponderous subjunctive) was now quite indefensible. To end the line I concentrated instead on *Carmes*, an unlovely (and short-lived) Latinism after *carmina(s)*, 'songs, odes' (as in Horace); compare *charmes* (as in Valéry). 'Airs' (as in Elizabethan lutenists) would do it. I still do not like the 'mysterious / Meaning' enjambement; but that is a knot in the wood, and I have other work to do.

La Ceppède usually rhymes his octaves *abba*; sometimes, as here, he uses *abab*. His sestets always begin the French way, with a couplet *cc*; the remaining lines vary between *dede* and *deed*. One sonnet (1:3:26) uses rhyme to heighten the familiar Old/New Testament typology – in this case the forbidden tree of Eden and the wood of the Cross. The *a*-rhymes are the masculine endings of past historic tenses, the *b*-rhymes are feminine past participles of the same verbs:

> Sathan par le bois vert nostre ayeule rauit:
> Iesus par le bois sec à Sathan l'a rauie.
> Le bois vert à l'Enfer nostre ayeule asseruit:
> Le bois sec a d'Enfer la puissance asseruie.

Here, exceptionally, I departed from a sonnet rhyme scheme. The only way to match these polarities was by rhyming in couplets:

> Satan by green wood our first mother snatched:
> Jesus by dry wood Satan's wiles has matched.
> Green wood to hell our first mother enslaved:
> Dry wood from hell's power all her kin has saved.

To get the right resounding ring at line-ends I took especial liberties with syntax. Throughout these translations my syntax is freer than I usually allow myself; I can only say it felt – and feels – right.

Two sonnets (1:2:67–8) are linked by the same rhymes to form a closely related pair: just as, says the first, the blood and spittle on Jesus' face make him look leprous, so, says the second, his redeeming blood and the spittle with which he healed a blind man will cleanse the leprosy of sin. These two were a particular challenge to translate, just as they must have been to write. Elsewhere, though not so rigorously joined, many sonnets are grouped round a single theme or image: there is an *Ecce Homo* triptych, the present sonnet is the first of three on the emblems of Christ's kingship (purple robe, crown of thorns, reed-sceptre), while another triptych celebrates the Cross, the axle-tree of the universe whose fruit, rather quaintly, *Est pour tous les bourgeois de la machine ronde* ('Is for all commons of the round machine').

Because I committed myself to following La Ceppède rhyme for rhyme (with the two exceptions I have mentioned) I took upon myself the – perhaps unnecessary – task of reworking those 1967 versions which did not do so. The present sonnet was one of them, and here I felt (translation is a very feeling process) that my earlier freedom had not generated enough steam: 'bloodstained' was awful, but I needed it for the echo of 'stained' in the last line, where there was no room for a longer word; 'globe/robe' is a good strong rhyme, but there was not enough reason for 'globe'; 'deign' was weak despite the cognate it rendered. (The reflexive form with *de*, by the way, is obsolete; and *brindelles* are today's *brindilles*.) With a little extra pressure, then, 'conceal' gave way to the more vivid 'hold . . . Hid', resulting in a new bottleneck in the last line. But the double genitive is in the original too (*du manteau de ta chair*) and I was encouraged by Hopkins' triple example, the last line of 'The Wreck of the Deutschland': 'Our hearts' charity's hearth's fire, our thoughts' chivalry's throng's Lord'. I don't like 'each', but you can't win them all.

What should one translate into? One's own tongue (of course), more or less as spoken in one's own place and time. More or less, because the best translation extends language; one's own place, because most of us need to hear our own tongue about us to keep our work fresh; one's own time, because we really have no choice. Here are lines 9–11 of the present sonnet rendered into mock-Baroque English by a translator who rightly insists on anonymity:

> Thy bloudie Hue oure sinnes doth signifie
> Which on the Lambe the Father will'd should lie;
> Christ to this load hath bowed his Backe submiss.

Pastiche is the last refuge of the bad translator. 'Doth signifie' just will not do, not only because of the lazy use of the auxiliary verb, but also because it does not translate *figure*: this means 'figures forth, is an emblem of' in the specific terminology of Christian types, whereas 'doth signifie' is at most no more than 'indicates, is a sign of' – a Protestant, not to say Evangelical, crudity. The spelling is broadly Elizabethan, yet 'submiss' can only be Milton on a bad day.

Dryden, as usual, got it right when he 'endeavoured to make Vergil speak such English as he would have spoken, if he had been born in England, and in this present age'. The language, the country, the age might all be wrong: a missionary once told me that he could not translate the Bible into his West African language without falling into heresy, and I too have my troubles making Finno-Ugrian folk poetry sound credible in a culture where oral tradition takes second place to literature. There are no archaisms in my La Ceppède, even though the old boy himself was not above the occasional *ains* or *cil*: I call Jesus 'you' like today's Christians and my rhymes have teeth. My only conscious anachronism is my syntactical freedom: I aimed at the 'strong lines' beloved of the Metaphysicals, and the odd inversion seemed the only way to match the poet's own essential knottiness, to let him breathe in our thinner air.

Why bother at all? Because I fell in love with the *Theorems*: they are the most radiant poetic expression I know of a Christian certainty I once enjoyed but have since lost. The sonnet as single throbbing image is La Ceppède's particular achievement: for me he is the great model, not Petrarch, not Shakespeare. Returning to him after many years, I translated about seventy sonnets in a few weeks, during which I had injections in preparation for a Middle East lecture tour: as I continued working in literally a high fever, I recalled how Britten had made his great settings of Donne sonnets in similar circumstances. I shall never forget the experience. And when the book came out, the solitary reviewer said I was more accurate than a prose crib. *Nunc dimittis*.

János Pilinszky's 'Desert of Love'
A Note
János Csokits

There are as many schools of translating poetry as there are theories of how not to do it. Ladislas Gara in his *Anthologie de la Poésie hongroise* (Paris: Éditions du Seuil, 1962) opted for the method, alien to French literary tradition, of recreating each Hungarian poem – style, versification, music and all – in French metrical structures. Gara imported this method from Hungary, where it is the only accepted way of translating poetry and where, in order to distinguish between ordinary and literary renderings, two terms are used for translation (*fordítás* and *műfordítás*). The latter form of literary art is highly regarded and some of its practitioners are held in particularly great esteem. One such poet was Árpád Tóth (1886–1928). His translation of Shelley's 'Ode to the West Wind', for instance, has been called one of the ten most beautiful Hungarian poems. Another celebrated translation by Tóth is Rilke's *'Archaischer Torso Apollos'*. Literary critics have drawn attention to the precision, style and music of this beautiful translation, in which almost nothing of the original form has been lost and even some of the respective rhyming words exactly correspond in meaning. And yet it is not Rilke. Besides the impossibility of 'recreating' a poem in another language, one must take into account the artistic temperament and personality of the poets involved. The dynamism and balance of Rilke's sonnet, written in his 'thing poetry' period, recalls to mind the substance and elegance of Greek marble, whereas the sound and texture of Tóth's language in this translation remind one of an impressionistic painting of a broken statue; it evokes the soft phosphorescence of decay, entirely absent from the German original. Árpád Tóth must have loved Rilke's sonnet very much, but their verbal chemistry was not compatible.

The question of compatibility arises every time one deals with translated poetry. In the case of János Pilinszky and Ted Hughes the characteristics separating their poetic worlds are at first appearance more obvious than those uniting them. The added difficulty of a two-way language barrier – Hughes does not speak Hungarian and Pilinszky had no English – seems to make the obstacles insurmountable. Appearances, however, are often deceptive: there must have existed sufficient common ground for the two poets to find each other's personal universe so attractive that both wanted to make an attempt at translating the other's works. To start with, Ted Hughes knew Pilinszky from a few raw literals of mine and a number of French translations only, but the appeal of Pilinszky's world was apparently so strong that he kept asking for more until we had an adequate number for the *Selected Poems*. Pilinszky had seen nothing but word-for-word translations of poems of Hughes, most of them in French (!), and that was enough for him to discover their spiritual kinship. Personal contacts no doubt confirmed his first instinctive recognition. He made it clear more than once: the works of no other contemporary western poet fascinated him as much as the poems of Ted Hughes. He planned to translate the entire Crow cycle, a book he greatly admired, – again on the strength of literals – but unfortunately he died before he could do it.

This very real affinity between the two poets made any salesmanship on my part totally unnecessary, and my role in the rendering of the *Selected Poems* consisted exclusively in linguistic mediation; that is, furnishing Ted Hughes with word-for-word translations and suitable notes. It was clear from the beginning that he wanted literal versions without metrics and rhyme schemes, but how much of the original stanza structure and line arrangement was I to keep? How far could I stray from poetic language without turning the text into flat prose? And what about the style and the tone? Hughes did not want smooth and polished renderings in what he called 'magazine English'; he had seen such texts and found them uninspiring. And because he could not read Pilinszky in the original I had to find a substitute for the verbal excitement a poem in another language offers to its translator. I thought it best to stick to the meaning and as far as possible to the spirit of the original. I tried to keep the poetic idiom of Pilinszky in English without exaggerated respect for the host language, hoping to preserve both the peculiar Hungarian flavour and the poet's pesonal style. Fragments and chunks of the original poetry survived in the literals, just enough to feed the curiosity of Ted

Hughes. By sticking to the original, the English text inevitably becomes odd, but this oddity seemed to appeal to the translator. I often wondered who was more surprised: Ted Hughes receiving the texts in what he politely called 'your odd English' or I getting back the corrected versions, still recognisably mine but their crudeness somehow transmuted into literary language. After this phase all I had to do was to see that the literals did not stray too far from the originals. Some of the translations travelled back and forth several times over the years, gradually reaching the point where we felt we could not come closer to the original.

I am convinced that my approach would never have worked without the special faculty of Ted Hughes to feel the quality, style and characteristics of a poem even in the crudest word-for-word translation. It is almost as if he could X-ray the literals and see the original poem in ghostly detail like a radiologist viewing the bones, muscles, veins and nerves of a live human body. The difference is that X-ray pictures do not show the human face, whereas Hughes can see and visualise the whole astral body of the poem. I saw the result of this operation in the corrections made to my literals and saw it happen several times. Pilinszky witnessed it, too, and was duly impressed. It is eery when it happens, one can almost hear the humming of a high tension line, but the effect is not that of a technical device; it has more to do with extra-sensory perception.

It is no accident that the fruits of our nine years' labour, the *Selected Poems*, are very much an X-ray Pilinszky. By losing their outer shell, the Hungarian language, these poems have lost the most distinctive feature of their appearance. What remains is the inner structure of sentences and ideas, a memory of stanzas and, underneath, the thoughts, feelings, emotions. Nothing has been lost of the all-pervading visions. Without the softening effect of the original metre and rhyme scheme the impact of some of these poems can be very painful; they sound harsher and Pilinszky's view of the world appears grimmer than in Hungarian. These X-ray versions, then, are evidently not for the reader in need of a verbal soporific or a musical therapy against life. There is no translation without some loss of the original, but by sticking to the 'linguistic poverty' of Pilinszky's poetry we remained faithful to the inner core of his message and its mode of expression: the unadorned language of the dispossessed.

Pilinszky was neither a traditionalist nor a modernist; he did not play with classical forms and was not interested in experiments with language. He had something to say and had to say it urgently like someone under sentence of death. No time to elaborate, to embellish. Never sentimental, his dry and precise sentences hit all the harder. As Ted Hughes has pointed out in his Introduction to the *Selected Poems*, Pilinszky's style is 'simple, unambiguous, direct'. His inner world on the other hand is in part hidden and extremely complex. As a result his style, his seeming simplicity, can be deceptive, and those short sentences without frills can easily trip the translator. I have selected one example of the many to illustrate this difficulty.

Here is the translation of 'The Desert of Love' (1952), one of Pilinszky's most enigmatic poems, a snapshot of a private hell in which time appears to stand still.

> A bridge, and a hot concrete road –
> the day is emptying its pockets,
> laying out, one by one, all its possessions.
> You are quite alone in the catatonic twilight.
>
> A landscape like the bed of a wrinkled pit,
> with glowing scars, a darkness that dazzles.
> Dusk thickens. I stand numb with brightness
> blinded by the sun. This summer will not leave me.
>
> Summer. And flashing heat.
> The chickens stand, like burning cherubs,
> in the boarded-up, splintered cages.
> I know their wings do not even tremble.
>
> Do you still remember? First there was the wind.
> And then the earth. Then the cage.
> Flames, dung. And now and again
> a few wing-flutters, a few empty reflexes.
>
> And thirst. I asked for water –
> Even today I hear that feverish gulping,
> and helplessly, like a stone, bear
> and quench the mirages.
>
> Years are passing. And years. And hope
> is like a tin-cup toppled into the straw.

The sentence in the eighth line, 'This summer will not leave me', is in Hungarian *Sosem felejtem, nyár van*. In my first word-for-word version in 1967 I translated it: 'I never forget it's summer', and in a footnote for Ted Hughes I added: 'The meaning in Hungarian is not absolutely clear – it can be interpreted differently as "I won't ever forget this summer" or as "I don't forget for a second that we are having summer now" – the latter explaining the phenomenon experienced by the poet.' In his first version Ted Hughes had: 'This summer will never leave me for a moment.' This sentence continued to bother me and after some reflection I wrote to him in January 1969: 'The whole difficulty comes from Pilinszky's use of "*sosem*" (never) . . . I feel he wants to say: "I don't forget for a minute that it is summer now" – meaning this fact explains the background of the scene of his experience. Could you, please, change this sentence in this sense. Otherwise it is misleading.' The change was duly made: it is the final version. Meanwhile, still troubled by the seeming straightforwardness of this statement, I worked out some variations of the two possible interpretations mentioned above. Interpretation I: (a) I will never forget this summer; (b) The memory of this summer will not pass; (c) This summer will always stay with me. Meaning: The memory of the past turns into present in the future. Interpretation II: (a) I don't forget for a minute it is summer now; (b) I am conscious of this summer all the time. Meaning: This is eternal summer, eternal present. In April 1972, still undecided, I referred the matter to Pilinszky himself, who at the time was staying in Paris. I gave him my two interpretations; here is his answer, first in Hungarian and then in English, translated by Ted Hughes.

> Ami a 'Szerelem sivatag' -át illeti: második értelmezésed a helyes. Egy olyan fekvésben azonban, amely a jelennek egyszerre ad múlt és örök jelen értéket. Örökké jelen lesz a jövöben is, miközben én magam megélem mulandóságomat. Valahogy úgy, ahogy egy múlhatatlan emlék, nem-múló-jelen csak még inkább mulandóvá tesz.

> As to 'The Desert of Love', your second interpretation is the correct one. But in this particular context the present takes on the value of the past and of the *eternal present* simultaneously. And in the future, too, it will be eternally present – while I myself live out my transitoriness. As a memory that cannot pass, with its insurmountable present, makes us even more transitory.

After this I was sure we could keep the sentence 'This summer will not leave me', but who could have guessed such depth in the simple statement 'I never forget, it's summer'? Those who know Hungarian will have noticed the poetic quality of the quotation – I mean the last two sentences. What makes it so beautiful, besides being profound and precise, is the way Pilinszky uses to the full the potentials of the verb *múlni* (to pass) and its derivatives. The music of this passage, its rhythm, alliterations and soft consonants, make it into a poem; it is certainly one of his memorable statements about his own poetry.

Finally, taking all this into consideration, how are the translators of literals valued? In Hungary, as in many other places, they are the pariahs of the realm of letters, unnamed and forgotten already this side of the grave. Pilinszky himself was unequivocal about their role. In an interview in 1972 he compared the translation of poetry to space flight. To the Hungarian poet to be translated he assigned the role of a space pilot, to the English poet doing the translation that of a co-pilot. As to 'the Hungarian poets, literators and sensitive non-professionals living abroad', who peddle the home-based poet's products because 'they are in love with it' and who prepare the literal translations for the foreign poet, Pilinszky compared these also-rans to booster rockets which at the onset of the second stage of the flight detach from the spaceship, 'and the Hungarian poet with his English co-pilot flies on'.

To understand Pilinszky's unflattering comment on translators of literals one has to bear in mind some of the traditional Hungarian views on the role of poets and poetry. Since the beginning of the nineteenth century the Hungarian nation has fallen into the habit of expecting its poets to act as gurus or Old Testament prophets in all matters connected with national survival, liberation from foreign occupation or domination, social progress, religion and culture. If not actually leading, the poet has at least the duty of pointing the way to the Promised Land. At a time of crisis, political guidance is expected from the best almost on a daily basis, and politically non-performing poets, however marvellous craftsmen, great lyricists or profound metaphysicians, are treated as second-raters. Pilinszky himself escaped this destiny only because he published six poems ('Harbach 1944', 'The French Prisoner', 'On the Wall of a KZ-Lager', 'Passion of Ravensbrück', 'Frankfurt 1945', 'On the Third Day') and the 'KZ Oratorio' which all deal with what the French call *l'univers concentrationnaire*. His admittance to the first rank, at first denied, rests exclusively on these deeply moving humanistic and Christian poems; hence the redeeming and misleading official epithet of 'antifascist', without which he could not be a poet of national importance. Even poems as great as 'Apocrypha' would not have gained him admittance to the Hungarian Parnassus, not even before 1945 or at the turn of the century. Only poets seen as fulfilling their prophetic mission have claim to national status in Hungary. Pilinszky was never involved in politics, he was an apolitical poet, but his human compassion for the sufferers and the victims of the deathcamps, artificially construed as a political stand, saved him from being ignored or relegated to the background.

Translating poetry is part and parcel of the poet's 'mission'. In the service of national culture Hungarian poets are expected to produce translations of quality, and in the past hundred and fifty years the majority of the best poets have indeed translated countless poems from foreign languages. The mission transcends national frontiers: according to Gyula Illyés (1902–83), who carried out his task with a prophet's fervour, one of the first duties of Hungarian poets living abroad is to translate and propagate the works written by their fellows at home. When the *Selected Poems* of Pilinszky were published in English, a Hungarian poet wrote to me, not without sarcasm, 'now you will be in the good books of Illyés' – meaning that I have at last discharged my duty as a poet in exile.

London, 1984

Postscript to János Csokits' Note
Ted Hughes

Among all the poems by Pilinszky that János Csokits and I translated, 'The Desert of Love' seem to be one of the most successful. Even now after such a long interval (and seventeen years since I first saw his literal version) I still do not see how I could take the poem further. A couple of places in it still trouble me slightly. 'Numb with brightness', in line 7, seems somewhat indistinct. I would have preferred 'numbed by' – but that releases a small avalanche of problems on into the next line. I see no way to recast the whole sentence and still retain what seems to me right about it. Then again, there has always seemed to me something inadequate about the last line, in my final version. That painful detail of feeling, focused in the tin cup, draws on the episode in the preceding verse, where the prisoner, tortured by thirst, begged for water and gulped it in such a way that the very sounds haunt him years after. But the consequent charge of anguish in that overturned cup is greatly sharpened, for me, by my experience of what a cup tends to do when you set it down in the straw with drink still in it. You think the straw is ideal for nesting the cup safely. What actually happens can seem almost diabolical. The straw begins to push up under one side of the cup and to sink away under the other side, till all at once the cup is over and your drink gone. There is something peculiarly shocking about it, when it happens. Fate seems to have a finger – and an especially malicious and petty finger at that – in such purposeful adjustments on the part of the straw. And the drink is so utterly gone, its disappearance is so total and irretrievable: not spilled onto a bare floor, from which it might have been lapped up, but vanished away down the thousand gappy lattice holes of the straw and in this case into the dung-soaked under-bedding. And the straw there, holding the empty cup, is now itself so proverbially empty, meaningless, inane. It is a potent little scenario. For me it is one of the line's most active secret components. It gathers the sense of Cosmic hopelessness into a familiar, intimate shock.

Yet my final version of the line suggests nothing of this. It merely indicates that the drinker dropped his drained cup into the straw, where it now lies on its side as an image of emptiness and degradation – a symbolic, filmic still. It serves its purpose, as a condensation point for the whole poem, and perhaps this is what Pilinszky intended. But I regret that János Csokits and I never questioned him about it. As it was, I tried hard to find some means of suggesting that compact drama of the way the straw behaved with the half-full cup of drink that the prisoner was trying to save for just a short while (or perhaps he only set it down to prolong his bliss). In the end I had to retreat to the single, static image.

When I look back at János Csokits' literal version of this line it assures me that my fantasy was superfluous (and probably illogical as well – and surely the prisoner was too thirsty not to have emptied the cup with those unforgettable gulpings). It confirms that I narrowly escaped injecting an embellishment into the structure of the text, and that my first principle of translating Pilinszky as literally as possible won out against my meddling self. It also shows me something else.

With all János Csokits' literal versions of Pilinszky's poems I came up against a happy difficulty, which is illustrated, I think, by his version of that last line. This difficulty lies in the fact that his literal renderings, very often, are all one could desire in a final version. When I go back through the whole poem in his literal version I see once more that the most effective lines in my final version have come through unaltered, or very little altered, from his crib. He produced, in other words, a mass of pure finds. And though we spent years tinkering with refractory lines and passages, I hung on to these windfalls to the end. To demonstrate what I mean, here is his literal version:

THE DESERT OF LOVE

A bridge, a hot concrete road,
the day is emptying out its pockets,
laying out in turn all its possession.
You are alone /by yourself/ in the catatonic twilight.

The country is like the bottom of a creased pit;
glowing scars in the dazzling darkness.
It is growing dusk. I am numb with brightness,
blinded by the sun. I never forget it's summer.

> It is summer and /it is/ flashing hot.
> They stand, /and/ I know their wings don't even quiver,
> the fowls, as burning cherubs
> in the planked /boarded-up/, splintered cages.
>
> Can you remember? First there was the wind;
> then the earth; then the cage.
> Fire and dung. And once in a while
> a few flaps of wings /wing-beats/, a few empty reflexes.
>
> And thirst. I asked for water /to drink/ then.
> Even today I hear the feverish gulps,
> and helplessly as the stone I bear
> and quench the delusions.
>
> Years are passing, years, and hope
> is like an overturned tin pot in the straw.

This is enough to show how lucky I was in having János Csokits as my guide. I am certain I would never have become as interested in Pilinszky as I eventually did, if my curiosity had not been caught in the first place by Csokits' swift word-for-word translations from the page at odd times during our long friendship. This facility of his had surprising qualities. His immediate English, as he translated, was always lucid and musical – quite often, in the way shown by the above, hitting on what might be called a poetic inevitability, in the shaping of a line. But even more exciting, for me, was the knack he had of projecting a raw, fresh sense of the strange original – the particular and to me alien uniqueness of the original. I know from experience with quite a few translators that this is a very rare ability. Most translators, inevitably, translate the strangeness of the original work into the standard of their own sensibility – and the best one can hope for is that their sensibility can adapt itself interestingly. But again and again János Csokits transmitted the characters of several quite different poets, while introducing me to modern Hungarian poetry. I still remember sections from various lyrics of his own that he translated, roughly, from the page as far back as 1961, and again their inner world is distinct and their flavour quite unique.

This faithfulness to the original is crucial in translating Pilinszky's poetry. All his poems can be called 'visions', in the sense that each one embodies a mystical experience, some confrontation undergone in an exceedingly peculiar and even super-normal state of illumination. They are spiritual disclosures, and to some degree they recreate the spiritual condition from which they are drawn – a compound of torment and ecstasy, an inner nakedness to some divine *fiat*, uniquely Pilinszkyan, which he expresses in a poetic medium that seems very pure, even chaste. This purity is perhaps no more than one aspect of his religious obedience to the experience. This sense of selfless, courageous testimony pushed to a near-saintly pitch is very strong in Pilinszky. It puts a translator under exacting obligations. There is no question of introducing anything from the translator's own poetical medicine bag. János Csokits' passion for exactitude, serving his passion for the originals, was perfectly suited to the task. And as I say, from my point of view his curious musical talent in English was a bonus. Reading over our translations now, and knowing how much the best things among them owe to him, I feel not so much like the co-pilot in Pilinszky's spaceship. As far as our translations are concerned, surely János Csokits is the co-pilot; I am quite sure my part is that of the troubled mechanic.

APPENDIX ONE

EGY KZ-LÁGER FALÁRA

Ahova estél, ott maradsz.
A mindenségből ezt az egyet,
ezt az egyetlen egy helyet,
de ezt azután megszerezted.

Menekül előled a táj.
Lehet az ház, malom vagy nyárfa,
minden csak küszködik veled,
mintha a semmiben mutálna.

De most már te nem tágitasz.
Megvakitottunk? Szemmel tartasz.
Kifosztottunk? Meggazdagodtál.
Némán, némán is reánkvallasz.

János Pilinszky:

ON THE WALL OF A KZ-LAGER

Where you have fallen there you remain.
From the universe you have <u>this place</u>,(1)
just this single place, (2)
but this one you have really <u>acquired</u>.

The country-side is <u>fleeing you</u>.(3)
Whether a <u>house</u>, a <u>mill</u> or a poplar,(4)
all <u>things</u> just <u>grapple</u> with you,
as if they were mutating in nothingness.

But now it is you who <u>wont give way</u>.(6)
(7) <u>Did we blind you</u>? <u>You keep us in sight</u>.(8)
<u>Did we rob you</u>? <u>You enriched yourself</u>.(9)
<u>Speechless, speechless</u> you accuse us.(10)

Postscript

Notes to My Letter of Philosophy: "On the Back of a K2 hope"

(1) - The second, third and fourth lines of the first stanza is one single sentence — the predicate, "acquired", is at the end of the fourth line. I had to choose whether to repeat the ~~field~~ expression "this one" or the word "place". I chose the second solution because this way there is a progression as in the original.

(2) - "Acquired" - or "obtained" or "secured".

(3) - The country-side fleeing him is the same idea as the one in "Harbach 1944" where the villages "go out of the way" or "avoid" the convicts. I did not want to use "runs away from you" because it is longer and too strong.

(4) - ~~grapple at~~ — In Hungarian you have this in singular like "all is just grappling with you" or "everything is just grappling" etc...

(5) - "grapple" or "struggle" — I think that struggle is too much. It is a slow, painful and ~~little~~ hesitant tussling.

(6) - "went his way" or "went onward". I prefer the first.

⑦ — "Did we blind you" or "have we blinded you"?
"Did we rob you" or "have we robbed you"?
I chose the first because I have the impression that
it is more compact and strong. — But you must
decide whether I am wrong about the tense.
Instead of "rob" you may use "loot". I think the
first is closer to the original.

⑧ — "You keep us in sight" — in the sense of "watching."

⑨ — "You enriched yourself" or "You became rich".

⑩ — Instead of "speechless, speechless" — "mutely, mutely"
is also possible. It is very difficult to render
the meaning of the last word without becoming
too long. The nearest thing would be — instead
of "you accuse us," — "you bear witness against us,"
or "you testify against us,", both too technical.
"You expose us," is not bad, but I feel it is
not telling as ~~strong~~ hard as, the "you accuse us".

On the wall of KZ-lager.

Where you have fallen, there you stay.
From the whole Universe, you have this one place
but this single place
but this one you have really secured.

          has abandoned you
The country side ~~of course it~~
~~Whether House, mill, poplar~~
Whether a house, a mill, or a poplar
Everything shuffles not ~~you~~
as if it were matters in nothingness.

But now it is you who wait more.
~~Have~~ Did we ~~failed~~ you? You go on waiting us.
~~Did up not you?~~
~~Have~~ Did we ~~failed~~ you? You have enriched yourself.
Speechless, speechless, you judge us.

On the walls of K.Z. Lager.

Where you have fallen, you stay. *is your*
~~For~~ In the whole Universe (you have) this one place
Just this single place
but this one you have really ~~secured~~. But this is yours for certain.

The ~~country~~ side *wonder* words, you
whether a have a mill, or a poplar
end they ~~toil~~ *struggle from* to be free of you
as if it were metal top in nothingness.

                                        stay.
But now it is you who ~~wait~~ move.
Did we ~~bid~~ you? You (so as) watch for us.
Yes Have we ~~robbed~~ you? You enriched yourself.
Speechless, speechless, you ~~bear~~ *witness* against
                              testify   us.

ON THE WALL OF A KZ-LAGER

Where you have fallen, you stay.
In the whole universe, this is your place.
Just this single spot.
But you have made this yours absolutely.

The countryside evades you.
House, mill, poplar,
each thing strives to be free of you
as if it were mutating in nothingness.

But now it is you who stay.
Did we blind you? You continue to watch us.
Did we rob you? You enriched yourself.
Speechless, speechless, you testify against us.

APPENDIX TWO

VAN GOGH IMÁJA

Csatavesztés a földeken.
Honfoglalás a levegőben.
Madarak, nap és megint madarak.
Estére mi marad belőlem?

Estére csak a lámpasor,
a sárga vályogfal ragyog,
s a kert alól, a fákon át,
mint gyertyasor, az ablakok;

hol én is laktam, s nem lakom,
a ház, hol éltem, és nem élek,
a tető, amely betakart.
Istenem, betakartál régen.

János Pilinszky:

THE PRAYER OF VAN GOGH

(1)
Defeat suffered in the fields.
(2)
Country conquered in the air.
Birds, the sun, and birds again.
What will remain of me by night?

By night only the row of lamps, (3)
the yellow wall of abode,
and from the far end of the garden, through the trees, }—(8)
the windows gleam, like candles in a row;
(5)
where I, too, have dwelt, and do not dwell,
(6)
the house, where I have lived and do not live,
the roof, which had me covered up. (7)
(4)
My God, you used to cover me in the past.

(from "Splinters")

Postscript

Notes to my literal of Pilinszky's "The Prayer of Van Gogh"

This one gave me a lot of trouble and I am not satisfied with the result, hence the number of points I have to take up with you. I am certain that this poem should be in the book — it is the only piece which can be considered as a natural link between Pilinszky's former and present style. But my literal will need a lot doctoring. I hope you can make head or tail of this!

(1) — The first word in Hungarian "Csatavesztés", literally translated "battlelosing". The first meaning is, as it says, the losing of a battle. The second, however, means "defeat". I have the impression that Pilinszky wanted to have the second meaning but also the atmosphere of the first meaning.

(2) — The first word in the second line is untranslatable. The dictionary can give only "description or interpretation" in English word. Translated literally "honfoglalás" would mean "countryoccupying" or "countryoccupying". It is employed only for the conquest by Hungarians, of their present country. The event took place in 896, after Christ.

(refer to "The prayer of Van Sösh" – continued)

(2) I don't think, however, that Pilinszky wants to have here any reference to this matter — he simply uses the word instead of request, or compassion, etc.

(3) He uses twice the word "van" — both for the lamps and for the candles.

(4) Difficult structure. The predicate, "gleam," is, in the original, at the end of the second line, but is valid also for the rest of the sentence which runs through the stanzas and continues in the next. I think the way I worked it out gives at least an idea of what goes on in the original.

(5) (6) In the third stanza, Pilinszky uses first the word "lakhat" (and "lakhom") then the word "élhet" (and "élhetem") which both mean exactly the same thing: the verb to say to be live, somewhere. "Élek" means, in English, "I live" where, "lakom" is rather "I dwell", but

(Note to "The prayer of Van Gogh" - Continued)

(5)(6) An Hungarian "lakom" is not as mannered or literary as "dwell" is in English. As a matter of fact, this is the word which people mostly use when they want to say that they live somewhere. When they use "élek" to say the same thing, they exactly mean that they are at home in that place, hence they really live [there] and not only "dwell" there.

Where he says "and do not dwell" and then "and do not live", he really means "and dwell no more" and "and live no more". But I couldn't say so in the text because it is a literal and philosophy does not use the word which would enable me to say "no more" or "any longer" in English.

(Note to "The prayer of Van Gogh Confined")

7th (f) The word *Pitäistäpä* here, in the last two lines, is the one usually employed for someone covering up someone — such as, a mother covers up (tucks in) her child in the bed, etc. He speaks here like a sulking child dissatisfied with the parental service.

I wish God had tucked him in, and covered him with whatever he wished to be covered with — — this would have spared (him and) us the labors of this translation ...

The Prayer of Van Gogh

Crushing defeat in the fields.
Occupying the air.
Birds, the sun, and again God.
By night(fall) what will be left of me?

At night only the row of camps gleaming,
the yellow wall of the room
and from the far end of the garden, through the trees,
like a row of candles, the windows.

Were I, too, have lived and do not live
the name, which was my home and is not
the one, which she (was) me
at they (it)? Then you sheltered me.

The Prayer of Van Gogh

Humbling defeat in the fields
to air claimed by invaders.
God, + the sun, and again God.
What will be left
by night fall what will be left of me?

If night only the row of lamps
the yellow wall of baked mud
and from the far end of the park, strange fig trees
like a row of candles, the windows

Where I, too, dwell do not dwell
the house which was where I lived do not live
the roof, which enclosed + sheltered over.
Oh God, then you sheltered me, enfolded me,
the roof which wrapped me like a mother
Ah God, then you enfolded me like a mother.

THE PRAYER OF VAN GOGH

Humbling defeat in the fields.
The air seized by invaders.
Birds, and the sun, and again birds.
By night what will be left of me?

At night only the row of lamps
the yellow wall of dry mud
and from the bottom of the garden, through trees,
like a row of candles---the windows,

where I, too, dwelt and do not dwell,
the house where I lived and do not live,
the roof which tucked me in—like a mother.
Ah God, then you covered me up, like a mother.

[handwritten annotations:]

in order not to repeat "like a mother,"
could you say here something like

"tucked me in gently" or
"tucked me in safely" ?

THE PRAYER OF VAN GOGH

Humbling defeat in the fields.
The air held by invaders.
Birds, the sun, and again birds.
By night what will be left of me?

At night only the row of lamps
the yellow wall of dry mud
and from the bottom of the garden, through trees,
like a row of candles, the windows,

where I too, dwelt and do not dwell,
the house where I lived and do not live,
the roof which tucked me in safely.
Ah God, then you covered me up safely.

Kafka and the Golem
Translating Paul Celan
John Felstiner

Einem, der vor der Tür stand, eines	To one who stood before the door, one
Abends:	evening:
ihm	to him toward
tat ich mein Wort auf –: zum	I opened my word –: ~~to~~ the
Kielkropf sah ich ihn trotten, zum	clod I saw him trot~~ting~~, ~~to the~~ toward
halb–	the half–
schürigen, dem	baked begot
im kotigen Stiefel des	brother ~~born~~ in ~~the~~ a
Kriegsknechts	dough boy's ~~hireling's~~
geborenen Bruder, dem	dung-caked, boot, ~~him~~
mit dem blutigen	~~with his blood~~ him with his
Gottes–	god–
gemächt, dem	~~on God's~~ like loins
schilpenden Menschlein.	~~handiwork, the~~ all bloody, the
	chittering manikin.
Rabbi, knirschte ich, Rabbi Löw:	Rabbi, I gnashed, Rabbi Loew:
Diesem	For this one –
beschneide das Wort,	circumcise *his* word,
diesem	for this one –
schreib das lebendige	write the living
Nichts ins Gemüt,	Nothing~~ness~~ on his heart,
diesem	for this one
spreize die zwei	spread your two
Krüppelfinger zum heil–	cripple ~~bent~~ fingers in a
bringenden Spruch.	~~sav~~ safe –
Diesem.	~~ing saying.~~ keeping prayer.
	For this one

....	....
Wirf auch die Abendtür zu, Rabbi.	And slam (shut) the evening door, Rabbi.
....	....
Reiß die Morgentür auf, Ra- –	Throw the morningdoor open, Ra- –

Because attentiveness or *Aufmerksamkeit* – as in a saying that Walter Benjamin took to identify Kafka's genius and that Paul Celan then took up in thinking of his own poetic practice: 'Attentiveness is the natural prayer of the soul' – because attentiveness mattered so critically to Celan, I try in translating him to make translating into the fullest possible and the closest act of reading and of writing.[1] A translator, I think, needs to become the reader *par excellence* – or perhaps I should say *par exigence*. Here I would borrow from Kafka's *Trial*, where Joseph K., trying to interpret the parable 'Before the Law', is told by a priest: 'The Scripture is unalterable and its interpretations often merely betray bewilderment at this.'[2]

At the enigmatic text before me now, '*Einem, der vor der Tür stand*', 'To one who stood before the door',[3] I feel a kindred bewilderment. I can at least perceive in this poem a dynamic linking divine creative speech to failing mortal clay. And I think I hear Paul Celan crying out for admission into a spiritual realm that we may (unknowingly) suppose he entered when in mid-career, a quarter-century after the catastrophe that took away his parents, culture and homeland, he took his own life by drowning. To begin tracing him through this poem, I think of what Franz Rosenzweig once said about his work on Judah Halevi: 'I myself understand a poem only when I have translated it.'[4]

Einem, in the dative, an indefinite pronoun initiating a subordinate clause followed by a colon; then a second dative, *ihm*, with a line to itself, leading to a dash and another colon: punctuation, line breaks, syntax and grammar already seem to compose the law of this poem, as if language and speech themselves formed a prior, primary reality governing anything the poem may refer to. Yet a translator's exactness with these technical elements does not dispel the reader's questions. Who is speaking, and to whom? Before what door, and when – Shabbat, or some other pivot in time? Maybe the fact of a door barring entrance to something matters more at first than the something behind it.

> To one who stood before the door, one
> evening:
> to him
> I opened my word.

'*ihm / tat ich mein Wort auf*'. Usually with *auftun* in the German Bible – in Job and Psalms, for instance – a divine or human speaker opens his mouth or lips, or doors and gates open up. In Celan's poem, a word is opened, but what word – or does the very act of opening, of speaking, matter most here?

Now if line by line I seem to be deferring and frustrating the interpretive impulse, I think Celan's poem requires just that of its reader-translator. We have not even come to the close of a sentence yet; and we have not yet come upon Rabbi Loew.

Having opened his word to someone standing before the door, the speaker saw him approach someone else. A broken, staggered syntax and an impasto of crude, animal-like images convey this scene. I sense here a derisiveness pulsing through all five adjectives with the same dropping cadence: *schürigen, kotigen, geborenen, blutigen, schilpenden* – a derisiveness I have tried to catch in fairly rough sound and rhythmic patterns:

> ... toward the
> clod I saw him trot, toward
> the half-
> baked
> brother begot in a
> doughboy's dung-caked boot,
> him with his god-
> like loins all
> bloody, the
> chittering manikin.

What is the 'clod', the *Kielkropf*, that spawns these phrases? A dialect term meaning changeling, abortion, monster or, colloquially, dolt; my word 'clod' indicates an earthy, soulless creature like the golem, but it loses the idea of something misbegotten and also weakens the bite of *Kielkropf*, with those two sharp k's that cut through again in *Kriegsknecht*. To regain a little in translation, instead of 'born' I have said 'begot' in a boot, for the verb's raw rhyme with 'trot' and its half-biblical, half-bestial overtones.

If Celan has the golem in mind here, he has certainly laded on more than its usual legendary traits. The word *half-schürig* – 'of the second shearing', i.e. imperfect – does tally closely with the biblical term *golem*, 'unformed', and also with the colloquial sense of 'golem', a dumbhead; both senses are perhaps audible in the English 'half-baked'. But Celan's next phrase gives a strange lineage to this creature the doorkeeper trotted toward, this 'brother begot in a / doughboy's dung-caked boots'.[5] Possibly some folk tale lies behind the image, with muck on a trooper's boot making do for the clay that formed humankind. Yet the *Kriegsknecht*, a 'mercenary', still baffles me. In sixteenth-century and later versions the golem as bodyguard or spy does defend Jews against their enemies, yet no source I have been able to find says that Joseph Golem actually served as a hired soldier, much less that he was born in the boot of one.[6] Provisionally, 'doughboy' will do for a common trooper, and the word jostles interestingly with 'dung-caked'. It also suggests the shaping of Adam, the miracle of creating human life that so powerfully underlies the golem tradition. In a kind of sacred parody written not long before this poem, and called 'Psalm', Celan begins by countering Creation: 'No one kneads us again out of earth and clay, / no one conjures our dust.'[7] This 'psalm', a quintessential expression of despair after the Jewish catastrophe, makes a bleak backdrop to the poem *'Einem, der vor der Tür stand'*, with its wretched creaturely hero.

Now why *Bruder*? Is this creature a brother to the 'one who stood before the door', the one who trots toward him? Is he something less worthy, an Esau perhaps, deprived of blessing, or even a Cain, the baneful side of humankind? Celan sees him with a bloody 'form', and here the word *Gemächt*, an unusual term, gives me pause. In Psalm 103:14 Luther uses it to translate the Hebrew *yetser*, 'frame': 'For He knoweth our frame; He remembereth that we are dust.' That Hebrew root occurs in Genesis 2:7, 'God *formed* man of the dust of the ground', and in *Sefer Yetsirah*, the third-century Book of Creation from which derived the earliest idea of magically fashioning a person such as the golem. So *Gemächt* signifies something made, and *Gottesgemächt*, 'God's handiwork'. But Celan's creature, created in the image of God, has blood on his frame. What is more, *Gemächt* can also mean something else: the male genitals; indeed for *dem blutigen Gottesgemächt* a French version of this poem has *le membre sanglant de Dieu*, 'God's bloody member'.[8] Although I cannot quite see Celan entertaining such an image, his poem (like the golem legend) certainly involves the question of (pro)creativeness as well as createdness. I try to resolve both senses of *Gemächt*, 'frame' and 'generative power', in the word 'loins'. I call them 'godlike' to reflect the Genesis story, and I break the word to replicate Celan's line-break, which (if only momentarily and prosodically) sunders God from his handiwork.

But why then 'bloody'? If this brother has something of Cain in him, then his 'brother's blood cries out from the ground' (Gen. 4:10). Or we remember that the Golem defended Prague's Jews against the Passover blood libel. Or perhaps bloody loins really signal the idea of circumcision that will decisively enter this poem in a moment; after all, the painful violence of 'his godlike loins all bloody' might possibly express Paul Celan's sense of having been inscribed in the Mosaic covenant. Fortunately a translation does not entail specifying one sense or another. I think the clod-brother-manikin in some way incarnates the animal and unredeemed side of human nature, and thus may reflect all those possibilities lodged in 'blood'. As in Psalm 139:16, the only biblical occurrence of the word *golem*, this creature is imperfect, Adam not yet touched by the breath of God. Then remembering that Rabbi Loew's homunculus cannot speak helps explain why this *schilpenden Menschlein* is called a chirping, or cheeping, or twittering, or chittering manikin.

Here the speaker stops, and moves from report – 'I opened my word', 'I saw him trot' – into direct speech. This brief transition –

> Rabbi, I gnashed, Rabbi
> Loew:

– becomes the poem's fulcrum, identifying as the Maharal of Prague the person who stood before the door and trotted toward the manikin. And in one unexpected verb, *knirschte*, 'gnash' or 'grate' or 'grind', the speaker takes on a desperateness that imbues everything he says from here on. Simply to utter the word 'Rabbi', which appears nowhere else in Celan's ten books of poetry, and to utter it twice, bespeaks for him a rare because openly Jewish urgency. In early 1961, when I believe he wrote this poem, Celan was acutely afflicted by a public charge of plagiarism against him and by its connection to recent German anti-semitism.[9] He might well have turned then to the wonder-working Prague Rabbi, the man whose golem fought against libel. And the name *Löw* itself, poised alone as an entire verse, may be calling up Celan's father Leo, in Russian Lev. Around the time of this poem Celan jokingly signed a letter 'Pavel Lvovitsch', Paul son of Lev.[10] As a boy he had not felt close to his father, a man whose Orthodox, Zionist persuasions represented a Judaism which, but for the Nazi war, he might have sloughed off.[11] So to single out the name *Löw* in this poem grounds a religious and historical urgency in a difficult private invocation.

After this invocation, again pointed by a colon, we hear twelve lines of direct speech for the duration of the poem. A much firmer syntax and grammar move these lines than in the poem's first half. And now a demonstrative pronoun, again a dative, opens the sentence:

> Diesem
> beschneide das Wort.

Celan builds so much into the dative with its verb that I have (reluctantly) added punctuation and emphasis to make this fulcral point decisive in English:

> For this one –
> circumcise *his* word.

Here again an enigmatic figure generates a cluster of possibilities. Given Celan's inexhaustible linguistic curiosity, a pun on *brit mila* – Covenant of the 'Word' as well as of circumcision – may inhabit the phrase *beschneide das Wort* (a pun audible only in the phrase's Hebrew overtones and thus not for German ears). 'For this one – circumcise *his* word', the speaker pleads, meaning not only the wordless golem but someone like Moses of 'uncircumcised lips' (Exod. 6:12), perhaps the poet himself in exile and wanting prophetic speech. The only English translation I know of renders this phrase as 'remove the word', since *beschneiden* does literally mean 'to cut off'.[12] Yes, Rabbi Loew removes the name of God from the golem's mouth every Shabbat, and ultimately tears away the aleph from *emeth*, 'truth', on the creature's forehead, leaving him *meth*, 'dead'. But an image of cutting off would deter the prayer rising in this sentence: 'For this one . . . for this one . . . for this one.' If only because Nazism construed circumcision as a fatal sign, I think

Celan would have wanted to 'circumcise the word', to bring his own German language itself, however murderously abused, somehow within the covenant. Jacques Derrida has called circumcision *une blessure lisible*.[13] Virtually every poem Celan wrote bears a 'legible wound'.

And no other figure of speech exposes that wound as acutely as paradox:

> for this one
> write the living
> Nothing on his heart

Again I regret having to use three words for Celan's inflected pronoun, especially now that the charged word *diesem*, flush left and filling a line of its own, begins to give a vertebral structure to this plea or prayer. As for the paradox of 'living Nothing', it may well be *emeth* written on the golem's forehead and then removed. But it also belongs to a larger dimension, as does the paradox of circumcision, the wound that sanctifies an organ of regeneration. 'The Nothing is the Nothing of God . . . from which all true Creation springs,' writes Gershom Scholem, whom Celan was reading at the time.[14] Yet a poet who had felt the pain of annihilations as if inscribed on his own back could not wholly regard *das Nichts* as sheer creative potential. For a survivor the paradox retains historical, experiential force, palpable even in the turn of Celan's verse, the sudden break after *lebendige*: 'write the living / Nothing on his heart'.[15]

And why 'write' it? Celan came to prize the kabbalistic theory of language and creation: 'Every word' – he marked this sentence once in Scholem's little book *The Secrets of Creation* – 'Every word is a name of God.'[16] Yet long before that Celan had felt his mother tongue become one and the same with life, with survival. 'In the midst of the losses,' he said after the war, 'this one thing remained: language.'[17] It was literally all he had left. He wrote – not as if, but because his life depended on it. So a poem that says *'schreib' das lebendige Nichts*, 'write' the paradox of life and death, only makes explicit an imperative implied in every poem.

Now a third *diesem*, holding to the spine of the poem, comes to enforce the dative case with its power of 'giving' to or going towards someone:

> diesem
> spreize die zwei
> Krüppelfinger zum heil-
> bringenden Spruch.

With no more syllables, an English version can attempt equivalence:

> for this one
> spread your two
> cripple-fingers in a safe-
> keeping prayer.

What English as always cannot do, however, is mimic the intimacy built up in *beschneide, schreib* and now *spreize*, three imperatives spoken in the second person singular. This form of address to Rabbi Loew seems slightly surprising, just as when Joseph K. uses it to a priest in *The Trial*'s cathedral scene.

Why then *two* fingers? For a while I tried various explanations: Do those bent fingers form the name of the Almighty, *Shaddai*, as in an ancient benediction? – but that would take three fingers![18] Do they symbolize the two-letter combinations recited by medieval golem-makers?[19] Finally on last Rosh Hashanah morning, much later than it should have, the correct image dawned on me: spread the third and fourth fingers of each upraised hand in the Priestly Blessing (Num. 6:24–7). 'The Lord bless thee, and keep thee': with these words in mind, I changed my 'sav-ing saying' – so as to cleave to Celan's *heil- / bringenden Spruch* – into 'safe-keeping saying', and then, for a better rhythm and sound, into 'safe-keeping prayer'. Yet the word 'prayer' may lose more than my prosody gains: namely the fact of 'saying', as in *Segensspruch*, German for 'benediction'. This whole poem has proceeded by virtue of language and speech: 'I opened my word', 'the chittering manikin', 'circumcise his word', 'write the living Nothing', and now a benedictive 'saying'. Well, perhaps in some other world the translation will come right!

We should still ask why these two fingers are not straight but bent, maimed, stunted, stumped, crooked. I tried all those adjectives, to stress the paradox in this blessing, and then realized that the cognate does it best: 'cripple-fingers' for *Krüppelfinger*. Images of a bruised, broken or contradicted faith abound in Celan's poetry, above all in the 1963 volume that includes this poem, *Die Niemandsrose* ('The No-One's-Rose').[20] The year before he had given an East German magazine *'Einem, der vor der Tür stand'* plus two other poems of a similar temper.[21] One of them begins:

> You prayer-, you blasphemy-, you
> prayersharp knives
> of my
> silence.
>
> You my words with me go-
> ing crippled, you
> my straight ones.

Such writing resists the need Celan's readers often feel to rationalize his harshest paradoxes. Likewise the appeal to Rabbi Loew comes to full stop in an opposition, a healing yet crippled word, the only kind of truth Celan could credit. Then a final verse, *Diesem*, gathers into one word the plea that blessing and safekeeping, light and graciousness, favour and peace be granted 'For this one', for a half-baked, misbegotten, bloody, cheeping handiwork of God.

After this highly liturgical period, *Diesem . . ., diesem . . ., diesem . . . Diesem,* a pause ensues, longer than any line- or stanza-break – and alas, the only thing a translation can perfectly convey. Clearly this silence marks off a time of waiting, of expectation. Then the speaker goes on, still in the intimate imperative of prayer:

> Wirf auch die Abendtür zu, Rabbi.
> . . . .
> Reiß die Morgentür auf, Ra- –

Not much defies translation here, except perhaps the German verbs' separable prepositions *zu* and *auf,* reserving their impact until the end of the phrase. English can try this with adjectives:

> And slam the eveningdoor shut, Rabbi.
> . . . .
> Throw the morningdoor open, Ra- –

Maybe my adjectives even take Celan's prepositions up a few decibels – not unjustifiably, I hope.

The poem climaxes here, if beseeching alone can make a climax. And wherever they may ultimately lead, these doors first lead us back to the beginning – not only to the poem's beginning, where 'To one who stood before the door, one evening . . . I opened my word', but to Genesis itself: 'And there was evening and there was morning: one day.' This poem of Celan's has at heart to do with the mystery of creation, or more truly, with mortal access to the mystery of creation and renewal. Is this evening encounter a Sabbath encounter? Does evening give way to morning? We can hope so. On another level Celan's plea to shut the *Abendtür* and open the *Morgentür* carries overtones of *Abendland* and *Morgenland*, Occident and Orient; in his letters of the time he turns away from 'this so golden West' toward Eastern Europe and his homeland.[22] But whatever they ask, the poem's last two imperatives, like the three before them, do not necessarily guarantee a response.

An earlier poem also speaks of two doors in a way that can darken our sense of Rabbi Loew's *Abendtür* and *Morgentür*.[23] Celan wrote 'Epitaph for François' in 1953, when a son born to his wife Gisèle died within hours of birth:

> The world's two doors
> stand open:
> opened by you
> at twinight.
> We hear them banging, banging . . .

The doors of life and of death stand dreadfully close to each other, as Celan already knew well enough. So when his later poem asks Rabbi Loew to 'slam the eveningdoor shut . . . Throw the morningdoor open', the hope, the force of this prayer must reside in the asking.

At this point another kind of source for the evening and morning doors comes to mind. It occurred to me, again much later than it should have but in fact on Yom Kippur, that Celan's final appeal in this poem echoes the Neilah prayer at sunset on the Day of Atonement: 'Open the gates to us when the gates are being closed, for the day is about to set. The day shall set, the sun shall go down and set – let us enter Your gates!' Whether Celan actually had this paradox of salvation in mind, or had it dimly in mind, matters only up to a point. If he did, it would firmly orient his poem, and would certainly make me grip my pen more firmly as I translate. But even the fact that earlier on Yom Kippur Psalm 103 is sung, in which God 'knoweth our frame', our *Gemächt* that is formed from dust – even this coincidence does not make Celan's poem a Yom Kippur cipher so much as it manifests the deeper coherence of his poetic imagination. He never made an explicit religious profession or wholehearted commitment, like Franz Rosenzweig, who converted *to* Judaism, as it were, after a Yom Kippur service. So I see the Neilah prayer as confirmation rather than source for the poem's closing lines.

Something unexpected and unliturgical happens at the very close of this poem. In the magazine version Celan had written *Reiß die Morgentür auf, Ra . . .*, with three dots after *Ra . . .*, a sort of trailing off or giving up. Later he changed that to *Ra* with a hyphen and a dash – not merely to prevent the interference of an Egyptian sun god supplanting a Prague rabbi, but to break off his own voice more abruptly. The hyphen ruptures a word, the dash ruptures speech. To translate effectively, need one only reproduce punctuation and not decide the vital question: whether this muting signifies an end or an onset, darkness or radiance, exile or entrance? I think again of Rosenzweig, his voice paralyzed for years, dictating as he died what 'the Lord has truly granted to me', 'the point of all points for which there . . .'[24] I think also of Kafka, speechless at the end from tuberculosis of the larynx. Of course the golem story itself, in which Rabbi Loew tears the holy name from his creature's mouth, furnishes close enough reference for the sudden end to Celan's poem. And by now the poet has grown into the golem-figure; in pleading 'For this one . . . for this one', he ends up pleading for himself.

Paul Celan's final silence remains open to the largest possibilities. Nightfall or morning: he had to tolerate that irreconcilable ambiguity at the heart of his Judaism, living as he did in exile while holding somehow to a spiritual expectation. So he put the hyphen after *Ra-*, breaking off a Jew's appeal in mid-voice. Yet the dash can point to something still to come.

Here the poem stops, and by rights this essay in translation ought to stop at the same moment. But throughout it all a presence has been hovering that I want to bring forward. Franz Kafka's parable *'Vor dem Gesetz'*, 'Before' or 'In Front of' the Law, first came into Celan's hands when he was sixteen or seventeen.[25] Then just after the war, in Bucharest, he translated it into Rumanian, and in 1959 he underscored some thoughts about it in Walter Benjamin's Kafka essay.[26] The parable begins quite simply: 'Before the Law stands a doorkeeper. To this doorkeeper comes a man from the country and asks for entrance into the Law. But the doorkeeper says he cannot grant him entrance now. The man thinks it over and then asks if he'll be permitted to enter later. "It's possible," says the doorkeeper, "but not now."'

Celan's lifelong, adherent kinship with Kafka starts with childhood, where they both felt the burden of an unsympathetic father caught between petit bourgeois and normative Jewish behavior; Celan once told a friend that Kafka's *Letter to His Father* had to be written over and over again in Jewish homes.[27] And Celan sometimes associated his mother, cherished throughout his poetry while the father appears only once, with Bohemia and Prague: he calls Bohemia his mother's 'three-year land' because she fled there during the first world war.[28] In Czernowitz, the Austrian Empire's eastern outpost ceded to Rumania after 1918, a German-speaking Jew could feel alien both nationally and linguistically, as likewise in Prague. Early in 1962, at the high pitch of his anxiety about post-war anti-semitism, Celan adopted a refrain from Kafka's story 'A Country Doctor' – *'s ist nur ein Arzt*, 'it's only a doctor' – and signed a letter with it: *'s ist nur ein Jud*, 'it's only a Jew'.[29] Both writers tried at times to counter their displacement as assimilated western Jews by gravitating toward eastern or hasidic Judaism, and Kafka even sketched in his diary a version of the golem theme.[30]

First and last, Celan identified with the writer in Kafka. Fleeing Bucharest in 1947, Celan carried a letter of introduction from his mentor, calling his poetry 'the only lyric pendant to Kafka's work'.[31] Later he would buy first editions of Kafka and give his French students Kafka to read and translate. Writing in April 1970 to an Israeli friend, Celan said his Kafka seminar was going well, and he quoted Kafka's remark about the difficulty of getting happiness from writing – 'happiness only if I can raise the world into the pure, the true, the immutable'.[32] Ten days later Celan took his own life.

At bottom, I think Celan saw in Kafka a radical, essentially human estrangement. He marked vigorously the diary passage where Kafka asks: 'What have I in common with Jews? I have hardly anything in common with myself.'[33] Yet he also knew that the seemingly nameless, causeless *Angst* of Kafka's protagonists, grounded though it was in Austrian bureaucratic Prague, had still to find its ultimate name and cause in Nazism. Celan's guilt at having survived when his parents did not, his loneliness in France, his corrosive suspicion that neo-Nazism and anti-semitism were preying upon him – these anxieties have a more drastic and specific basis than Kafka's.

Despite – or I should say because of – this historical rift between the two writers, Celan's poem 'To one who stood before the door' compellingly recalls the voice of Kafka's parable *'Vor dem Gesetz'*. 'You're very friendly to me,' Joseph K. tells the priest in *The Trial*, 'With you I can speak openly.' Then K. hears the parable in which a man waits many years, beseeching a doorkeeper for entrance into the Law. The man grows old and finally almost blind and deaf. 'But now in the dark he perceives a radiance that streams inextinguishably from the door of the Law.' Gathering all his years of trial into one question, the man asks why, since everyone strives after the Law, no one but himself has come demanding admission. 'No one else could obtain admission here,' the doorkeeper shouts at the dying man, 'because this entrance was meant only for you. I will now go and shut it.'

In rehearsing Celan's poem with Kafka in the wings, I see the poet stationing himself within the frame of the parable and hear him opening his word to a guardian of the Law. Maybe this guardian trots over towards the only sort of person eligible for entrance into the Law, one of those animal-like creatures ridden with guilt in Kafka's stories. And now the crude name 'Kafka' itself seems to crop up in Celan's text. Possibly the double k's in this poem's *Kielkropf* and *Kriegsknecht* are hidden signatures – I should have translated: 'toward the *klutz* I saw him trot, toward the half-baked brother begot in a *kossack*'s dung-caked boot'.[34]

'For this one' Celan's poem intercedes, commingling the golem legend with Kafka's parable: for him some radiance or *Glanz*, as the parable says, may finally break from the door. Kafka's word *Glanz* sends me momentarily back to another poem Celan wrote just after his first son's death.[35] Entitled 'Assisi', it has 'animals trotting' toward Saint Francis, and the poem ends: *Glanz, der nicht trösten will, Glanz. / Die Toten – sie betteln noch, Franz*. 'Radiance that will not comfort, radiance. / The dead – they still go begging, Franz.' Speaking at once to the saint and to his lost son François, Celan also addresses the Franz whose parable promises radiance at the moment of death. The later poem, 'To one who stood before the door', also begs some of that radiance for a golem, a speechless creature revertible to clay and dust.

Finally the dative *Diesem* drops away and the poet speaks for himself. Just as we do not actually know whether Kafka's doorkeeper shuts the door or leaves it open, Celan can only ask for the eveningdoor shut, the morningdoor open. And as in Kafka we are never to hear the last word. In fact it literally breaks off.[36] 'Throw the morningdoor open, Ra- –', our poem ends, with that much prayer and no more. Let me close now with a motto from Kafka's notebook that holds equally for Celan and also, if I may say so, for his translator: *Schreiben als Form des Gebetes*, 'Writing as a form of prayer'.[37]

Notes

This essay originated as a paper for the Association for Jewish Studies, Boston, 16 December 1985. I wish to thank Gisèle Celan-Lestrange for her generous assistance in my work; Mary Lowenthal Felstiner for her critique of this essay; and Sigrid Mayer, Jerry Glenn, Al Hoelzel, James K. Lyon for their helpful counsel.

1. Walter Benjamin, 'Franz Kafka', in *Schriften*, ed. Th. W. Adorno and Gretel Adorno (Frankfurt, 1955) 2:222. For a translation of this and other essays see Benjamin, *Illuminations*, ed. Hannah Arendt, trans. Harry Zohn (New York, 1969) p. 134. Celan cited the sentence in his speech 'Der Meridian' (1960): Celan, *Gesammelte Werke* (Frankfurt: Suhrkamp, 1983) 3:198. (This collected edition, in five volumes, is hereafter referred to as *GW*.)
2. *Der Prozeß* (1925; Frankfurt, 1979) ch. 9, p. 185. All translations in this essay are mine.
3. *GW*, 1:242–3.
4. Letter to Margarete Susman, 22 Aug. 1924, in Franz Rosenzweig, *Briefe und Tagebücher*, 2 (1918–29) ed. Rachel Rosenzweig and Edith Rosenzweig Scheinmann (The Hague, 1979) p. 982.
5. Kafka's 'man from the country', who approaches the doorkeeper in 'Before the Law', evidently derives from the Hebrew *'am ha'arets*, 'the common people; an ignoramus', or literally a person of the land, and more literally of the earth: see Heinz Politzer, *Franz Kafka: Parable and Paradox* (Ithaca, NY, 1966) p. 174.
6. See Gershom Scholem, 'The Idea of the Golem', in *On the Kabbalah and Its Symbolism*, trans. Ralph Manhein (New York, 1969) pp. 158–204. Celan owned the German edition, *Zur Kabbala und ihrer Symbolik* (Zurich, 1960). On the golem legend see also Micha Josef bin Gorion, *Der Born Judas* (Wiesbaden, 1959); Sigrid Mayer, *Golem: Die literarische Rezeption eines Stoffes* (Bern, 1975).

7. *GW*, 1:225.
8. Celan, *La Rose de Personne*, trans. Martine Broda (Paris, 1979) p. 71.
9. For biographical material see John Felstiner, 'Paul Celan: The Strain of Jewishness', *Commentary* (April 1985) 44–55.
10. Letter to Reinhard Federmann, 23 Feb. 1962, in 'In Memoriam Paul Celan', *Die Pestsäule* 1 (Sept. 1972) 18.
11. For material on Celan's early years see Israel Chalfen, *Paul Celan: Eine Biographie seiner Jugend* (Frankfurt, 1979).
12. 'To One Who Stood at the Door', trans. Cid Corman, *Origin*, 3rd Series 15 (Oct. 1969): 34.
13. Derrida, 'Shibboleth', in Geoffrey Hartman and Sanford Budick (eds) *Midrash and Literature* (New Haven: Yale University Press, 1986). This paper was originally given in French at the International Paul Celan Symposium, University of Washington, Seattle, 14 Oct. 1984. Derrida also makes a connection between the opening of a door in this poem and Elijah, since the person holding the infant during circumcision sits on 'Elijah's Chair'.
14. *Von der mystischen Gestalt der Gottheit* (Zurich, 1962) p. 128. In his 1958 poem 'El Golem', Jorge Luis Borges twice makes his subject rhyme with 'Scholem': Mayer, p. 77.
15. For the word *Gemüt*, 'mind', 'soul' or 'spirit' would perhaps do better than 'heart'. Something of a poeticism, the word occurs only this once in Celan's poetry. I settle on 'heart', maybe by contagion with Judah *Lev* ben Bezalel, *Lev* being Hebrew for 'heart', or with the 'circumcision of the heart' (Deut. 10:16, 30:6).
16. *Die Geheimnisse der Schöpfung: Ein Kapitel aus dem Sohar* (Berlin, 1935) p. 29.
17. 'Ansprache anläßlich der Entgegennahme des Literaturpreises der freien Hansestadt Bremen' (1958) in *GW*, 3:185.
18. Joshua Trachtenberg, *Jewish Magic and Superstition* (New York, 1979) p. 80.
19. Scholem, *On the Kabbalah*, pp. 185–6.
20. *Die Niemandsrose* (Frankfurt, 1963).
21. *Sinn und Form* 14, 5–6 (1962) 701–3. The third poem was *Es war Erde in ihnen*', which begins:

> There was earth inside them, and
> they dug.
>
> they dug and dug, so their day
> went by, their night. And they did not praise God . . .

22. Letter to Alfred Margul-Sperber, 8 Feb. 1962, in 'Briefe an Alfred Margul-Sperber', *Neue Literatur*, 7 (1975): 57.
23. 'Grabschrift für François', *GW*, 1:105.
24. Rosenzweig, p. 1237.
25. Chalfen, p. 67. A recent article on the presence of Kafka in Celan's work does not mention 'Einem, der vor der Tür stand': Dietmar

Goltschnigg, 'Zur lyrischen Kafka-Rezeption nach 1945 am Beispiel Paul Celans', *Literatur und Kritik*, 197–8 (1985) 316–26.
26. *Zeitschrift für Kulturaustausch*, 3 (1982) 286.
27. Otto Pöggeler, 'Kontroverses zur Ästhetik Paul Celans (1920–1970)', *Zeitschrift für Ästhetik und allgemeine Kunstwissenschaft*, 25:2 (1980) 226.
28. Celan, 'Es is alles anders', *GW*, 1:285.
29. Kafka's story 'A Country Doctor' appeared in the same collection – *Ein Landarzt* (1919) – as the parable 'Before the Law'. The parable later formed part of *The Trial*, ch. 9. Celan's letter to Reinhard Federmann, 23 Feb. 1962, in 'In Memoriam', p. 18.
30. Kafka, *Tagebücher 1910–1923*, ed. Max Brod (Frankfurt, 1973) p. 310 (20 April 1916). Kafka reportedly liked the atmosphere of Prague's old Jewish quarter evoked in Gustav Meyrink's novel *Der Golem* (1915): Gustav Janouch, *Conversations with Kafka* (New York, 1953) p. 47. Johannes Urzidil says that one Friedrich Thieberger was a Hebrew teacher of Kafka's: 'Two Recollections', *The World of Franz Kafka*, ed. J.P. Stern (New York, 1980) p. 60; Thieberger later published *The Great Rabbi Loew of Prague* (London, 1955). Marthe Robert, *As Lonely as Franz Kafka*, trans. Ralph Manheim (New York, 1982), deals beautifully with Kafka's vexed Jewishness.
31. Letter from Alfred Margul-Sperber to Otto Basil, printed in part in *Plan* (Vienna) 6 (1948) 423; reprinted in Milo Dor, 'Paul Celan', in *Über Paul Celan*, ed. Dietlind Meinecke (Frankfurt, 1973) p. 282.
32. Kafka, *Tagebücher*, p. 333 (25 Sept. 1917).
33. Kafka, *Tagebücher*, p. 219 (8 Jan. 1914).
34. In a diary entry of 27 May 1914 (*Tagebücher*, p. 234) Kafka remarks: 'I find the letter K ugly, it almost sickens me yet I write it down, it must be characteristic of me.' Celan's poem 'In Prag' (ca. 1966) bears mention in relation to 'Einem, der vor der Tür stand'. Against a somewhat ghastly background, 'In Prag' speaks of the Hradcany Castle Hill, where alchemy was practised, and then of 'bone-Hebrew/ ground to sperm'.
35. 'Assisi' (1954), *GW*, 1:108.
36. In a 1966 poem ('Frankfurt, September', *GW*, 2:114) that quotes Kafka and plays on 'jackdaw', his name in Czech, Celan also recalls Kafka's tuberculosis of the larynx – the *Kehlkopf* – and his final story, 'Josephine the Singer'. The poem ends:

Der Kehlkopfverschlußlaut singt.	The glottal stop sings.

37. Kafka, 'Fragmente', in *Hochzeitsvorbereitungen auf dem Lande*, ed. Max Brod (Frankfurt, 1966) p. 348.

Brief Afterthoughts on Versions of a Poem by Hölderlin
Michael Hamburger

I have never kept any notes about the process of translating or felt any need to record the unconscious or conscious choices active in the process. So anything I can say about specific translations now is a reconstruction, as unreliable as any retrospective conjecture as to why one did one thing rather than another. Most of my later translations were done in a single session, with no variant drafts, only the odd correction made before or after first publication. One reason may be that I have been translating for forty years, and have come to know in advance whether I can translate a poem or not. There have been abortive efforts, of course, but I have thrown away the evidence. More often than not, the real preparation for my versions has been done not on sheets of paper that would serve as evidence of my choices and rejections, but in my head, over the years and decades, by living with a poem, assimilating it, grappling with its peculiarities.

That has been so with Hölderlin, the most difficult of the poets I have attempted to translate, because the most remote from English conventions and modes. Always dissatisfied with my Hölderlin versions, I returned to them again and again over the decades. If I were to make another attempt now – and that is unlikely – it would have to be different in kind from my earlier ones. In fact it would have to be the kind of translation I have never wished to produce – an imitation – and that would be an admission of defeat. It has also taken me more than a decade to translate as many poems of Paul Celan as I have been able to translate, but for slightly different reasons: not so much because Celan's poems are unlike any that have been written in English – though they are – but because I have had to immerse myself again and again in the totality of his work before this or that poem became translatable; and that has been a question of interpretation, of intelligibility, requiring some help from specialised Celan scholarship. After struggling with Hölderlin scholarship, on the other hand, I came to the conclusion that my guesses were as good as another man's; and my first versions, done when I was almost wholly ignorant of the most rigorous Hölderlin exegesis, differ only here and there from my later ones as far as interpretation is concerned.

The worksheets of my earlier Hölderlin versions – begun at school, at the age of fifteen or sixteen – were destroyed, like all my early manuscripts, but I do have a notebook into which I copied the finished drafts of these versions in 1941–2. This includes the poem whose stages I shall trace here in my renderings, 'Hälfte des Lebens' – called 'The Middle of Life' even in this earliest extant version, though the literal rendering would be 'Half of Life'. Since it is a free-verse poem, my successive versions of it were not subject to the radical reworking required for Hölderlin's odes and elegies when I had decided – between my first book of 1943 and the second of 1952 – that I must try to render their refractory metres. Here are the German text of the poem and my earliest extant version:

HÄLFTE DES LEBENS

Mit gelben Birnen hänget
Und voll mit wilden Rosen
Das Land in den See,
Ihr holden Schwäne,
Und trunken von Küssen
Tunkt ihr das Haupt
Ins heilignüchterne Wasser.

Weh mir, wo nehm' ich, wenn
Es Winter ist, die Blumen, und wo
Den Sonnenschein,
Und Schatten der Erde?
Die Mauern stehn
Sprachlos und kalt, im Winde
Klirren die Fahnen.

THE MIDDLE OF LIFE

With yellow pears the land,
And full of wild roses,

> Hangs down into the lake,
> O graceful swans,
> And drunk with kisses
> You dip your heads
> Into the hallowed sober water.
>
> Alas, where shall I find when
> Winter comes, flowers, and where
> Sunshine,
> And the shadows of earth?
> The walls stand
> Speechless and cold, in the wind
> Weathercocks clatter.

The wording of the version printed in 1943 in my first book collection, *Poems of Hölderlin*, is identical with the fair copy, except for a comma after 'kisses' and a hyphen between 'hallowed' and 'sober'. That hyphen is a concession to my awareness that the contraction *heilignüchtern* has a peculiar significance and weight in Hölderlin's poem, since it is a marriage of opposites pregnant with all the conflicts and conciliations of his working life, his thinking about poetry and the differences between ancient and modern sensibilities, Dionysos and Juno, Saturn and Jupiter, and much else. Nevertheless that hyphen did not please me.

This version remained unchanged in the 1952 book; but in my copy of that book I pencilled in changes that were to be implemented later. Since no other edition of my verse translations could appear before 1966, many of the emendations went into the prose version published by Penguin Books in their Penguin Poets series in 1961. This is the prose version of 'The Middle of Life':

With yellow pears and full of wild roses the land hangs down onto the lake, you lovely swans, and drunken with kisses you dip your heads into the holy and sober water.

Alas, where shall I find, when winter comes, the flowers, and where the sunshine and shadows of earth? The walls loom speechless and cold, in the wind weathercocks clatter.

The hyphen has been eliminated again. 'Lovely' has been substituted for 'graceful', because 'lovely' renders more of the many shades of meaning in the now archaic German word *hold* – 'dear', as well as 'beautiful' and 'graceful'. (Hölderlin was called 'Holder' in his youth by his friends.) 'Loom' has been substituted for 'stand', though the semantic gain – more menace – had to be weighed up against the sonic loss – that of the harsh 's' and 't', when it is harsh consonants that dominate the second half of the poem, as liquid and gentle ones do the first. (That consideration may have been operative in my choice of 'lovely', with its two 'l's.) 'Drunken', instead of 'drunk', is the one change pencilled into the 1952 version that did not outlast the interim prose rendering. Most probably I adopted it because it is so close to the German *trunken* – and close rhythmic correspondence was something I aimed at in all my successive versions, because rhythm is more essential to poetry than metre and the rhythm of this poem has a rightness that left me less freedom than Hölderlin's metrical verse – and rejected it again because it is too 'poetic'.

Whatever the reasons, 'drunken' was dropped again in what has remained my last version of the poem, as printed in the *Poems and Fragments* volume of 1966 and reprinted in its recent new edition (1980). (The poem, by the way, was originally a fragment – part of the draft of an unfinished longer poem – but Hölderlin made it a finished poem when he sent it out for publication with a batch of other short poems, the *Nachtgesänge*, the last poems he ever submitted for publication.) My last version reads as follows:

> THE MIDDLE OF LIFE
>
> With yellow pears the land
> And full of wild roses
> Hangs down into the lake,
> You lovely swans,
> And drunk with kisses
> You dip your heads
> Into the hallowed, the sober water.
>
> But oh, where shall I find
> When winter comes, the flowers, and where
> The sunshine
> And shade of the earth?
> The walls loom
> Speechless and cold, in the wind
> Weathercocks clatter.

Changes of punctuation – elimination of commas – in the first half have to do with my recognition that Hölderlin's use of syntax in poetry broke the rules of syntax in prose. He wrote an essay to explain the need for that. Yet I would not or could not go so far as to reproduce the 'architecture', as he called it, of the first line, most probably because I could not find a two-syllable verb that would have completed that line both semantically and rhythmically, as Hölderlin did, by placing the verb *before* its normal position in a prose sentence. Even Hölderlin resorted to the archaic two-syllable *hänget* (hangeth), but that form was still close enough to usage to be acceptable to him as a functional word. (What enacts the 'hanging' rhythmically in the first two lines is not the iambic metre but the feminine line endings, the trochees within the iambic line, and I have lost one of those, as well as the transposed verb that enacts it semantically within the first line.) To get the internal rhyme of *trunken/tunkt* I should have had to substitute 'dunk' for 'dip', and that would have been more than a little grotesque in the context. If I considered 'tipsy' for 'drunk' it must have struck me as inappropriate for swans that are swimming, not walking. The elimination of 'alas' needs no comment, though the rhythm demanded a redundant, because too logical, 'but'; and one that Hölderlin avoided, despite the prevalence of linking 'ands' and 'buts' in his other Pindaric hymns and fragments of that period. Nor could or would I attempt a closer approximation to the marriage of opposites in *heilignüchtern*, because in English a telescoping of the two words would have been much odder than in German. ('Holysober' would have conveyed little but oddity to anyone not versed in Hölderlin's thinking.) As for 'shade' in place of 'shadows', the German *Schatten* is ambiguous and could be either singular or plural. The comma after *Sonnenschein* in the German text could point to 'shadows' rather than 'shade', but I have taken it as a musical rest, a brief pause, rather than as a grammatical notation. My interpretation of the controversial last line has remained constant from the first version to the last, though no one can be sure that Hölderlin's *Fahnen* are not flags, either flapping in the wind with a sound so sinister that Hölderlin rendered it as a metallic or glassy clank, or frozen stiff.

Many other considerations that I have forgotten may have gone into the successive versions. All of them aimed at closeness to an original that has no parallel in any poem written in English around

1803. Aware as I am of the shortcomings of my sort of translation – mimetic translation one could call it, if one is not biased against it as Robert Lowell was when he wrote of 'taxidermists' – I still believe that there is something to be said for trying to convey the uniqueness of a text by translation, as opposed to writing a poem of one's own after cannibalising the more digestible parts of an existing text. There is no point in reopening these perennial questions of aim and kind here. (I touched on them in the Preface to my *Hölderlin: Poems and Fragments*.) That it is the cannibalisers who draw attention to themselves again and again is not astonishing, when the opposite procedure is a disappearing act.

Translating Martial and Vergil
Jacob Lowland among the Classics
Extracts from a talk by James S Holmes to the University of Iowa Translation Workshop, January 1984

I began life as an Iowa farm boy and went to high school – the high school no longer exists, near Clemons, north of State Center – where it was quite unheard of anyone wanting to learn a foreign language. And I remember a group of us tried to pressure the school into giving us a course in, of all things, Latin, and there just wasn't the possibility, because there simply wasn't a teacher to teach Latin. Nor was there anyone to teach another foreign language either. When I went to college – I got a BA, along the road, in Oskaloosa, from William Penn – I had the good fortune of having a brilliant Central European refugee as a teacher of German, who was really wasted on us. There he was, one of the world's authorities on Dante, teaching first- and second-year German. And we were all – practically all of us – Iowa farm kids. And for some reason or other, from the very beginning, learning another language – I was, of course, terribly hooked on poetry – got all tied up with immediately trying to translate poems from that other language into English. Of course my first attempts were miserable, but he encouraged me greatly. And then, when I went on to graduate school and suddenly to my own surprise got interested in Old English, not just as a linguistic exercise, but as a body of poetry that is very remote and still one of our roots, I started translating some of the shorter Old English poems, carefully avoiding Pound at the same time. So, it was natural that when, by a fluke, I ended up as a Fulbright teacher in Holland, one of the first things I did was to start asking around who the leading poets were, whom I should be reading, and actually, within a year, publishing my first two translations of poetry from the Dutch – in *Poetry Quarterly*, out of London. [. . .]

I've always had the problem, translating from the Dutch, that you feel – even though I don't believe in such things as definitive translation – *this* translation will probably be the only one ever made of this poem in the near future. So you have an important responsibility to the poet, to the text. [. . .] It was a very liberating thing for me, therefore, when I was here in Iowa City in '75, as a member of the International Writing Program, and working a lot with the Translation Workshop, that I could make all sorts of crazy experiments, because what I was producing was just part of the workshop and not something for publication, nor with that feeling of responsibility to the poet, that this is probably going to be the only translation of the poem he'll ever see. [. . .] And actually, since that time, I've been more experimental. In fact, for quite a different reason, I've developed an alter ego who also writes poetry, Jacob Lowland, and Jacob Lowland is a much less moral person than Jim Holmes, or James Holmes. He believes in doing all sorts of crazy things [. . .] But I want to emphasize that you have to know what is there, in the first place, before you embark on these kinds of experiments. And never just rely on your dictionaries; research is essential. I've been living with a Dutch guy for thirty years, so I have my resource person at hand, and his English is very good and my Dutch is pretty good, but still, after thirty, thirty-five years, I often have to ask him the meaning of things, I still get caught out. [. . .]

Some of you may have seen the *Penguin Book of Homosexual Verse* that came out last year. It's not a very good anthology. It has a lot of very perverse – if I may use the word in this context – translations in it. But it's the first anthology that has ever been issued which gives an overview of poetry about erotic relationships between men and men, or men and boys, since the Greek Anthology, many ages ago. And one of the things that I've been concerned with is showing again today that there is a tradition which runs counter to the tradition we're all presented with in our literature courses, simply because our literature courses, certainly since the Renaissance, have been dominated by male, straight versions of what literature is, very Christian in background, and very moral behind the aesthetic. A few years ago I decided that I wanted to teach a seminar which combined gay concerns with translation . . . and what I did was to choose some of Catullus' poems. Catullus is known to most of you, if you know him at all, as one of the great love poets of all times, for his quite anguished, tortured poems to and about Lesbia. But perhaps before, perhaps after, but possibly at the same time as he was having an affair with Lesbia, he was also having one with a boy named Juventius. So I thought it would be an interesting study to see what translators in English, from the Renaissance on, have done with those poems of his to this boy. It turned out that there have been ups and downs, that there are periods when it's quite easy to translate classics which refer to man–boy relationships, as long as they *are* classical and not contemporary. And actually one of the major problems of translating Catullus through the ages has been not his homosexual feelings, but his obscenity, the street language. Only since about 1965 has it been possible for people to use such language in poetry and get it published. It's not a question of what poets dare to do, often, but of what publishers dare to publish, because of the censorship laws. [. . .]

Well, one of the results of that project was that, while I was looking around for translations everwhere, I found myself at a certain point trying to work out a way of dealing with the Latin line when translating it into English. In most of the traditional English renderings of Latin and Greek texts you either get terribly long lines that just seem to break down in the middle, or else things get left out, or else there are half as many lines again as in the original. My solution for Catullus was to make every line in the Latin two lines in the English. So you get a sort of loose trimeter pattern in English; two trimeter lines would correspond to one line in the Catullus. And the discipline of working line for line, in this way, seemed to be very fruitful, for me at any rate, in getting some kind of form and concision into the translation. So I now have a sheaf of about twelve poems of Catullus, and hope one day to write an article about translating these poems, one in particular . . .

I hadn't done anything more with Latin until this past summer. I picked up a book called *From Daphne to Laurel*, which is a very interesting anthology of how English-language translators – English means British; the Americans were quite neglected! – how British translators have dealt with the classics, from the Middle Ages up to today. It's arranged not by poets but by translators, chronologically, and a number of the poems are actually translated several times in the course of this anthology. A fascinating book . . . Well, I came across a poem that I didn't know, in an anonymous late seventeenth-century version, by someone who brought out a book of Martial translations. I'm fascinated by this poem. It was August. I was having office hours. Office hours in August, in Europe, where we don't have summer school, is a time when you do things for yourself. It's warm – not hot like here – but warm enough to have you not do things you *ought* to be doing. So I sat down and started to make a translation, a new rendering – from the *English*, the seventeenth-century English – and I took it home with me, and I thought on my way home, well, I'd better get out my Martial and check what he really said, instead of what so-and-so says. And that's the next stage. But – and I'm sorry I don't have that seventeenth-century English version with me – let me just read the literal English translation that you have of number 69. I should also warn you that the edition I have of Martial, though it's also Loeb Classical Library, is a recent reprint, and the only edition that we found here is the earlier, twenties one. Also, you may not know very much about Martial. Martial was a first-century Silver Age poet, who was not the most obscene of all the Latin poets but falls into that category. My edition is quite a good contemporary one. It uses . . . well, it doesn't use quite the four-letter words that we might, but it's fairly explicit, though it still employs somewhat archaic words. The version you have, we found when we checked it out, whenever things get a bit too rough, shifts to Italian! In fact one of the poems that I translated at that time, the whole poem, exists only in Italian here. Anyway, the translation of the particular poem I'm going to read is pretty much the same in both editions. [. . .] The poem's about a certain Mamurra. All these epigrams refer to someone by name. That's one of the rules of the classical epigram. Either it's the name of a person being spoken about, or the name of a person being addressed. Most of the time it's the person being addressed. But this one is simply about Mamurra.

MARTIAL BOOK IX, LIX
Mamurra, long and often wandering in the Saepta, here where Golden Rome flings about her wealth, inspected and devoured with his eyes dainty boys, not those the outer stalls made public, but those who are guarded by the platform of a secret stand, and whom the people do not see, nor the crowd of such as I. Then, sated with the view, he had tables and round covered table-tops laid bare, and must needs have their high-hung glistening ivory

supports brought down; and after four measurements of a tortoise-shell couch for six, he said with a sigh that it was too small for his citrus-wood table. He took counsel of his nose whether the bronzes smelt of Corinth, and condemned even your statuary, Polyclitus; and, complaining that the crystal vases were disfigured by a small piece of glass, he put his seal on ten murrine articles, and set them aside. He weighed antique tankards, and any cups made precious by Mentor's handiwork, and counted the emeralds set in chased gold, and every larger pearl that tinkles from a snow-white ear. Genuine sardonyxes he looked for on every table, and offered a price for some big jaspers. When at the eleventh hour, fagged out, he was at last departing, for a penny he bought two cups – and bore them off himself.

Now there are some things I should tell you about this fairly good English text, although the more recent version is somewhat less high-flown, a little bit more straightforward. This is about a man, Mamurra, who is wandering around window-shopping (that's actually the title of the sevententh-century poem: 'Window-shopping', so the concept existed even then). Mamurra is a name that goes back to the time of Catullus, and I suspect that Martial knew that. Julius Caesar's friend, his lover until he died, was named Mamurra, and Catullus absolutely hated him. Apparently Catullus' father was a friend of Caesar's, and Caesar, though a dictator, was not quite like modern dictators and could take quite a bit of criticism. Catullus' satyric poems against Caesar are really vitriolic, and even more so about his friend. [. . .] Peter Wigham, in the Penguin translation of Catullus, translated Mamurra with a pun, as O'Toole. Anyway, Mamurra is wandering around Rome, in the district where the most expensive shops are, and he's window-shopping, as we say. [. . .] In the late seventeenth-century English version he is in the wealthier section of London, shopping but not buying anything, just looking around. When I started I decided that I wanted to translate this so that it communicated in the present day, to gay people in the present day; that was the first decision I made. This meant I was going to make a lot of changes in what were traditionally called in literary studies (though not any longer) 'realia', concrete cultural items, that functioned then and no longer function today. It's a very risky business, of course, and many people would say that's not translation anymore. I suddenly thought of the fact that there used to be a place in San Francisco which was called The World's Largest Gay Department Store. And I was reminded too of the fact that it had one department, not of used furniture, but of *abused* furniture. Stocks, cages for slaves, and so on. And that set me off. Instead of letting him go to various shops, I'll situate him just in the gay department store, I thought. There was also an area in the store where you could cruise other guys, but I turned that into a place where you could buy slaves – slave isn't understood in quite the same way that it was in Rome, but you can play with that sort of thing. So one idea led to another and I ended up imagining what sort of a person this might be. He wanders around a gay department store, looking at all these things and commenting on them. He's the aesthetic queen type, with a special way of talking. And this led to the translation which you have in front of you, called 'Window Shopping'.

When I started translating, or adapting, I stayed in the same iambic pentameter form that the anonymous translator in the late seventeenth-century had used. My first versions were all in rhymed couplets, iambic pentameter. Later I decided that it would be more effective to break up the pentameter line. Sometimes it breaks in the third foot and sometimes somewhere in the middle, where it seems to work most effectively. So these are in fact iambic pentameter couplets, broken into four-line stanzas instead of two-line couplets.

WINDOW SHOPPING

O'Toole in *ennui*
   (life is *such* a bore)
goes shopping
   in the Gay Department Store.

First to the Slave Department.
   With his eyes
he eats 'em up:
   not those on show for guys

like you & me,
   but prime-time types locked tight
in special rooms
   tucked out of common sight.

None's *hot* enough.
   Now Stocks & Pillories.
He checks out this one, that.
   None of them *please*.

He measures all the slings,
   twice, three times, four.
None of them *fit*.
   When *will* you have some *more*?

Now on to Art.
   There's this new set of draw-
ings just in from Finland.
   Look! A *flaw*!

O *Tom*, how *could* you!
   Time to contemplate
the silver cockrings.
   Silver! Silver *plate*!

He *loves* the harnesses,
   has three of them
laid by, *adores* a belt
   (each studded gem

selected & set in
   by Rob Himself),
counts every stone,
   then moves on to the shelf

with rings & earrings.
   Oooh, the *diamond*'s nice.
The *big* one.
   Oh? *That* much? At *half* the price . . .

Exhausted after four hours' stay,
   he'll buy
two jars of Lube &
   really have to *fly*.

Now obviously everything's new here, everything's different. I should say something first about a few of the references, because though they'd be known in the gay world, they'll not necessarily be known to you! 'Tom of Finland' – that's not his true name, which is an unpronounceable Finnish one; he's never worked under his own name because Finnish laws on homosexuality were, until a few years ago, very strict – is an artist known throughout the gay world, but completely unknown outside of it. 'Rob Himself', Rob of Amsterdam, runs an art gallery in Amsterdam and is Europe's best-known leather and accessory maker for gays in the leather scene. 'Lube' is a lubricant, which has largely replaced Crisco. It's the sort of thing that you would buy the way you pick up some small item after you've been shopping around for hours. [. . .] The surprising thing now is that, with all the liberties I've taken, I've at the same time given you a line-for-line version – that is, two lines for one, though of course there's some running over, and you have to tuck things into one line because English syntax doesn't correspond with Latin. And whenever something has been substituted, it's always something that has a relation to the original, a translation of a cultural item which functioned in the Roman world into a cultural item akin to it which functions in the contemporary gay world.

Now when I translated, when *Jim Holmes* translated, Catullus, he felt that using rhyme for Latin poetry, for classical poetry in general, was barbaric. Well, it is! Rhyme came into European poetry in the early Middle Ages, from India by way of Persian and Islamic poetry. And I've always felt that we really shouldn't use it when translating classical poetry. However, I was led – not I, in this case, because these poems were translated by Jacob Lowland! – Jacob Lowland was misled, perhaps, in the first place, by this beautiful seventeenth-century neo-classical couplet pattern. Now Jacob Lowland, unlike Jim Holmes, loves to rhyme, and so he had a lot of fun doing this. And at a certain point I became convinced that probably rhyme is the right vehicle for dealing with these very taut, witty epigrams of Martial, quite different from the poetry of Catullus. So that perhaps what we need to do, when choosing forms for translating classical poetry, is to approach each poet differently. You can't reproduce Latin verse forms. We tried it in the sixteenth century, in English, and it just doesn't work. I don't think that the many translations of the Iliad and the Odyssey, for instance, into hexameters work. The hexameters get in the way – for me, at any rate. Many have chosen simply to use free verse, but free verse lacks the discipline, it seems to me, that these poets were imposing on themselves. And it is important to suggest that there is such a discipline. For each poet I try to see if I can find a formal principle which will reflect that poet's style, and I think that I, or Jacob Lowland, was right to decide that Martial needs rhyme.

Well, it was primarily this poem that I wanted to deal with, but since in the photocopying it also worked out that we copied both the Latin and the literal in English and Jacob Lowland's translations of Number 57 too, we might as well just look at that for a moment. In this case we have a line-for-line correspondence. It's a shorter verse that Martial is using here, so I, or Jacob, put that into a sort of four-beat, four-accent line, with rhyme – somewhat comlicated rhyme. Here is the literal.

MARTIAL BOOK IX, LVII
Nothing is worn smoother than Hedylus' mantles: not the handles of antique Corinthian vases, nor a shank polished by a ten-years-worn fetter, nor the scarred neck of a broken-winded mule, nor the ruts that intersect the Flaminian Way, nor the pebbles that shine on the sea beach, nor a hoe polished by a Tuscan vineyard, nor the shiny toga of a defunct pauper, nor the ramshackle wheel of a lazy carrier, nor a bison's flank scraped by its cage, nor the tusk, now aged, of a fierce boar. Yet there is one thing – he himself will not deny it: Hedylus' rump is worn smoother than his mantle.

This is a traditional form in the epigram – Martial does it a number of times – listing all these things that it is not, and then saying what it is; not something we do in poetry today. The items he lists would be known to any Roman, so I've tried to replace them with things which would have some association for us today. The roads that intersect the Flaminian Way, for instance . . . They didn't have paved streets, and at the intersections it got pretty bumpy. Now that doesn't happen to us in our cities, except in New York City, because the streets are not repaired there . . . Actually I didn't really think of that at the time, but you could have done something with the New York City potholes. Anyway, I simply moved it out into the country. It's an image which probably doesn't even work for young people today, out in the country, because even the country roads are better now, but I have terrible memories of deep ruts in spring, riding those country roads. It's the same with 'the bison's flank scraped by its cage'. I don't think that the idea or sight of bisons in a cage would signify much to us.

That's why I changed the bison to a lion. Or the 'tusk of a fierce boar'. Now I don't suppose any of us ever even saw a wild boar. So I introduced a billy-goat instead. And that got me into another difficulty: butt-prone billy-goats. This meant I couldn't talk, at the end, about Harry's butt being worn, and so, as I had to have a single-syllable word, I resorted to the briticism 'bum' . . . though I could have said 'can', I suppose. Likewise with 'the handles of antique Corinthian vases', trying to think in terms of an image people could associate with, I ended up with the 'stein', which is not quite on the same aesthetic level as a Corinthian vase. So there are a lot of risks taken here. [. . .]

You certainly wouldn't treat the next poet we're going to be talking about, Vergil, in this way. It depends on an understanding of Martial and what he's trying to do. And he's usually pretty straightforward and down-to-earth. There are a few poems when he ascends to other poetic heights, and there you wouldn't go in for this sort of thing. Let me read you my version now. Obviously I've changed Hedylus' name to Harry, and the only basis I have for that is they both begin with an 'h'. I mean they bear no other relation to each other. But what do you do with Latin names that have no resonance at all, when you're working in this kind of a modernization? [. . .] By the way, I generally consult a friend who is at this moment working on his dissertation on Martial. So I think he picked up most of the errors I made. We talked about these names and he wasn't familiar with them; he said they were just names, very often of friends or enemies and so forth, and they had no special symbolic or other significance.

HARRY'S COAT

Nothing's worn smoother than Harry's coat:
not the handle on a long-used stein,
a slave's wrist polished by years of rope,
a city dog's neck, rubbed by the line,
the ruts that cut country roads in spring,
the gleaming pebbles on ocean beaches,
a hoe for suburban gardening,
the shiny seat of a beggar's britches,

rickety wheels on a market cart,
the bare-scraped flanks of a zoo-caged lion,
the horns on a butt-prone billy goat.

Wait! There's one thing I wouldn't deny him:
his bum's worn smoother than Harry's coat.

I might mention a couple of things: the whole succesion of 'Nil, non, nec, nec, nec' and so forth, that I wasn't able to retain; and one last-minute change that I made. I had: 'Wait! There's one thing, he wouldn't deny it: / his bum's worn smoother than Harry's coat.' This is closer to the Latin, but I finally changed it to 'I wouldn't deny him', because it's a better rhyme with 'lion'. I suspect I may, in a later edition, change it back to 'deny it'. [There is some discussion about the danger of built-in obsolescence in this kind of translation. In particular, the 'hoe for suburban gardening' is mentioned. Holmes continues . . .] Of course, if this is supposed to be America today, this no longer works. That's the sort of bind you get into when you do cultural translations. But I still liked it. That is, it expresses my *dislike* for suburban life. [. . .]

Anyway, as I was saying, these are all experiments. After I'd been working on Martial for a while they came out in a small special publication, for a conference, a colloquium that I was organizing last November. About eight of these poems are in it. I'd also been interested, for some time, in the Second Eclogue of Vergil, which plays an important, I'd almost say central, role in western European poetry. Vergil began as a young poet, by writing a series of Eclogues, and most people think that this one is probably his first, although it's number two in the series. It's probably the first poem he ever decided was good enough to publish, and it has a personal tone that his later writing doesn't have. In the Aeneid he becomes, as it were, the poet of the Roman state, something like Robert Frost in his later years – the official poet of these United States. Well, that's the role that Vergil came to play and his later poetry is extremely impressive, but here a clear personal note is sounded. You will notice, as we read through it, echoes that you may think I introduced from the English tradition, but actually they're echoes within that tradition from this poem, especially in the eighteenth century, Gray's Elegy, for instance. The poem itself also echoes the Alexandrian poets, especially Theocritus. It's about a shepherd who is in love with a boy named Alexis, but Alexis doesn't pay him any attention. Probably this is also a personal theme. The legend, the myth, is that Vergil was in love with a slave boy named Alexis and that Mycaenas, his patron, gave him this boy as a slave, and that they stayed together for the rest of their lives. It's not certain this is true, but it appears pretty early on in the literature, and most of the classical critics and writers think that, in fact, it is true. We'll take a look at the literal version you have. [. . .]

Now Vergil, even in these Eclogues, writes in a high style, as opposed to a low style. These terms are too much bandied about in western literary history, but you have at least three styles: the high style, the middle style and the low style. Satyric epigrams you wrote in the low style, and epic you of course wrote in the high style. Vergil's poetry, on the whole, is written in the high style. He would never have thought of using some of the words that Martial or Catullus use. In fact Vergil, Catullus and Cicero were more or less contemporaries, and you almost get the feeling that Catullus was deliberately using words that were not supposed to be used in poetry and in literary Latin. Cicero, at almost the same time as Catullus was writing poems using street language, gave a list, in one of his books, of words that should never be used in proper writing, and Catullus uses all of them. Martial does too. Vergil would never have done this. His poem about his love for Alexis is quite unerotic, in the sense that it doesn't get down to the physical details at all. And he writes it in the classical verse form, the high style, in hexameters. It seemed to me that to reflect this traditionalism of Vergil, the high style, and the sense of extending a tradition, not only a Latin tradition but also a Greek one, required something like blank verse in English.

As I've said, one of the problems with most of the traditional English translations is that for every four lines of Latin you have to have about six lines of English, if you're going to put it in the iambic pentameter. And on the other hand there is a problem with the high style in Latin, that it's chock full of information, and if you translate all this information, things move very slowly indeed. So I wondered whether I couldn't force myself to be concise and sprightly and moving along, if I tried to translate line for line. And that's what I did here. For every line in the Latin there is a line in the English, which means that in many cases I've simply left things out; but it also means that I was obliged to look for the most compact way of saying things, and that often I was able to use one or two words where most of the translators up to now have used half a line. Let me just read it to you in English. This is pretty traditional verse that I hope is twentieth-century verse as well.

VERGIL, ECLOGUE TWO

The shepherd Corydon's aflame for Alex,
his lord's delight. No hope for Corydon.
All he can do is haunt the spots where beeches
spread their high shade, and sing, caught in love's ardor
these artless shreds of song to woods and hills.
Cruel Alex, don't you like my songs at all?
Have you no pity? You will be my death.
  Now is the hour when cattle seek the shade,
when even lizards creep beneath the brushwood,
and Thestyl brews a thyme-and-garlic drink
for farmhands fazled by the searing heat.
Yet while the orchards echo the cicada
I trace the paths you've walked, in blazing sun.
  Would it have not been better to put up with
Amaryl's sulks and airs? Or with Menalcas,
swarthy though he may be – and you so fair?
O pretty boy, don't count too much on color!
the privet's white flowers fall, dark hyacinths stand.
  You scorn me, Alex. You don't even ask
what kind of man I am, what flocks I have.
A thousand lambs of mine range Sicily's hills;
summer, winter, I never lack fresh milk.
  And I can sing, as once Amphion sang
calling the cows home from the Theban hills.
  Nor can you claim I'm ugly. At the sea
the other day I saw my own reflection.
I can match Daphnis – unless mirrors lie.
  If only you would come and live with me
under a simple roof, here in the country,
to hunt the deer, to herd the goats with switches.
  With me to teach, you'll learn to play like Pan
(Pan who taught how to wax-seal reeds together,
Pan who looks after sheep and after shepherds),
and not be vexed, if a reed chafes your lip:
Amyntas was so keen he shrank from nothing.
I have a pipe with seven graded stalks:
Dametis gave me it as he lay dying.
He said to me: You are its second slave.
Those were his words. Amyntas was quite jealous.

Then this: I found two baby chamois, trapped
in a wild dale. They've white spots on their coats.
They suck the ewe twice daily. They're for you,
though Thestyl nags at me to let her have them.
And so I will, since you snub all my gifts.

    O pretty boy, come. Can't you see the nymphs
laden with lilies for you, see the naiads
picking you poppies and pale irises,
tying narcissi fast to pimpernels,
with cinnamon and other herbs twined in,
and marigolds to mark the hyacinths.
And I'll pick quinces, with their white, frail blossoms,
the chestnuts Amaryl loved when she was mine,
and waxy plums (yes, let plums too be honored).
Then you, you laurels, and your friends the myrtles:
set side by side, you sweetly blend your scents.

    Corydon, you're a yokel. Alex doesn't
want gifts from you: Iollas can give better.
O, O! What have I done? I've let the south wind
ruin my flowers, wild boars muddy my springs.

    Alex, why run from me? there have been gods
who've made the woods their home. And Paris. Let
Athena live in town, for me the forests.

    The lion chases the wolf, the wolf the kid;
the kid frisks off in search of clover blossoms.
And I chase you. Each drawn by his own dream.

    The oxen pull the plow home, blade hung high;
the westering sun casts shadows double-long.
Yet love still burns me up – and what can stop it?

    O Corydon, Corydon, what's this madness?
You've left the vines half-pruned, their elms untrimmed.
Instead of this, why not do something useful?
Go weave a basket out of twigs or reeds.
If Alex scorns you, there are other boys.

[. . .] One of my problems in translating this was that it has been such an important poem historically, and that you do have to preserve some of the echoes that we all know from English literature. I should say a bit more about the importance, in western literature, of the Eclogues in general. They became a norm for aspiring young poets in the Renaissance, if not in classical times.

The way to begin as a poet was to write pastorals, eclogues, and the Neo-Latin poets of the Renaissance all did that. Also, at least one of those pastorals had to be about a shepherd's love for a boy rather than for a woman. It's very interesting how this became a part of the western European tradition. The classical tradition of boy-love and Christianity, with its prohibition of sexuality, run parallel to each other all through the Renaissance. For instance, Spenser's first book, *The Shepherd's Calendar*, is a series of twelve pastorals, one for each month. [. . .] Spenser had a passionate friendship with Gabriel Harvey, his mentor. And Harvey was quite jealous of Spenser's heterosexual interests. They shared a room at Oxford, in the long university tradition of having 'unlawful loves'. Even Pope began in this way with his first publication. It was a series of eclogues or pastorals, and one of the eclogues is about his relationship with an older poet, his mentor.

But aside from this tradition you get the other one, which goes all the way through English poetry. And that does leave the translator with a certain responsibility. You really need to get that echo in there, I think. So at various places, especially towards the end, I try to reflect this tradition. But take also the passage that begins at line 8: 'Now is the hour when cattle seek the shade . . .' You can find that sort of thing in various pastoral poems, as well as the description of the noonday heat and then, at the end, the sunset: 'The oxen pull the plow home, blade hung high' – which is not literally out of Gray, yet the resemblance is there. And the 'O Corydon, Corydon' also became a standard quotation and is parodied and copied all through later Latin poetry; you even find it, now and then, in the vernaculars. So that sort of thing *needs* to be reflected, I think, to show that the poem has a long tradition behind it in our language, and in western literature as a whole. But somehow it has also to be language that people can respond to today. The translator is torn between these two requirements. I've tried to achieve a balance. I didn't feel, in this poem, that I could change names and realia in the way that I did with Martial. I should add, as a postscript, that this version has not yet been checked by my classicist friend, so it is not final, just a version at a certain stage. [. . .]

[Further discussion follows about making a text modern, the danger of 'premature ageing' if there are too many contemporary references. The 'Window Shopping' poem is mentioned in this connection. Holmes comments . . .] That doesn't worry me at all.

I'm quite willing for translations to age very fast. In fact, I'm quite willing for my own poetry to age very fast. I'm very much concerned with communication *now*. [. . .] Urban poetry, with this sort of reference to a concrete time and place, ages very fast. But we make the effort to read eighteenth-century poetry about London, and figure out the details . . . Actually, for original poetry, I don't think it's such a problem. I think that people who are really interested in poetry, and who have an historic sense, will do that work . . . I believe firmly in new translations for every generation . . . It's a somewhat different situation with a translation now of a poet now. The translation *can* age in the same way as the poem. But with the translation now of an older text, the translation will date, while the text will remain. Look at the history of the translation of the classics. I think you'll agree that the translations before Pound can only be read historically now; we can't read them as living poems any more. And I think that's something that as translators we simply have to accept. [. . .]

Translating Nerval
A Reply to a Letter by Richard Holmes
Peter Jay

Greenwich, July 1984

Dear Richard,

Belatedly your letter brings me in from the garden, thinking again of you and of Gérard, of how his poems perennially flourish for us both. Your marsh columbines are settling in well, and the hollyhocks which I've raised from seed are now planted out. Sometimes I think they represent the nearest I'll ever come to Nerval, and yet 'hollyhocks' sound nothing like *roses trémières* . . . so what do they really have in common?

Once more I've been over the translations, trying to tidy loose ends, hoping here to translate more and interpret less, there to translate less and interpret more . . . above all, tuning each poem, each line, to as Nervalian a 'noise' (in Peter Levi's sense) as I can. It's a treacherously difficult business, combining freedom and constraint (restraint?) in ways only those, perhaps, who've tried to get under the skin of foreign poems in order to 'English' them can fully understand. *Vers Dorés* could be read as an evocation of the platonic idea of translation – 'Under the skin of stones a pure soul grows'; but poetry is as impure as any art form, and translation of poetry is doubly so.

Nerval's practice in his Heine versions was to write the best poetry he could, following the general drift of Heine's lyric movement. I think he was much freer with Heine, who befriended him, than I've dared to be with him, but then I've not been able to visit him and make his acquaintance. Principles in translation are *ad hoc*, they derive from your contact with particular poets or poems; they're the summary of your part-solutions to an individual nexus of problems. Theory is an attempt to codify and evaluate principles from the evidence of many different, often contradictory practices. I've been less methodical than I'd care to admit, were I a scholar or theorist; but I've not yet come across any theoretical precept that's helped me make a line of any translation ring true. In the end, I've had to be 'freest' when most awed by the *force majeure* of Nerval's inspiration – but I still maintain that many translators of poetry, whether or not they are poets 'in their own right', don't try hard enough to cut to the bone of a poet's words. Liberation can come from sustained meditation on the very words.

The long-acknowledged problem of translation's demands for double loyalties, and the strain it puts on them, has vexed me greatly over the years. It's a classic dilemma, or paradox. Isn't it sometimes like trying to serve two masters – the two languages to which allegiance is owed – or having two concurrent love affairs? Perhaps it's not often as compromised a performance as that, but simpler analogies with close human relationships are pertinent. I'm thinking of the tensions between lovers with strong personalities who, in striving to pull together, succeed largely in pulling apart. The conscious motivation may be towards principles of balance and fidelity, but the wholly or partially repressed impulse may be to do with possessive control, domination, and resistance to subservience. Or desire for it. Don't we talk of 'getting into' a poem, of 'mastering' or 'getting on top of' a passage that seems impenetrable or unyielding, and so on? The metaphors of sexual politics are inevitable. You translate a poet because you're 'attracted' to the work, but if the attraction is superficial or false you will be rejected.

> Celle que j'aimai seul m'aime encor tendrement

One of those quintessential Nervalian lines, in your sense, utterly simple and memorable, like a rune or a charm. I've found myself repeating it at times, as if to thwart its imagined opposite. An ultimate loyalty is invoked. I've used it as a line for eternal love against the failures of temporal love; for life in the face of everything, against death in the face of nothing. Still I find new resonances in those words. Is the tone of the line accepting and resigned, or can you hear defiance and despair there too?

'We should read whole poets, and always whole poems, yet it is sometimes possible to dislodge the universe with one line.' (Peter Levi again, in *The Noise Made by Poems*.) Gérard succeeds in doing so with more lines than almost any poet I know. Apart from lines 3–4 of 'El Desdichado', these eruptive lines are all end-stopped, like self-contained poem within the poem. His great lines astonish you both in and apart from their context – but they never make the rest of the poem fall flat.

Before I had really begun to wrestle with the *Chimères*, my provisional version of that line was: 'My only love still loves me tenderly'. Your work, and Norma Rinsler's, convinced me of the inadequacy of that as translation, however enamoured of its sound as English I might be. Painfully I struggled through (the surrounding lines were also in flux) to the literal 'She I loved alone still loves me tenderly'; then, 'She I alone loved loves me tenderly still'. Neither are pretty, especially the slurred 'she-I-alone', and neither are rhythmically anything to write home about, but both are fairer to that critical *seul*, even though they still limit its senses. The word is so delicately placed in Gérard's line as to suggest both 'she whom I loved when I was alone' and 'she whom I was the only person to love'.

Tracing the nuances of Nerval's *seul* in these poems is a job for someone. In English you have to juggle with combinations of 'only', 'one' and 'alone' – 'sole' would be an unfortunate homophone – in shifting contexts. Sooner or later you begin to curse the English language for not being French, or French for not being English; and you're right back to the basic conflict of loyalties. Well, I had given up and gone back to 'My only love . . .', and we were about to cohabit when I suddenly deserted her for 'Alone my love still loves me tenderly'. I'm begging this one to make a go of it with me. Fickle? No wonder people talk of abandoning rather than finishing a translation!

Mostly, though, it's been a process of nagging away at the parts which secretly I knew would not quite do, but could see no obvious way to improve. It's ridiculous how long it sometimes takes for the obvious to become clear! Thanks, by the way, for guiding me away from 'For the Muse *enrolled* me as a son of Greece'. I had to laugh at your 'scouts!' in the margin. Less obvious was my dissatisfaction with what I had for:

Je pense à toi, Myrtho, divine enchanteresse . . .

'I think of you, Myrtho, divine enchantress' is accurate and acceptable, and yet when 'ponder' presented itself I knew it was what my line needed. As for the contortions I'd put myself through before arriving at the present version of the close of '*El Desdichado*', you may recall how ingeniously I was contriving, over several years, to avoid a straightforward solution.

Yes, it's a strange and intricate business. It fascinates me. I find translation, at least the translation of poems as rich and deep as those of Gérard, much harder than writing anything of my own, though God knows that's hard enough and I do it all too little. Translating absorbs most of my desire for making verses. But of course this gives me every excuse for writing next to nothing else: perfectionism disguising fear or failure, lack of talent, what have you. In my mellowest moments, I feel that the ultimate necessity of poems is in the lap of the gods. But with other people's poems that have become necessary to *me*, I feel strongly drawn to translate them, to describe and share my sense of their value, hoping (less modestly?) to make them needed in English.

Maybe it's something like that for you, in your biographical-critical work? We could both be said to be writing vicariously, but we don't see ourselves as parasitic, frustrated artists. Why should the jibes like 'X is a translator, and it shows' sting? But they do. Perhaps biographers get credit for critical insight, but poetry translators often aren't accorded even that much, and they are generally denied 'originality' (that romantic concept, unknown to the sensible ancients) by reviewers who take no interest in their problems.

'But I digress.' How much distance one needs from poems, how much closeness to them! I don't think anyone can reconstruct the real reasons for decisions made in the course of a poetic translation, any more than you can describe in sufficient detail the internal course of the choices made in a poem's growth. Even manuscript evidence, I suspect, is misleading: decisions, associative or imaginative leaps, are made *off* the page as often as on it. How to account for one's passions dispassionately? No, I wouldn't believe myself. The danger to avoid is of mounting a critical defence of a translation, with the dubious benefit of hindsight, in the guise of a *methodology*. Actually it's sheer luck, mostly, that leads to those decisive strokes that give you hope that a poem will begin to come good. 'Luck' is my word, 'inspiration' would be a more traditional way of putting it . . . but the point is that it's unaccountable, finally. I'm as happy as the next person to run the risk of the 'intentional fallacy' – we all *have* intentions – but mine with Gérard's poems was mainly to make them convincing in English. What a nerve all that implies!

La rose qu'elle tient, c'est la *Rose trémière*.

'What was your intention there, M. Nerval?' '*Enfin*, I meant to write an unforgettable line, and to give translators of my poems sleepless nights.' Wasn't it you, Richard, who told me that Gérard wrote somwhere to the effect that poetry is what *survives* translation?* Worth remembering for the next time somebody trundles out Frost's definition of poetry as being what is lost in translation. It has a chance of being an equally useful half-truth.

I've rid myself of the etymological fantasy that *rose trémière* has the slightest undercurrent of anything like fear or trembling, and much as we both love hollyhocks, the word as well as the flower, we've agreed that 'The rose she's holding is a hollyhock', or near offer, won't do. *Pace* Derek Mahon, of whom more in a moment.

That line, and the poem *Artémis* as a whole, is an extreme example of the delight and torment of verse translation. The strains have told on me here more than anywhere, because to negotiate the extraordinary pressures of this poem, which is the mid-point of *Les Chimères*, translation has to be most strict to be most liberating. Every phrase, every line – so dense, yet so fluid – must be given maximum freedom to let its meanings expand. 'What's freedom but the rule of poetry?' is an apposite, if slightly riddling, question to quote in this context.

Derek Mahon's bold idea, starting the poem with 'Thirteen o'clock, and the first hour once more', leads you very firmly in the path of one interpretation. By excluding some possibilities, he gives his poem a sharper but a narrower focus. And what about his fifth and sixth lines?

> The goddess carved on the provincial clock
> Of childhood loves you as she always did.

What a fine poet he is! But this looks less like a matter of making

---

* 'Honneur sans doute au rythme at à la rime, caractères primitifs et essentiels de la poésie. Mais ce qu'il y a de plus important, de fondamental, ce qui produit l'impression la plus profonde, ce qui agit avec le plus d'efficacité sur notre moral dans une œuvre poétique, c'est ce qui reste du poète dans une traduction en prose; car cela seul est la valeur réelle de l'étoffe dans sa pureté, dans sa perfection.' – Nerval quoting Goethe (*Dichtung und Wahrheit*) as the authority for his manner of translation, in the 1840 preface to his final version of *Faust*.

forced choices among ambiguities, than of his having concluded that Gérard's own choice of words and images offers no chance of dialogue: so he has compensated by making a fictional Nervalian poem with detail drawn from the commentaries. There's a fine Odilon Redon picture of the Sainte Gudule clock-tower in Brussels, which illustrates Mahon's version of Gérard's hidden allusion; he didn't haul in the clock just for rhyming with our friends of the *Rosa Althaea* family.

Oddly enough, I was thinking of Derek Mahon in connexion with Nerval long before I heard that he'd made a version of *Les Chimères*. (I think of Derek Mahon too every time I hear birdsong on an empty stomach: 'For who, unbreakfasted, will love the lark?') Along these lines: if one wanted to imagine the 'ideal' translation of *Les Chimères* in the twentieth century, to what writer in English would you assign it? Yeats, perhaps? Not the mystical Yeats of the pernes and gyres, but the hard-headed, sober Yeats whose touch with pentameters was so sure, who could write the simple, prosaic bridging passages as well as the heart-stopping one-liners. Yeats is not often Nervalian in tone, though: he's both grander – prone to a strutting magniloquence that the modest Gérard would never have affected – and, frankly, crazier. In his writing Nerval is remarkably sane, isn't he? Crazy in a mild but inoffensive way it may be to take a lobster for a walk on a lead, but it isn't mad to intimate that lobsters know the secrets of the deep. (And as you've pointed out, it's an example of his mischievous sense of humour, too.)

Nerval is far from being a wild romantic. In an age of excessive gestures, his was not an excessive life-style. In his writing he puts on no airs and graces, he says exactly what he has to say as it should be said. Yeats, by contrast, does love to cut an impressive dash. Lines like:

> That we descant and yet again descant
> Upon the supreme theme of Art and Song

– bellow them in your thickest brogue – spoil for me an otherwise beautiful and moving short poem, 'After Long Silence'.

If not Yeats, then what other poets have the requisite control and freedom of line? I keep coming back to two of the best poets now writing in traditional forms in England or Ireland: Geoffrey Hill and Derek Mahon. Mahon has been to school with Yeats profitably, and we have his version. I wonder if you will think that he permits himself too much enjambement, making the flow of the poems a little choppy; and that some of his liberties – 'My star' for *Ma seule étoile* is one that springs to mind – don't help? But he does make fine sonnets, and that matters. Is Geoffrey Hill, I wonder, moving in the direction of Nerval? That is probably too much to read into his marvellous poem on Charles Péguy.

If you discount the possibility of sonnets in English alexandrines, the whole thing stands or falls on the credibility of a Nervalian pentameter in English. It has to be a clear and supple line, allowing modulation in verbal texture from the plain and relaxed to the compressed (but not muscle-bound). Gérard's lines have such balance, such a fine sense of pace, so little straining for effect. It has to be a line capable of singing, but not in the style of grand opera.

> La *fleur* qui plaisait tant à mon cœur désolé

A haunting line, with its unhurried tempo, total economy of means, its poise – look at how he places those internal rhymes, so unobtrusively yet firmly; they seem natural to the language in a quite unstudied way.

I can't get much closer to this. It's something to do with the specific gravity of the verse. How do you measure the moral density of language? Poetry is words in a particular suspension of language, but the only gauge we have is the experience of our ears, and of our hearts. Nothing as scientific as the hydrometer you gave me, which is in regular use for predicting the results of my efforts to turn water into wine (I hope to surprise you with the Italian Classico in October). But in translating, as in any writing, one doesn't proceed by recipes or prescriptions, but by intuition and work, the intuitions often growing out of the work, as if it were the catalyst that causes yeast cells to become active.

> Et dans l'éclair furtif de ton œil souriant

Eighteen years have passed since 'And in the furtive lightning of your smile' came to me like a gift, promising that one day the rest of *The Chimeras* might grow from it.

And yet there's hardly a line in my version that I don't feel might be bettered, had I but world enough and time. I've gone as far as I can now in entering the Nervalian spirit, but that may not be far enough for the poems. I'd rather swim than sink in them. Returning to less dangerous matters of technique, I've never doubted that a decent version of the *Chimères* has to be in the form of sonnets, tackling them head-on with all the compromises that differences between the state of the French sonnet in the 1840s and the English sonnet now must entail. (Poor Gérard was not only plunged in the waters of Cocytus, he has been thrice Californianised, God rest his soul.)

Depending on how you look at it, it was either a natural or a forced decision to use half-rhyme, assonance and other rhyme-substitutes. Compared to French, English is poor in full rhymes, but we also inhabit the last quarter of the twentieth century and must use what comes to hand. Joseph Brodsky, a strict believer in what Dryden called 'metaphrase'– extreme literal and formal fidelity, not to say subservience – when it comes to other people's version of his Russian poems, might consider even this too soft an approach. Do you know his poem 'Plato Elaborated'? These lines, in George Kline's version, suddenly struck me as apropos.

> There would be a café in that city with a quite
> decent blancmange, where, if I should ask why
>   we need the twentieth century when we already
>   have the nineteenth, my colleague would stare fixedly
>   at his fork or his knife.

All the paradoxical questions about the nature and purpose of translation are implicit in those lines. The 'impossible' dimension of time-travel, for example . . . and what can I say about the blancmange? Give the poor fellow a spoon!

I still find myself envying Gérard his simplicity and ease of technique, hard-won though I'm convinced it must have been. His poetry *is* inimitable, yet translation is a kind of mimicry. Should I have gone more the way of Robert Lowell, or of Derek Mahon? Did Nerval agonise over such problems in his Heine and other versions, or did he just do the best job he could? Something of the austere, dark ease and compulsion of Geoffrey Hill's technique in his sonnets might have helped me. Yet Hill is more brilliant and more polished than Nerval in some ways, as well as more contorted and self-conscious.

In formal matters, Gérard was not obsessively concerned, for example, to maintain correspondence in his rhyme-schemes from one quatrain to the next, and some of his own rhyming is loose enough. (I say this to encourage myself, *mon brave!*) He could write low-key prosaic lines when they're necessary, which is more often, especially in the 'Christ' sequence, than one remembers. The poems don't bombard you with one stunning line after another – he's too good, too sure of his aim, to show off in that way.

It would be worth studying Nerval's enjambements, there are few enough of them, and they're very forceful in '*El Desdichado*', for instance. I've had to increase their number, especially in narrative passages. English pentameters lose their rhythmical tension very quickly unless, to apply a famous remark to a different context, the lines are turned across their endings with just the right variation. Defending his use of 'English Heroic Verse without Rime', Milton wrote that 'true musical delight . . . consists only in apt Numbers, in quantity of Syllables, and *the sense variously drawn out from one Verse into another,* not in the jingling sound of like endings . . .' (my italics).

It's also a question of rhythmical alertness, and we still have a lot to learn, as some young poets are beginning to realise, from Yeats and Auden. French is a language with a more even distribution of stresses or word-accents than English, which tends to have stronger stresses and is much more monosyllabic. The French alexandrine flows with enough melodic variation, if the poet pays attention – as Gérard always does – to the tone and colour of his interplaying vowels and consonants, and to his variation of pitch. Pitch, of course, is another aspect of language in which French and English habits differ. It's worth remembering that even in 'English' pitch is not at all uniform; think of the widely different cadences of any Irish, Scottish, Welsh or 'regional' English poet reading his work aloud. With poets like Heaney, MacDiarmid, Hughes, Harrison or Bunting, to name only a few impressive readers I've heard, pitch is either local or personal, at any rate not 'standard'. And there must be no less diversity in American English, Caribbean English and so on.

Are English pentameters harder to write well now than alexandrines in French were in the nineteenth century? Is it a relevant question? English alexandrines are a rarity, and they're hardly ever convincing. I remember taking some translation classes at Oxford with the classicist Richmond Lattimore, who died recently. He had published versions of a few Nerval poems.

> I am the dark, the widowed, the disconsolate.

If only lines as good as that could be sustained!

> Here in the midnight of the grave, give back, of late
> my consolation, Pausilippe, the Italian
> sea, with that flower so sweet once to my desolate
> heart, and the trellis where the vine and rose are one.

He's trying for a rapid line with a French sense of light accentuation, but aren't the pentameters crying out to be released? Give or take a few words, like this:

> Here in the midnight of the grave, give back,
> of late my consolation, Pausilippe. [. . .]
> that flower so sweet once to my desolate heart
> and the trellis where the vine and rose are one.

English sonnets for French sonnets, sonnet-cycle for sonnet-cycle: the challenge was to anglicise form-and-matter in their integrity. 'Tied to the heart of matter is a word . . . /*Ne le fais pas servir à quelque usage implie!*' An injunction to be taken seriously.

I shall have some final, nagging questions of detail to put to you when you're back. (Sorry, but the golden curls have been shorn from 'Myrtho'!) And there are questions . . . Was Gérard a gardener? Can we find something mystic and Vergilian in Samuel Palmer, or in Turner? By the way, the Corot painting you mentioned is a beauty: let's use that pastoral scene, so evocative of the landscape of Gérard's childhood. I suppose childhood is where it all begins: but that's another story, which I hope you'll get back to telling one day.

A bientôt,

Peter

Translating Penna and Cernuda
Working Papers
James Kirkup

FROM JAMES KIRKUP'S NOTEBOOKS

Translation

I keep as close to the original as possible, though careful to avoid a word-for-word literalism.

I dislike those modern poets who seek to impose their own (often inferior) individual style and vocabulary on some helpless foreign poet.

I try to let the foreign poet speak out in his own way, with his own voice, at the risk of my English occasionally sounding a little strange. Indeed, I prefer my translator's English to have a touch of the foreignness inherent in the foreign tongue itself.

Translation into English is a problem of English, not of the foreign language.

SANDRO PENNA'S 'SERA NEL GIARDINO'

ORIGINAL
SERA NEL GIARDINO

La sera mi ha rapito
i rissosi fanciulli.
Le loro voci d'angeli
in guerra.
          Adesso in seno
a nuove luci stanno
là sull'opposte case.

Resta sul cielo chiaro
d'un eroe s'un cavallo
incisa macchia muta

sotto la prima stella.

FINAL VERSION
EVENING IN THE GARDEN

Evening robbed me of
the boys scrapping.
Their angel voices
playing war.
          Now at the heart
of renewed illuminations
there they are again, in
the houses across the way.

On the candid sky
the mute inscription
of a hero on horseback

beneath the first star.

Evening in the Garden

Evening abole someday took
the forest light goes with their quarrels
Their cruel voices at war.

Fresh illuminations
there at the heart
the leaves across the way
they are, in

On the clear sky is left
the music inscription
of a hero on horseback

under the first stars.

SANDRO PENNA'S 'IL MIO AMORE È FURTIVO'

ORIGINAL	FINAL VERSION
Il mio amore è furtivo come quello di un povero. Ognuno può rubarlo. Ed io dovrò lasciarlo.	My love is as furtive as a poor man's passion. Anyone can steal it from me. I must get rid of it.
Per ciò, fiume silente, per ciò, mio dolce colle, io non posso chiamarlo amor semplicemente.	And so, silent river, and so, my gentle hill, I cannot simply call it love.
Ma tu, colle dorato, e tu, mio fiume molle, sapete che il mio amore davvero è un grande amore.	But you, hill of gold, and you, my lazy river, you know that my love is in all truth a great love.
Il pericolo odiato per adesso non c'è? Ma voi sapete, amici, che nel mio cuore è.	That hateful danger seems for the moment absent? But, my friends, you know it is always in my heart.
Piangere mi vedrete, o voi sempre felici, non come piango già, non di felicità.	Weeping you shall see me, O you, forever happy ones – and not weeping as I do now, with happiness.
Fuggono i giorni lieti lieti di bella età. Non fuggono i divieti alla felicità.	

My love is furtive
as a poor man's love.
Anyone can steal it.
I must get rid of it.

And so, silent river,
and so, my feeble will,
I cannot simply
call it love.

But you, hill of gold,
and you, my indolent river, molle
you know that my love lazy
is truly a great love.
        davvero — in all truth
That hateful danger
for the moment absent?
But, friends, you know
it is stirring in my heart.
        waking
Weeping you shall see me,
O you, forever happy —
and not weeping as I do now, all
weeping with happiness.
X

SANDRO PENNA'S 'QUANDO TORNAI AL MARE DI UNA VOLTA'

Quando tornai al mare di una volta,
nella sera fra i caldi viali
ricercavo i compagni di allora . . .

Come un lupo impazzito odoravo
la calda ombra fra le case. L'odore
antico e vuoto mi cacciava all'ampia
spiaggia sul mare aperto Lì trovavo
l'amarezza più chiara e la mia ombra
lunare ferma su l'antico odore.

Whenever I returned to that former sea of mine,
at evening, in the sultry back streets
I would look for the companions of the past . . .

Like a crazed wolf I would sniff
the warm shadows between the houses.
That ancient, vacant smell would drive me to
the vast, open sands of the high seas.
There I would discover a less clouded bitterness,
and my moon-shadow clinging to that ancient smell.

Whenever I returned to that tower
                                    sea
                                    kept stretc-
at evening, in the sul try towel
I would look for the event windows
              of the past ---

        @rafael
Like a wounded wolf I would sniff
the warm shadow between the covered
that ancient,   be empty smell would
                     bring me to
the verge, often bound the high-
                                  was.
Pie   dlycoon
There I would trifled a clearer lea
          cloudy lightness,
and very north- shadows clinging
             to that excrement swell.

SANDRO PENNA'S 'MA SE OGNUNO DORMIVA IL TRENO E IO'

Ma se ognuno dormiva il treno e io,
demoni affettuosi alla deriva,
vegliavamo su lui. L'alba richiama
gli angeli sonnacchiosi. Basse e lente
cavalcate di nebbie: la pianura
etrusca. Con un piglio leggero la sua guancia
ricerca ora una luce e vi si accosta.
Si fila verso il giorno se la terra
appare lentamente. Ed egli parla . . . O numi,
egli viene quaggiù per lavorare.

Though the rest were sleeping, the train and I –
affectionate demons with nothing else to do –
stayed awake, keeping watch over him.
Dawn calls up somnolent angels.
Slow, low cavalcades of mist:
Etruscan plain. With a slight movement
his cheek now seeks the light and stays there.
We are speeding towards day, but earth is slow in coming.
And he speaks . . . merciful gods,
he's coming to work here.

Though the rest were sleeping, the train opened affectionate adieus with neither blue to the barque of which toward the hair, down walls and arms but angels. Slow, low between rocks of mint. Emerson Plain. With a light movement in clock, now seeks the light & stays there with every letter slowly, we are speeding towards day.

And he speaks -- merciful poets, he's coming to work hard.

LUIS CERNUDA'S 'ADÓNDE FUERON DESPEÑADAS'

¿ADÓNDE fueron despeñadas aquellas cataratas,
Tantos besos de amantes, que la pálida historia
Con signos venenosos presenta luego al peregrino
Sobre el desierto, como un guante
Que olvidado pregunta por su mano?

Tú lo sabes, Corsario;
Corsario que se goza en tibios arrecifes,
Cuerpos gritando bajo el cuerpo que les visita,
Y sólo piensan en la caricia,
Sólo piensan en el deseo,
Como bloque de vida
Derretido lentamente por el frío de la muerte.

Otros cuerpos, Corsario, nada saben;
Déjalos pues,
Vierte, viértete sobre mis deseos,
Ahórcate en mis brazos tan jóvenes,
Que con la vista ahogada,
Con la voz última que aún broten mis labios,
Diré amargamente cómo te amo.

ADONDE FUERON DESPEÑADAS
Where have they ~~been cast away~~ Vanished, those
        ~~Gods'~~   cataracts —
So many kisses, that pallid history
Presents now to the pilgrim as so
             many ~~poisonous~~ perfidious signals
In the desert, like a glove, forgotten,
That asks where its hand has gone?

You know the answer, Pirate!
Pirate ~~cast away~~ running riot on
                   sultry coral reefs,
Bodies crying out beneath the body
                 that visits them,
And they are thinking only of a caress,
Thinking only of one desire
Like a block of life
Slowly melted by the chill of death.

Other bodies know nothing at all, Pirate,
So leave them alone.
Spend, spend yourself on my desires

Cling to me in my arms, to yours,
And with lost eyes
With the final shout issued from my lips
~~Silently~~ I shall tell you ~~that~~ how
         ~~much~~ I love you.

WHERE HAVE THEY VANISHED AWAY

Where have they vanished away, those cataracts –
so many lovers' kisses, which pallid history
presents now to the pilgrim as so many venomous signals
in the desert, like a glove, forgotten,
that asks where its hand has gone?

You know the answer, Pirate;
Pirate running wild on sultry coral reefs,
Bodies crying out beneath a body's visitations,
and they are thinking only of a caress,
thinking only of one desire
like a block of life
slowly melted by the chill of death.

Other bodies know nothing at all, Pirate;
so leave them alone.
Spend, spend yourself of my desires,
cling to me in my arms, so young,
and with lost eyes
with the final shout issued from my lips
bitterly I shall tell you how I love you.

Revising Brodsky
George L. Kline

I

On two previous occasions I have expressed myself, briefly, in print on the principles and practices involved in translating the Russian poetry of Joseph Brodsky, with his help, into English. The first piece was called 'Translating Brodsky' (*Bryn Mawr Now*, Spring 1974), the second 'Working with Brodsky' (*Paintbrush*, Vol. 4, No. 7-8 [1977] – accompanied by my translation of 'A second Christmas by the shore'). All that needs to be recapitulated here is that Brodsky and I are in full agreement on the principle that translations of formal poetry, such as the Russian, must convey as much as possible of its *form* – its meter, assonance, alliteration etc. – and, where this is possible without recourse to padding or other artificialities, its rhymes and slant-rhymes as well.

A more accurate, if unwieldy, title for the present essay, which focuses on the 'nuts and bolts' of putting Brodsky into English, would be 'Revising my Translations of Brodsky with Brodsky's Guidance and Help'. I am not, of course, as the briefer title might suggest, discussing revisions of Brodsky's Russian texts. In the infrequent cases where the text from which I had made an earlier translation (usually for journal publication) was revised by the time I undertook a revision of the translation (for book publication), my only job was to take the change into account. An example is Brodsky's decision to revert to an earlier variant of '*V ozyornom krayu*' ('In the Lake District'), which markedly differs in lines 10–12. (See *A Part of Speech*, p. 67.)

In what follows I shall discuss the revisions, for publication in Brodsky's *A Part of Speech* (New York: Farrar, Straus & Giroux 1980; Oxford: the University Press, 1980), of four poems, taken in order of their composition. I list them here, with the pages on which their revised English versions appear in *A Part of Speech*: 'A Second Christmas . . .' (1971) p.10; '*Nature Morte*' (1971) pp. 43–6; 'Letters to a Roman Friend' (1972) pp. 52–4; 'Plato Elaborated' (1977) pp. 129–31.

Brodsky had of course approved the earlier versions (here called 'initial versions') of all of these translations before their first publication, in 1977, 1973, 1974 and 1979 respectively. But in the intervening years his command of literary English had deepened and become richer and more subtle. Furthermore, when the proofs of *A Part of Speech* began to cross his desk he took fresh critical looks, in some cases with the counsel of English or American poets or critics, at translations which he had last scrutinized several years earlier. Our negotiations were carried out partly in person at Brodsky's apartment in Greenwich Village, New York, but mostly by telephone between that apartment and my home in Ardmore, Pennsylvania.

The discussion that follows will *not* include those infrequent cases in which Brodsky made unacceptable suggestions for revision because he misunderstood an English word. For example, in '*Sreten'e'* ('Nunc Dimittis'), stanza 10, he at one point proposed 'subject for striving' where the Russian is *predmét prerekánii* (literally, 'object of strife' or 'occasion of conflict'). He had mistakenly assumed that 'striving' is a synonym for 'strife'. Similarly, I shall not discuss in detail those relatively rare cases in which Brodsky assumed that certain kinds of Russian word-order, in particular inversions, will work in English. For example, he objected to my rendering of *i tri chelovéka vokrúg / mladéntsa stoyáli, kak zýbkaya ráma / v to útro zatéryany v súmrake khráma* ('*Sreten'e*', stanza 2) – 'The three of them, lost in the grayness of dawn, / now stood like a small shifting frame that surrounded / and guarded the Child in the dark of the temple' – on the grounds that 'guarded' has no counterpart in the original and that 'grayness of dawn' is an insufficiently direct rendering of *v to útro* (literally, 'on that morning'). But I had to reject his proffered revision on account of its painful word-order: '. . . frame that surrounded / that morning the Child in the dark of the temple'. In the end we compromised on '. . . frame that surrounded / the Child in the palpable dark of the temple'.

A technical note: I shall use accents to mark stresses of transliterated Russian words. In many cases a word's stress makes a crucial difference to the functioning of a rhyme or slant-rhyme in Russian.

II

The untitled poem *'Vtoroye Rozhdestvo na beregu . . .'* ('A second Christmas by the shore', 1971) contains four eight-line stanzas, rhymed *AbbACddC*, with a mixture of pentameter and tetrameter iambic lines, the last line of each stanza being iambic dimeter. It was the second quatrains of the second and third stanzas which proved problematic. In each case the passage in question begins in the middle of the first line of the quatrain; that is, the fifth line of the stanza.

Here is the Russian text of the first passage and the initial version of my translation, as published in *Paintbrush*, 1977.

> ... я пальцами черчу
> твое лицо на мраморе для бедных;
> поодаль нимфы прыгают, на бедрах
> задрав парчу.

> . . . My finger finds
> your face on poor man's marble. In the distance
> brocaded nymphs lope through their jerky dances,
> flaunting their thighs.

The Russian masculine C-rhymes are *cherchú/parchú* and the feminine *d*-slant-rhymes *bédnykh/bédrakh*, the corresponding English slant-rhymes being 'finds/thighs' and 'distance/dances'. Brodsky had a minor objection to the verb 'lope', arguing that it suggests smooth, graceful movement and thus clashes with the adjective 'jerky'. I offered to substitute 'leap', and he agreed. He had a stronger objection to the verb 'finds', both because of the somewhat dubious slant-rhyme 'finds/thighs' and because 'finds' – though I *meant* it to be elliptical for 'tries to find' – suggests assurance and attainment rather than uncertainty and quest.

My answering revision provided a phonetically – though not of course visually – exact rhyme, 'limns/limbs', and the bonus of an internal slant-rhyme with 'nymphs' (in line 3). Thus the first revision:

> . . . My finger limns
> your face on poor man's marble. In the distance
> brocaded nymphs leap through their jerky dances,
> flaunting their limbs.

However, Brodsky found 'limns' too exotic, even though – as I recall – he did not contest my claim that 'my finger limns / your face' is a close equivalent of *ya pál'tsami cherchú / tvoyó litsó*. His weightier objection was that 'limbs' is less specific and vivid than 'thighs'. I had to agree. So I tried another tack. The second revision read:

> . . . My finger maps
> your face on poor man's marble. In the distance
> brocaded nymphs leap through their jerky dances
> flaunting their hips.

In addition to the slant-end-rhyme 'maps/hips' this version also provided a slant-internal-rhyme with 'leap'. But Brodsky was not impressed. He did not much like the verb 'maps', considering it too technical and not clearly suggestive of the primary meanings – 'trace, draw, outline' – of the Russian *cherchú*. He deplored the loss of 'thighs' and looked somewhat askance at the slant-rhyme 'maps/hips'. So I moved on to the third revision:

> . . . My fingers trace
> your brow on poor man's marble. In the distance
> half-naked nymphs leap through their jerky dances
> in stiff brocades.

This version has certain advantages over the second revision, including avoidance of the word 'maps', alliteration of 'naked' and 'nymph', and use of the plural 'fingers' (so that the verb 'trace' will be a monosyllable; 'my finger traces' would have ruined both meter and rhyme) – which corresponds to the Russian plural *pál'tsami*. But it also has at least two disadvantages, which Brodsky was not slow to detect: the word 'face' has been replaced by the inexact and slightly precious term 'brow' – this to avoid the jarring internal rhyme 'trace/face', jarring because the rhyming words are separated by only the single monosyllable 'your' – and the term 'half-naked' is unspecific compared to the expression 'flaunting their thighs'. (The Russian *na bédrakh / zadráv parchú* means literally, 'having hitched their brocade [skirts] up on their thighs'.)

My recollection is that at this point Brodsky took matters into his own hands. He was a bit desperate, as the *second* set of corrected page proofs was overdue at the printer's. He substituted 'tries' for 'finds', reverting otherwise to the initial version. I was not then, and am not now, entirely satisfied with 'tries', although I recognize that (a) it provides an exact rhyme with 'thighs', and (b) 'tries / your face' is meant to be elliptical for 'tries / to draw [or "trace"] your face'. But I am not sure that this will be any more evident to readers of Brodsky (in English) than that the 'finds / your face' of my initial version was meant to be elliptical for 'tries / to find the outlines of your face'. As I indicated earlier, the Russian of this passage is straightforward and unelliptical: *ya pál'tsami cherchú tvoyó litsó* (literally, 'I draw [or "trace" or "outline"] your face with my fingers').

In any case, the final version turned out to differ in only two words from the initial version: 'leaps' had replaced 'lopes' and 'tries' had replaced 'finds'. Here is the result, the fourth revision and final version:

> . . . My finger tries
> your face on poor man's marble. In the distance
> brocaded nymphs leap through their jerky dances,
> flaunting their thighs.

There were also problems with the second quatrain of the third stanza:

> . . . падает предмет,
> скрипач выходит, музыка не длится,
> и море все морщинистей, и лица.
> А ветра нет.

In the 1977 *Paintbrush* version (initial version) I had rendered this as:

> . . . Things fall, the fid-
> dler leaves, the music dies, and deepening creases
> spread over the sea's surface and men's faces.
> But there's no wind.

Brodsky disliked the slant-rhyme 'fid-/wind', though not primarily because of the breaking of the word 'fiddler'. (In Russian the masculine C . . .C end-rhyme is exact: *predmét/net*. The feminine *dd* end-rhyme is slant: *dlítsya/lítsa*, and tolerably reproduced by 'creases/faces'.)

To eliminate the bothersome slant-rhyme I had to recast lines 1, 2 and 4 as follows in the first revision:

> . . . The fiddler goes,
> the music dies, things fall, and deepening creases
> spread over the sea's surface and men's faces.
> But no wind blows.

However, this changed the order of the 'events' catalogued in the original: *pádayet predmét / skripách vykhódit, múzyka ne dlítsya* (literally, 'an [or "the"] object falls, the fiddler goes out, the music does not continue'). Brodsky insisted on retaining the original order. He also found the expression 'the music dies' measurably closer to cliché than the Russian *múzyka ne dlítsya*. We decided to change 'dies' to 'ebbs', which also seemed to go well with the sea-imagery of the following line. To restore the order of the listed items I rewrote the stanza as follows; this is the second revision and final version:

> . . . Things fall, the fiddler goes,
> the music ebbs, and deepening creases
> spread over the sea's surface and men's faces.
> But no wind blows.

Note that the move from version 1 to version 2 involves changing the first line from tetrameter to pentameter and changing the second line from pentameter to tetrameter. This is not a momentous change; in the Russian text *both* of these lines are pentameter.

This was a compromise which Brodsky and I could both accept. But I confess to a lingering nostalgia for the simple and direct line 'But there's no wind' – a precise equivalent, moreover, of the Russian *A vétra net*.

III

The long poem '*Nature Morte*' (1971) had already been published in two English versions prior to *A Part of Speech*: in the *Saturday Review* in mid-1972 and then in *Joseph Brodsky: Selected Poems* (London: Penguin, 1973; New York: Harper & Row, 1974). Working from the latter version we encountered two stanzas which gave us headaches.

Here is the first troublesome passage (section III, stanza 1) and my initial version:

> Кровь моя холодна.
> Холод ее лютей
> реки, промерзшей до дна.
> Я не люблю людей.

> My blood is very cold –
> its cold is more withering
> than iced-to-the-bottom streams.
> People are not my thing.

Brodsky questioned 'withering/thing' because, though it is an exact rhyme, the syllable '-ing', being unstressed, provides a somewhat unsteady *masculine* rhyme. I should perhaps add that the translation is rhymed throughout *XAYA*, where *X* and *Y* indicate non-rhyming masculine endings. In other words, only the second and fourth, but not the first and third, lines are rhymed. The rhyme scheme of the Russian is *ABAB*.

But the main objection was to the 1960s American slanginess of 'people are not my thing', rendering the straightforward and unslangy *Ya ne lyublyú lyudéi* (literally, 'I don't like people'). On the other hand, if the slang is found acceptable, the use of 'thing' can perhaps be justified in this particular poem, which is marked by a pervasive contrast between persons and things as well as a contrapuntal depiction of persons – including, at the poem's climax, the crucified Christ – as thing-like *natures mortes*.

I began by changing the second line to 'its cold is fiercer than' and deleting the 'than' at the beginning of line 3. I then suggested a series of alternative fourth lines, each with a final word, or syllable, that slant-rhymed with 'than'. They included 'I dislike everyone', 'People I cannot stand' and 'People don't turn me on'. This last, of course, suffers from the same smell of the 1960s as the initial version. I tended to favor the second, despite its slightly awkward inversion. Thus my preferred first revision, at least for a time, was:

> My blood is very cold –
> its cold is fiercer than
> iced-to-the-bottom streams.
> People I cannot stand.

When this failed to pass Brodskyean muster, I offered a hybrid second revision:

> My blood is very cold –
> its cold is more withering
> than iced-to-the-bottom streams.
> I dislike everyone.

This was not acceptable either, mainly, I think, because of the dubious slant-rhyme 'withe*ring*/every*one*'. So in the end we returned, reluctantly, as a *pis aller*, to the initial version.

The other troublesome passage was section VI, stanza 3. Here it is with my initial version:

> Я неподвижен. Два
> бедра холодны, как лед.
> Венозная синева
> мрамором отдает.
>
> I do not move. My thighs
> are like two icicles.
> The blueness of my veins
> has a cold-marble look.

Brodsky's objection was threefold: (a) the slant-rhyme 'icicles/look' is not very successful; (b) 'icicle' suggests something long, thin and pointed, as well as hard and cold, but it is only these last two qualities which are conveyed by the Russian *kholódny, kak lyod* (literally, 'cold, like ice'); (c) the line 'The blueness of my veins' scans as straight iambic trimeter. It thus *begins* with an iamb, whereas all of the Russian (trimeter) lines of this poem begin with either trochees or amphibrachs. The typical line is either a trochee followed by two iambs: ´/˘´/˘´; a trochee, an amphibrach and an iamb: ´/˘˘´/˘´; or, finally, an amphibrach followed by two iambs: ˘´˘/˘´/˘´.

In an attempt to meet Brodsky's threefold objection I recast the stanza as follows in my first revision, the final version:

> I do not move. These two
> thighs are like blocks of ice.
> Branched veins show blue against
> skin that is marble white.

This met with Brodsky's approval, although I suspect that he was not entirely happy with the slant-rhyme 'ice/white'. (But then, in other poems of the 1970s, he permits himself such bold slant-rhymes as *plével/Séver*, *Síti/kísti/susúde*, *bezuchástno/Chárlza*, *pobédakh/razbítykh* and *skórosti/vózraste*.)

IV

In my translation of '*Pís'ma rímskomu drúgu*' ('Letters to a Roman Friend', 1972), published in the Los Angeles *Times* in mid-1974, the troublesome passages, though fairly numerous, were short. Most of them involved only a line or two.

Brodsky corrected my initial misconception, which he had failed to catch when he checked the 1974 version, of his line *Na rassókhsheisya skaméike – Stárshii Plínii* (literally, 'On a dried-off bench [was] Pliny the Elder'). I had pictured Pliny the *man* sitting on the bench; Brodsky meant that a *book* by Pliny the *author* was lying there. He proposed to substitute 'On the garden bench a book of Pliny's rustles' for my line 'On a bench now dry I glimpse Pliny the Elder'. He was willing to sacrifice the specificity and vividness of the recently wet bench (dried, presumably, by the strong sea winds referred to in the first stanza of the poem) for an adjective – 'garden' – which merely specified the location and 'function' of the bench. The verb 'rustles' has no counterpart in the Russian text; but when the poet himself adds such words to a translation, any padding involved is, at the least, 'authorised padding'!

I did not object to 'rustles' or 'garden', but I did object to 'a book of Pliny's' as misleadingly suggesting 'a book *owned* by Pliny' rather than 'a book *written* by Pliny'. Brodsky accepted my proposed change, a very minor one, to 'a book of Pliny'; we both recognized that, had the meter been able to accommodate it, 'a volume of Pliny' would have been better yet.

In section III, stanza 2, the last line – *Dázhe zdes' ne sushchestvúyet, Póstum, právil* (literally, 'Even here, Postumus, there are no rules') – was changed by Brodsky in correcting proofs to 'Here too, the rules are proved by their exceptions' (replacing my 'Rules here, Postumus, are proved by their exceptions'). Since the meter of this poem is trochaic hexameter, I was baffled as to how he intended this line to scan. A telephone conversation quickly established that

Brodsky had been treating 'here' as a two-syllable word, pronounced 'he-yer'. I insisted that this would not work in English, and he finally agreed to revert to my initial version of the line in question. (There were a few other attempted revisions which I had to abort for the same reason. For instance, Brodsky changed my line 'close beside the wall of our provincial city' to 'just near [i.e. "ne-yer"] the wall . . .' When I protested that 'near' cannot be treated as a two-syllable word, he agreed to the compromise formulation 'hard against the wall . . .'

The final two lines of section VIII, stanza 1, read in Russian as follows: *Zaberí iz-pod podúshki sberezhén'ya, / tam nemnógo, no na pokhoróny khvátit* (literally, 'Collect my savings from under my pillow. There isn't much there, but it will be enough for the [i.e. "my"] funeral'). My initial version of these lines was: 'Take my savings, then, from underneath my pillow – / not much, but enough for funeral expenses'. Brodsky proposed changing the final line to 'though not much, it'll make my funeral look decent'. I did not like either 'it'll' or 'look decent' and made a counter-proposal: 'though not much, they'll pay the cost of my interment'. At first Brodsky was not sure about 'interment', but he finally acceded to this version.

V

Section 1, stanza 2, of *'Razviváya Platóna'* ('Plato Elaborated', 1977) reads as follows:

> Чтобы там была Опера, и чтоб в ней ветеран-
> тенор исправно пел арию Марио по вечерам;
>   чтоб Тиран ему аплодировал в ложе, а я в партере
> бормотал бы, сжав зубы от ненависти: «баран».

The rhyme-scheme is *AAXA*; that is, there are triple masculine end-rhymes and the third line of each stanza is unrhymed.

It was decided in our earliest exchanges, during the revision of my drafts for publication in the *New Yorker* (where the translation appeared in the 12 March 1979 issue) that the key Russian term *barán* (literally, 'ram') could not be rendered by 'ram', 'sheep' or even 'old goat'. After rejecting several alternatives – the only one I now recall is 'jerk' – we settled on 'creep', which I rhymed with 'keep' and slant-rhymed with 'overripe' as follows in the initial version:

> There would be an Opera House, in which a slightly overripe
> tenor would duly descant Mario's arias, keep-
> ing the Tyrant amused. He'd applaud from his loge, but
> I from the back rows would hiss through clenched teeth, 'You
> creep!

In the Russian text the word *barán* is doubly highlighted: as the last word in the stanza and as the third of the masculine triple rhymes. It forms an exact end-rhyme with *veterán*, a slant-end-rhyme with *vecherám*, and an exact internal rhyme with *Tirán* – which tightens the identification of *barán* with *Tirán* ('creep' with 'Tyrant'). In addition, the internal rhyme *Tirán/veterán* suggests that not only the tenor but also the Tyrant is a long-time practitioner of his trade. Unhappily none of the usable English equivalents of *barán* retains the internal rhyme with, or even an echo of, 'Tyrant'.

Between the appearance of the *New Yorker* version and the final preparation of the texts for *A Part of Speech* an objection had been raised to 'creep' – as being too slangy, or too 'American', or both. I devised various substitutes in response to this criticism. The first used 'ass' (in the expression 'You ass!') and slant-rhymed it with 'obese' and 'pleas-'. In this first revision the stanza reads:

> There would be an Opera House, in which a somewhat obese
> tenor would duly descant Mario's arias, pleas-
> ing the Tyrant no end. He'd applaud from his loge, but
> I from the back rows would hiss through clenched teeth, 'You
> ass!'

The ensuing objection was not, as might be assumed, to the breaking of the word 'pleasing' for the sake of the rhyme on 'pleas-'; this sort of thing, after all, occurs in the initial version as well, with 'keep-'. Furthermore it is a device which Brodsky uses himself; for example, *pro-pórtsiyu* (pro-portion) rhymes with *peró* (pen), *polú-bezúmnykh* (half-crazy) with *porú* (time) and *ne-pokidáyemyi* (un-forsakable or in-separable) with *mne* (me). These examples are from other poems of the 1970s; in 'Plato Elaborated' the closest thing to this is the breaking of the compound term *veterán-ténor* and of the French expression *ménage-à-trois* (*menázh-a-trua*), broken after *menázh-* to rhyme with *shpionázh* and slant-rhyme with *nash*, in the penultimate stanza. Rather, as I recall, the main objection was that 'obese' involves padding (!), since the Russian text makes no reference to the tenor's size or shape – although he is described as a 'veteran' and is presumably middle-aged, so that he may reasonably be assumed to have gained some avoirdupois, as tenors typically do.

In an attempt to meet these objections and still avoid 'creep' I revised the stanza further. This is my second revision:

> There would be an Opera House, in which a seasoned class-
> ical tenor would duly descant Mario's arias,
>   pleasing the Tyrant, who'd applaud from his loge, but
> I from the back rows would hiss through clenched teeth,
>   'Jackass!'

Here 'Jackass' rhymes with 'class' and slant-rhymes with 'arias'. It was the last of these, as I recall, which met with less than wholehearted approval on Brodsky's part. Along the way I considered several other slant-rhymes for 'Jackass' (or 'You ass'), among them: 'a *moss*- / backed tenor', 'a *senes*- / cent tenor', 'and old war*horse* / of a tenor', and even 'a *seas*- / oned classical tenor'. None of these worked out.

After agonizing reappraisals it was decided – very late in the proofreading process – to revert to the *New Yorker* version. Thus the third revision turned out to be identical with the initial version; the exile of 'creep' had been revoked!

VI

Working closely with a Russian poet who has a deep and subtle, even if fallible, command of one's own language – the language into which one is struggling, with that poet's help, to transpose his work – is a unique experience, always stimulating, sometimes illuminating, occasionally humbling or frustrating. Even in those cases where the process of revision comes full circle – as in the passages in my translations of Brodsky's *'Nature Morte'* and 'Plato Elaborated' discussed in Sections III and V above – one learns just which alternatives will *not* work, and why. And this, in its way, is as valuable as the heady experience of attaining, with the poet's help, clear improvements in one's imperfect English versions of his more recalcitrant Russian texts.

Translating Anna Akhmatova
A Conversation with Stanley Kunitz
Transcribed from a conversation between Stanley Kunitz and Daniel Weissbort in New York City, May 1982

Weissbort: How did the project originate, the co-operation with Max Hayward, because I know you worked on other projects with him?
Kunitz: I had worked previously with Max on the Voznesensky translations. In '64 Arthur Gregor, who was poetry editor of Macmillan at that time, approached me, asking whether I would be interested in doing a translation of Akhmatova, and offered a contract. I got in touch with Max and he was agreeable and we signed . . . It took us eight years to complete the project, because we had to wait for Max's visits to this country to go over the material, and both of us had other commitments, and finally there was a changing of the guard at Macmillan and Arthur no longer was with the firm. Since nobody remaining at Macmillan seemed particularly interested in the project, I secured a release from the contract and switched over to my own publisher, Atlantic Monthly Press. That's the history . . . It wasn't till '72 that we turned in the final manuscript. The book was published in '73 and there's still a lively demand for it.
W: Could you say something about your work procedure?
K: Max went over all the available poems of Akhmatova and made very precise transliterations . . .
W: The entire *œuvre*?
K: The ones that he thought would be of any interest. And these transliterations were word for word, with no literary pretensions, but adequate for letting me choose the texts I wanted to translate. In the end I came across a few poems by myself that I

felt were needed to complete the book, and these I added to the table of contents.

Along with the transliterations, which were accompanied by a phonetic approximation of the Cyrillic text and indication of the stresses, Max sent me another version in readable English prose. During our sessions together he would read the poems aloud to me in Russian. This was of the utmost importance, for the soul of a poem, I have always felt, is in its sound. When I read my versions back to him, above all I wanted them to *sound* right.

In general, whatever I did with the text was acceptable to Max. He did not claim to be a poet and he certainly did not want to be a critic of my poems. Only in a few cases did he feel that I had misconstrued the sense or the tone. He did not leave me much room for error, since his prose renderings were meticulously accurate and his marginal glosses on difficult passages examined ambiguities or supplied relevant biographical or historical information. Sometimes he would say of a word, 'This is truly untranslatable, but here are some of the possibilities.'

W: He was an ideal collaborator, in that he didn't interfere with your own inspiration or insights.

K: Right! He was not defending the territory of Slavic linguistics! [Laughter.] And he was happy if what I gave back to him came out sounding like a poem!

W: Had you read, before the proposal was made for a collection of Akhmatova, much of her work in translation?

K: I had seen several translations. Not, I think, a full text, but isolated poems. And I felt most of them were not very promising. [Laughter.] But I sensed that behind those poems there was a tone of voice, an urgency, a moral and political passion that excited me. And I also felt that the more I read her poems, the more I understood that in a curious way, in the fulfillment of her destiny, she had become as allegorical figure. She was the history of Russia of her time.

W: To what extent was Max able to convey more impalpable aspects, I mean the tone, the general feeling of what kind of poet she is, how it all works in Russian?

K: We had very little conversation in that area. Max's introduction was not written until after we were through with the work. So I didn't have the benefit of his insights to begin with. I did read whatever I could about her and the other poets of that era. The rest was largely intuition. I might add that though I gave a lot of

Translating Anna Akhmatova

myself to her, she more than paid me back. I learned something from her about transparency of diction, directness of approach to a theme, the possibility of equating personal emotion with historical passion.

W: That was what I was going to ask you, what you felt you had gained . . .

K: And actually, by the time I had finished those translations, I felt that I had been profoundly affected in my own life. Not that I think my work sounds anything like Akhmatova.

W: No, not something one would immediately discern stylistically . . .

K: But it did modify me a few millimetres!

W: Do you, in fact, know any Russian?

K: So little that I might as well say no.

W: This method, one might say, is the standard method of translating in Russia itself. You have a scholar or linguist, working with a poet.

K: Akhmatova herself did that.

W: Some people have expressed doubts about a method where the final translator, the poet, has no immediate contact with the original language, but did you feel any doubts about this?

K: I trusted Max implicitly. And I knew that if I had any doubts about a reading, he would be able to help me. I also felt that if I'd had an ordinary, rudimentary grasp of Russian – equivalent, let's say, to my grasp of French or German – it might have been more of a hindrance than a help. Because I had the benefit in this case of sharing the erudition, the linguistic brilliance, of one of the great Slavists. That's the work of a lifetime, and I doubt that most poets in English are going to spend a lifetime acquiring that much command of another language.

W: Yes, that's quite true. It sometimes happens by chance, or historical accident, where bilingualism occurs.

K: Max had the notion that since I do have East European ancestry, my genes knew more Russian than I did. He'd say, 'Oh, you really caught that. How did you do it?'

W: You said you were attracted to the way Akhmatova linked the personal and the political. She also worked, in her early days, in very classical form . . .

K: And wrote very feminine, domestic poetry.

W: Yes. But I wonder whether the constrictions of that very formal classical meter and rhyme scheme, in particular, run somewhat contrary to your own . . .

K: To a degree, but I too had started as a formal, metrical poet. Of course, I went through a radical change. Akhmatova remained more of a formalist, but her late poems are certainly more open stylistically than her early work. Actually, I sensed a certain correspondence in our development.

W: There has been a view, much put around lately, that translators of formal poetry, especially formal Russian poetry, have tended to ignore the formal side. It seems to me that your Akhmatova translations represent a very nice balance between formal demands and semantic accuracy, even if not of the literal, verbal kind. Verbal accuracy, literal accuracy is, in any case, often a contradiction in terms. Strictly speaking, it is impossible!

K: The genius of each language is unique. Each poem is also unique, with its individual inflection, rhythm, pitch, pacing, auditory pattern, etc. So much of it can only be implied in translation. What is most readily translatable is the matter of a poem, its substantive ground, which there is no excuse for betraying, even in the absence of equivalents. All the rest – its music, its spirit, its complex verbal and psychic tissue – one tries to suggest as best as one can. It's foolish to argue for the exact reconstruction of a poem in another language when the building blocks at one's disposal bear no resemblance to those of the original.

W: Do you think the absolutist demand for the 'exact reconstruction of a poem', as you say, expresses the unrealistic, idealistic ambition to somehow transform English into a kind of Russian – in this case a Russified English, which is somehow, magically, both English and Russian and therefore is not obliged to compromise between them?

K: There's a kind of purism in literature that is just as destructive as fanaticism in religion. I equate the two.

W: To return to Akhmatova herself, I am often struck by her very precise sense, for a lyric poet, of time and locale – place.

K: Her awareness of time and place is consistent with her exercise of the dramatic imagination. Among modern poets she vies with Yeats in her mastery of the dramatic lyric.

W: She brings an enormous amount of her life into the poetry.

K: I admire her ability to capture a scene, to introduce a dramatic confrontation, and with such economy of means. Her poems hardly ever sprawl. She has a fierce attention to her destination.

W: Were these aspects that you found . . .

K: Yes, congenial . . .

W: Can you trace influences, if I might put it that way, in your own work, subsequent to translating Akhmatova, of her example? I guess what I'm trying to say is this: there are, on the one hand, your actual translations of Akhmatova and, on the other hand, there is something which occasionally happens when a poet translates another poet, or perhaps which always happens, if it is a real meeting, in other words, a kind of translation through the translator's own work, a kind of transcendence . . .

K: Mainly what my work with Akhmatova did for me was to [pause] keep me alive to the possibility of translating human situations, conflicts, disturbances into poems that go beyond the personal, that can be read as existential metaphors. She confirmed my image of the poet as a witness to history, particularly to the crimes of history.

W: Let me, perhaps, stress a slightly different aspect of that same question. Supposing you were another poet reading your, Stanley Kunitz's, translations of Akhmatova, having a similar congeniality for Akhmatova; would merely reading the poems, in someone else's translation, have as potent an affect as translating them yourself? In other words, does translation imply a higher degree of assimilation? Obviously we both believe it does, but I would be interested in your comments.

K: Yes, I'm sure this happens in any extended work of translation. Not so much if you translate individual poems, but if you take on the whole body of a poet's work and move, as one tries to do, into the dominion of that poet's imagination. To do that is to extend the boundaries of one's own imagination, to become, in a way, magnified.

W: I was wondering also, because the point has sometimes been made about Lowell's translations for instance (at least his *Imitations*), that rather than opening himself to another poet, he somehow . . .

K: . . . used the poet as a springboard.

W: Yes. Would you say that's fair criticism?

K: Fair enough. But you have to understand that this is what he set out to do. He did not demand of himself any great fidelity to the original text. He thought it was more important to produce a poem by Lowell. And that's what he did. My intention is quite different. I insist on the premise of affection for the original text and loyalty to it, *insofar as it is compatible with the production of a new poem in English*. Sometimes these are quite incompatible directives. Sometimes you have to sacrifice a grain of fidelity, simply because it sounds rotten in English.

If you study Max's transliterations of Akhmatova, you can see that certain lines, taken literally, sound preposterous or silly. Every language reflects a set of social conventions and has its roots in the character and history of a people. In a poem that deals with human affections, it is the culture that determines how much expressiveness is tolerable in an exchange between persons. What sounds genuine and moving in one language may strike the reader in another language as bombastic or insincere. I found such instances in Akhmatova's poems. There were also opposite cases, where the literal English version of a line came through as so flat and unevocative that the intensity had to be stepped up one notch in order to save the poem from collapsing. Occasionally a closure that Max assured me was quite grand and resonant in the Russian tongue had so thin a sound in English that I felt obliged to modify the text in order to get the vibrations right. These were not easy or wilful choices.

W: Perhaps we might now turn to an actual translation. You mention one of these poems as being particularly problematical. Might we perhaps look at that one? I believe it was the poem 'We're all drunkards here . . .'

K: Oh yes, a famous one, the poem used against her by the establishment, because its opening line indicates how immoral, how corrupt the whole society of bohemian poets was: 'We're all drunkards here, and harlots.'

W: It's also, I suppose, a particularly striking example of dramatic writing.

K: Yes, she captures a scene. She has what Henry James called a scenic imagination, which he believed to be the secret of the novelistic art. What he learned to do was to select a few crucial encounters or conflicts which required elaboration in great detail, and then to bridge them with summaries. Poetry dispenses with the bridges, but the gift of the scenic imagination is indispensable for the writer of dramatic lyrics.

W: Yes. Her life is the bridge. You said that this poem was, perhaps, one of the few poems where there was some controversy between you and Max.

K: That's too strong a word. But I think it was the only poem where we had some debate about the interpretation. And if we can go over it, I'll point out where. I may be able to locate the letter in which he comments on that.

W: He has something in his Introduction explaining the circumstances of 'The stray dog' and so on. The poem is on page 51 of the book.

K: Yes, here it is: 'When it was first published in the journal *Apollon* in 1913, this poem was titled "Cabaret Artistique".' Max discusses it in the Introduction on pages 13 to 14. [Pause] Maybe I should comment on what happens in my version of the poem, as compared with the original. Well, maybe I should read Max's version, stanza by stanza, and then comment on what I've done with it.

This is Max's rendering into English. [Reads MH's literate, stanza 1: see Appendix 1.] My version reads . . . [reads final version, stanza 1]. 'Wretched', I think, is stronger than 'unhappy'. 'Unhappy' is a dead word. He says 'flowers and birds / Yearn for the clouds'. Well, in English it's too short a line and too vague in its feeling. I want to suggest the tight metrics of the original, the concentrated power of the stanzaic structure, without becoming a slave to the prosody. My use of off-rhyme, as in 'together / gather', gives me a measure of freedom.

Max's version. [Reads MH's literate, stanza 2.] The trouble here is that the English paraphrase doesn't sound like Akhmatova. It's overly naive, even ingenuous.

W: Yes, that's right. In Akhmatova it seems lucid and simple, but not ingenuous.

K: In fact, she is confiding her sexual motivation for wearing so narrow a skirt. In 1913, to say that in a poem took a bit of courage, no doubt. [Reads final version, stanza 2.] I want those lines to sound mature and bold and feminine all at once – qualities I associate with Akhmatova.

W: It's curious, because in the second line, where Max translates it quite literally, 'The smoke above it is so strange', that's exactly what the Russian says and it is so beautiful, so expressive, and yet so dead when literally translated.

K: Which is why I change it to 'strange shapes above you swim'. For the sake of a little metaphorical life.

Next stanza. [Reads MH's literate, stanza 3.] My version, 'The windows are tightly sealed', ties in with the preceding skirt-image and has the advantage of economy and energy, linear tension, in contrast to the literal rendering, 'The windows are blocked up for ever'. 'What's outside? Sleet or thunderstorm?' Each language has its own natural order. The acceptable locution in English is 'thunder or sleet'. 'What's outside?' is awkwardly sibilant. I prefer 'What brews?' because it harmonizes with 'your eyes' in the second line following and because it has an appropriately ominous inflection.

W: Which I think may be in the Russian, because it uses the word *tam*, meaning literally, rather indeterminately, 'there', in this case 'outside', rather than some more precise expression for that.

K: It could be argued, I suppose, that the line 'How well I know your look', preceding 'your eyes like a cautious cat', is an arbitrary insert lacking textual justification. The truth is that, since Max's paraphrase in this passage was considerably more economical than the Russian, I had to invent something to meet the demands of the given stanzaic structure. My interpolation, hinting at the intimacy of the male–female relationship, is quite unintrusive. Indeed it is implicit in Akhmatova's text. The important consideration for the translator in this case is to present the poem as an aesthetic whole, conveying the sense of its formal order in the midst of great emotional agitation. I have seen a free-verse translation of this very poem relying on word-for-word correspondence with the original that missed this point entirely.

To turn to the last stanza – here is Max's translation. [Reads MH's literate, stanza 4.] No doubt it works beautifully in the Russian, but in English paraphrase it's a let-down. This is what I did with it. [Reads final version, stanza 4.]

In my reading of the poem it's the kind that seethes with violence from the start and needs to erupt violently at the last. Poetry in English rests on the power of its verbs. Hence the strong verb 'rots' in the final line. My original version was even stronger: 'But that one dancing there, / I hope she'll rot in hell'. An expression of jealous rage seemed to me to be the gist of the conclusion. But Max demurred, complaining in a letter, which I have here, that this was carrying things too far. [Laughter.] He wrote: 'I am a little unhappy about "I hope she'll rot in hell". I believe that we discussed this before. Her feelings about Glebova-Sudeikina were obviously mixed, but basically she was very friendly. There are other poems in which she more or less absolves her from blame over Knyazev (who was killed, as you remember, in a brawl) and takes it on herself. The same is true of her dedication to O.S. in the poem. I think, therefore, it would be best not to put this so strongly, particularly as there is no warrant for it in the original. Literally: "That one dancing there will surely be in hell". In other words, just a plain statement, not a wish or hope.' Max almost convinced me. I changed the line to the version as published.

W: He just felt this was not the kind of thing that Akhmatova would say?

K: In her later poems, which were darkened by her sense of political betrayal, she was perfectly capable of denunciation. But this was an early poem, personal and ambivalent, so that the corrected version is probably truer to the original.

I think we should go back now and comment on Max's notes to the poem [see MH's transliteration]. For example, in stanza 2, end of the stanza, the word *stroinyey* is rendered as 'graceful', but the gloss tells more: 'This word refers to elegance of figure. It suggests tall, graceful, slim, well-built etc.' It was the gloss that led me to the adjective 'trim'.

W: The photographs one has seen of her seem to bear out that impression.

K: In the next stanza his note on the second line, 'for ever blocked up are the windows', reads: 'This has a rather more concrete sense than in English, since Russians seal up their windows in a most elaborate way against the cold in winter.' Without that explanation I doubt I would have arrived at 'The windows are tightly sealed.'

W: Ah yes, so it came from the note, rather than from the literal translation.

K: We can see another example in the opening line of the last stanza, literally 'Oh how my heart longs!' Max comments, 'The verb [*toskuyet*] means to be full of misery, apprehension, foreboding etc.' My solution was to distribute those connotations through the line: 'O heavy heart, how long'.

W: Yes, *toskuyet* is one of those highly problematical words which all languages, to the despair of translators, contain. It cannot be translated literally!

K: Shall we talk about the poem that pays homage to Pasternak? It's one of my favorites. What it intimates about the role of the poet in the modern world needs to be understood and reinforced. The temptation is to regard poetry as primarily a verbal skill. In her view of poetic genius Akhmatova stressed the importance of character in relation to history. In this poem to her friend, written in the time of the Stalin terror, Akhmatova pays what I would suppose to be the ultimate tribute to a fellow poet, in that her images are drawn from Pasternak himself. There's a delicacy about that gift, that gift of reciprocity, that touches me infinitely.

So now, to get back to the translation. I wanted to infuse it with a lyrical tenderness, but that was hard to manage, given the amount of information that needs to be conveyed. To include all that information and yet to ride the wave of a melodic line – this was the challenge that had to be met.

Take the literal version, for example, of the opening stanza. [Reads MH's transliteration: see Appendix 2.] It is out of Max's gloss again that I get my direction. The paraphrase itself won't do. [Reads MH's literate, stanza 1.] I have to fight for a rhythm. [Reads final version, stanza 1, pausing after line 2.] See, I like those heavy stresses, that jamming effect. [Reads on.] I think it was 'ice frets', Max's phrase, that gave me the clue to the music I wanted to hear. Then the next stanza. [Reads MH's literate, stanza 2.] Out of that I get . . . [reads final version, stanza 2]. I've kept the images almost exactly, but the rhythm has been transformed. It's back into the lyric mode.

And then the next stanza. [Reads MH's literate, stanza 3.] Some of that comes through. [Reads final version, stanza 3.] Consider the phrase given to me: 'He is timidly making his way over pine-needles'. I give it back as 'It means he is tiptoeing over pine-needles'. The difference is in the lightfootedness. Poetry is always trying to embody gesture in language.

And the next stanza. [Reads MH's literate version, stanza 4.] When Max wrote the note he wasn't sure about the reference to the 'Daryal Stone'. He noted, 'This probably means the Caucasus, but I'll have to check.' Well, it does. As I discovered for myself, Pasternak had a lodge in the Caucasus, in the Daryal Gorge. [Reads final version, stanza 4.] Again, I tried to establish the rhythmic base. My ear rejects 'Accursed and black, from some funeral or other', but accepts 'from another funeral'. Somehow, the whole meaning is changed.

And then the next stanza. [Reads MH's literate, stanza 5.] Again one senses that something quite noble in the original has suffered a diminishing. How to restore its luster? [Reads final version, stanza 5.] Here I'm working with the complex of feelings behind the language, as given, rather than with the literal sense. Since we know that a literal translation of poetry is a delusion, is it permissible to substitute on occasion an equivalent for what one believes to be the true intention of the poet? I think so, but it's a risky procedure, and arguable.

W: Yes, it comes up again and again. Whereas a poet-translator will often have the audacity to do that, someone else lacking that confidence will not.

K: Oh yes. But poets are born to dare. [Laughter.] Who would complain if I had kept to the rendering, stanza 6, 'Of verse reflected in new space'? Yet I am sure that 'reverberating' is the right verb in that line. At least in English it's right. And then the blessing: 'He has been rewarded by a kind of eternal childhood', in the last stanza. That's a good line as it stands. But 'With the generosity and sharpsightedness of stars'; what a mouthful! 'And he has inherited the whole of the earth / And he has shared it with everybody.' I couldn't let this poem die like that. So . . . [reads final version]. I know I've taken chances, but not with the spirit behind the text, and so I believe that I've been faithful, in my fashion, to Akhmátova.

W: Well, finally, I was wondering whether you had any other translation projects, or whether you had done any translations since the ones we have been discussing.

K: No . . . Oh, I've done a few random translations, but I'm going on seventy-seven now, which is hard for me to believe [laughter], and I still have poems of my own to write, which is also hard to believe. So I can't afford to spread myself thin.

W: Did you do much translation in the past, before your work with Max?

K: Not intensively, though very early I translated from the Spanish and French, some Baudelaire in particular. And in recent years I've done a few Mandelstam poems, and a rich poem of Ungaretti's, which I include in my collected volume. And I've done a few things of Bella Akhmadulina, some of which are still in my files. Incidentally, I've always felt that I should do more with Mandelstam, and maybe one of these days, despite my reservations, I might try my hand at it.

W: Well, of the many versions there have been, perhaps the closest to coming into poems in English are Merwin's, which are among the earliest.

K: I feel about Merwin's that they have a grace and something magical too about them, but that maybe they are more elusive than they ought to be. I might be wrong. One wants to strike at the terrible crystal, but in Mandelstam's case the difficulty is in finding where the crystal is.

APPENDIX ONE: WE'RE ALL DRUNKARDS HERE

MH's transliteration

A *Fsye mi brázhniki zdés, bludnítsi,**
   All we-are tipplers here. harlots,
B *Kak nevéselo vméste nám!*
   How cheerless together we-are!*
A *Na stenákh tsvetí i ptítsi*
   On the-walls flowers and birds
B *Tomyátsa po oblakám.*
   Long for clouds.

A *Ti kúrish chórnuyu trúbku,*
   You smoke black pipe,*
B *Tak stránen dimók nad nyéy.*
   So strange-is smoke above it.
A *Ya nadéla úskuyu yúbku,*
   I-have put-on narrow skirt,
B *Shtob kazátsa yeshchó stroinyéy.**
   So-as to-appear even-more graceful.

A *Nafsegdá zabíti okóshki:*
   For-ever blocked up / are / the windows:*
B *Shto tám, iźmoros il grozá?*
   What's there, sleet or thunderstorm?*
A *Na glazá ostorózhnoy kóshki*
   To eyes of-careful cat*
B *Pokhózhi tvoyí glazá.*
   /Are/ like your eyes.

A somewhat unusual word since it is used in the Biblical Great *Whore* of Babylon. *Harlot* just about gets the oldfashioned flavor.

This is a simple colloquial phrase meaning quite simply: 'What a miserable time we're having.'

You is in 'thou' form and she must be addressing Gumilyov, as in most of these early lyrics.

This word refers to elegance of figure. It suggests tall, graceful, slim, well built etc.

This has a rather more concrete sense than in English, since Russians seal up their windows in a most elaborate way against the cold in winter.
izmoros can mean either sleet or hoarfrost.
There means 'outside'.
'Careful' here means wary, prudent.

Translating Anna Akhmatova

A *O, kak sértse moyó toskúyet!*
   O, how heart my longs!*   The verb means to be full of
B *Nye smértnovo-l chasá zhdú?*   misery, apprehension,
   Am-I deathly hour awaiting?   foreboding etc.
A *A tá, shto seychás tantsúyet,*
   But she, who just-now
     is-dancing.
B *Nepreménno búdet v-adú.*
   Certainly will-be in-hell.   [1 January 1913]

MH's literate

We're all drunkards here, and harlots,
How unhappy we are together!
On the walls flowers and birds
Yearn for the clouds.

You puff on a black pipe,
The smoke above it is so strange,
I have put on a narrow skirt,
{ To set off my figure even better. }
{ To seem even slimmer yet. }

The windows are blocked up for ever:
What's outside? Sleet or thunderstorm?
Your eyes are like
The eyes of a cautious cat.

Oh, how my heart is heavy!
Can I be waiting for the hour of death?
But she who is dancing here now
Will certainly go to hell.

Final version

We're all drunkards here, and harlots:
how wretched are we together!
On the walls, flowers and birds
wait for the clouds to gather.

You puff on your burnished pipe,
strange shapes above you swim,

I have put on a narrow skirt
to show my lines are trim.

The windows are tightly sealed.
What brews? Thunder or sleet?
How well I know your look,
your eyes like a cautious cat.

O heavy heart; how long
before the tolling bell?
But that one dancing there,
will surely rot in hell!

APPENDIX TWO: BORIS PASTERNAK

MH's transliteration

Ón, sam sebía sravńivshi s kónskim
  glázom.
He (who) himself himself compared
  to horse's eye,
Kosítsa, smótrit, vídit, uznayót,
Squints, looks, sees, recognises,
I vót uzhé rasplávlenim almázom
And then already a-molten diamond
Siyáyut lúzhi, izniváyet liód.
Shine puddles, frets ice.*

V lilóvoi mglé pokóyatsa zadvórki,
In lilac haze repose backyards,
Platfórmi, bróvna, lístia, oblaká
Platforms, logs, leaves, clouds.
Svíst parovóza, khrúst arbúznoi kórki,
Whistle of-locomotive, crunch
  of-watermelon rind,
V dushístoi láike róbkaya ruká,
In perfumed kid-glove timid hand.

Zvenít, gremít, skrezhéshchet, biót
  pribóyem –
Ringing, roaring, grinding, crash
  of breakers –

* Ice frets (eats its heart out)– example of P's fondness for the pathetic fallacy, using colloquial, homely images. Or, on the contrary, raising the ordinary to a higher level: puddles shine like molten diamonds.

I vdrúg pritíkhnet, – éto znáchit, on
And suddenly there-is-silence, –
  this means he
Puglívo probiráyetsa po khvóyam
Timidly is-making-his-way over
  pine-needles,
*Shtób ne spugnút prostránstva chútki
  són.*
So-as not to-startle space /out of its/
  light sleep.

    Light in sense of easily awakened from.

I éto znáchit, on schitáyet zórna
And it means he is-counting grains
V pustíkh kolósiakh, – éto znáchit, on
In empty ears, – it means he
K plité daríalskoi, próklatoi i chórnoi,
To slab of-Darial, accursed and
  black,
Opiát prishól s kakíkh-to pokhorón.
Again has-come from some funeral.

I snóva zhót moskóvskaya istóma
And again he-is-racked
  by-Moscow's fever,
Zvenít vdalí smertélni bubenéts –
Rings in-distance deadly sleighbell –
*Kto zabludílsa v dvúkh shagákh ot
  dóma,*
Someone has-got-lost two paces
  from home,
Gde snég po póyas i vsemú konéts . . .
Where snow / is / up-to waist and
  everything is-finished . . .

    Fever translates *istoma*, a difficult word meaning vaguely discomfort of the spirit caused by the excessive demands of the environment, or life in general – as a result one is uneasy, bored, fretful etc.

Za tó shto dím sravníl s Laokoónom,
For his having smoke compared
  with Laocoon,
Kladbíshchenski vospél chertopolókh,
(For having) sung-of graveyard
  thistles,
Za tó shto mír napólnil nóvim zvónom

For his having world filled
  with-new sound
V prostránstve nóvom otrazhónikh stróf
In space new reflected of-verses.

On nagrazhdión kakím-to véchnim
  détstvom,
He-is rewarded with-kind-of eternal
  childhood,
Tói schchédrostiu i zórkostiu svetíl
With-the generosity and
  sharpsightedness of-stars,
I vsiá zemliá bilá yevó naslédstvom,
And all-of earth has-become his
  heritage,
A ón yeyó so vsémi razdelíl.
And he it with all has-shared.   [19 January 1936]

MH's literate

He, who has compared himself to
  the eye of a horse,
Peers, looks, sees and identifies,
And, at once, like molten diamonds
Puddles shine, ice eats its heart out.
  / broods, pines, frets /

In lilac mists repose backyards,
Platforms, logs, leaves, clouds.
The whistle of a locomotive, the
  crunch of a watermelon's rind,
A timid hand in a perfumed kid
  glove.
{   breakers crash   }
{ Ringing, roaring, grinding, the crash of breakers – }
And suddenly silence, – that means   And silence all at once,
  that he   release,
Is timidly making his way over   It means he is tiptoeing
  pine-needles,   over pine-needles
So as not to startle the light sleep of
  space.

And it means, he's counting the grains
In empty ears, – it means that he
Has come again to the Daryal Stone,
Accursed and black, from some funeral or other.

<blockquote>This probably means the Caucasus, but I'll have to check.</blockquote>

And again Moscow, sweltering, burns,
The deadly sleighbell rings in the distance –
Some one's lost two steps away from home,
Where snow's up to the waist and all is finished . . .

For having compared smoke with the Laocoon,
For singing of graveyard thistles,
For filling the world with a new sound
Of verse reflected in new space,

He has been rewarded by a kind of eternal childhood,
With the generosity and sharpsightedness of stars,
And he has inherited the whole of the earth
And he has shared it with everybody.

Final version

> He who has compared himself to the eye of a horse
> peers, looks, sees, identifies,
> and instantly like molten diamonds
> puddles shine, ice grieves and liquefies.
>
> In lilac mists the backyards drowse,
> and depots, logs, leaves, clouds above;

that hooting train, that crunch of watermelon rind,
that timid hand in a perfumed kid glove . . .

All's ringing, roaring, grinding, breakers' crash —
and silence all at once, release:
it means he is tiptoeing over pine needles.
so as not to startle the light sleep of space.

And it means he is counting the grains
in the blasted ears; it means
he has come again to the Daryal Gorge,
accursed and black, from another funeral.

And again Moscow, where the heart's fever burns.
Far off the deadly sleighbell chimes,
someone is lost two steps from home
in waist-high snow. The worst of times . . .

For spying Laocoön in a puff of smoke,
for making a song out of graveyard thistles,
for filling the world with a new sound
of verse reverberating in new space,

he has been rewarded by a kind of eternal childhood,
with the generosity and brilliance of the stars;
the whole of the earth was his to inherit,
and his to share with every human spirit.

Voice; Landscape; Violence
Sonnevi into English in Helsinki
Rika Lesser

Back in the good old days, when perhaps I translated poetry more quickly and prose more slowly than I do now, I thought it was absurd to write about the problems of translating any particular poem. For one thing, I am the sort of poet-translator who likes to bear in mind the entire body of work of the poet I am translating. For another, I am the sort who prefers to show only clean sheets to the public, and I do not mean winding sheets. Either the poem lives in my English or I will not publish it. No breast-beating, hair-tearing, garment-rending explanation of lamentable choices can breathe life into a *corpus delicti*.

Back in the good old days I mainly translated dead poets. Of this century, but safely underground. For the last three or so years I have also been translating living poets. I have heard some of my colleagues sing the praises of this practice: You sit down with the poet – you may even be translating one another's work – with an imperial quart of scotch, a tape recorder and perhaps a dictionary or two. And the poet you are translating says, 'Oh yes, that's much better in your English. Perhaps I'll change it myself in the next edition.' Now and then, with much less to swallow, I have had this experience. But I am wary of this – what shall I call it? – this lifeline. On Judgment Day the translator alone may hang from it.

Quite recently I have embarked upon two new projects of poetic translation from the Swedish language, both matters of elective affinity and not money. One is a selection of poems by the Finland-Swedish modernist Rabbe Enckell (1903–74) that will center on his nineteen-page masterpiece '*O spång av mellanord*' (from *Andedräkt av koppar* [The Breath of Copper], 1946). Aside from three short poems put into English by one of his fellow Finland-Swedes and eighteen lines of '*O spång*' excerpted and unidentified by its Swedish/English binational editor and translator, the poems of Rabbe Enckell are unavailable to English readers. The other project is translating poems by the living and much celebrated Swedish poet Göran Sonnevi (born 1939). Larger selections of Sonnevi's poems have found their way into English print in translations by Robert Bly, John Matthias in collaboration with Göran Printz-Påhlson, and others.

It is fairly easy to describe how I am proceeding with Enckell. Thirty or so of his books are lined up in chronological order on a shelf above my writing table here in Helsinki. I read them (or reread the ones I was able to get hold of in the States) one by one – taking notes of the prose works, drawing up lists of poems I may translate and include in my selection – between taking stabs at the *real work*, line after line of the four-hundred line '*O spång av mellanord*', which is still only in first draft. Later on I may consult Enckell's manuscripts and correspondence in the archives of the Swedish Literature Society of Finland. In connection with other poems I may stare long at his paintings, to be seen in collections here or in the homes of members of his family, who have readily opened doors to aid me in what will be a years-long effort. When I return to New York in the fall I even plan to study Finnish. Not that Enckell ever wrote in Finnish, but because I no longer find it tolerable to return again and again to this country while utterly ignorant of the majority language. The landscape may not look any different to me when I can read Finnish, but I may well look at it and think about it in a different way.

Although I am much farther along with an English version of one of Sonnevi's poems, it is somehow more difficult to describe this process or procedure. Perhaps it is because he is alive and still very productive and therefore I cannot devour and digest his works in my usual fashion; his next book may cast more light on an earlier book or books, which could make me read them and translate poems from them in a different way. Perhaps it is simply because there is so much more uncertainty about every aspect of a massive new undertaking, so much more inertia to overcome. Certain aspects of this inertia have a history which I can and shall relate, before unraveling some strands of the text still very much in question.

When I lived in Sweden in 1974/5 and was just beginning to work in earnest on Ekelöf's '*Vägvisare till underjorden*' (Guide to the Underworld), Sonnevi was all the rage. I read as much of him as I could stand to at the time, and recall arguing with his many advocates about the merits of his work. If I wanted my fill of linguistics or the natural and physical sciences I could easily pick up the appropriate texts in those fields and read them, as I had in the past. Although opposed to American participation in the Vietnam War in particular (and in general to any land's intervention in the governance of other peoples) I was simply not 'Swedish' enough – then or now – to *enjoy* his blatantly political poems. And it seemed to me that the poems he was writing about music had been written fifty years earlier, and better, by Rilke. This strong negative reaction kept me from reading much Sonnevi between 1975 and 1981.

In September 1982 we both ended up on a translation panel in New York, one of the many events under the banner of Scandinavia Today, this one in particular sponsored by the Academy of American Poets and the American–Scandinavian Foundation. After the several American poets and translators and their Danish, Finnish, Icelandic, Norwegian and Swedish counterparts had finished speaking, the Scandinavian poets read their own poems in their own languages and in English; the order was alphabetical, by country. It was a long afternoon at the Guggenheim. By the time Sonnevi was about to read I was pacing in a glass booth above the auditorium with Bly's bilingual selection ready for marking. And then Göran began to read his poems.

Read is not the right word, neither is intone or incant – there are no elements of melodrama, no pretentions of grandeur in Sonnevi's reading, his singing, voice. It is quiet and melodic; the word intonation takes on an entirely new meaning once you have heard his voice. It rises at the end of each enjambed and often brief line; the stress on each word is extraordinary, the stress on the first word of a new line even more extraordinary. Still more crucial is the underlying rhythmic pattern or the shifting of rhythmic patterns. And the pauses of different durations, the beauty of the various silences. I can scarcely describe the sensation transmitted through the labyrinth of my inner ear when that voice entered for the first time. It was sensual, nearly erotic. Like a knife . . . through water? 'So that is how to read them!' I thought as the voice went on. But why had I not discovered this reading the poems on the page, even when I read them out loud?

Göran Sonnevi and I spent the next couple of days taking long walks around New York City. Between observing the differences in our respective flora and fauna – especially the tails of squirrels – we talked long about poets, poetry, poetics. The key issues we argued were the overriding importance of rhythm, the sound of one particular voice, and how much or how little of these factors can be conveyed by a poem's graphic or orthographic representation.

Over the next year or so I read (or reread) all of Göran's books, keeping his voice in mind; but before I could take a stab or two at any of his poems he surprised me with various versions, in Swedish, of one of my poems from *Etruscan Things*. It was the last poem in the book, 'Degli Sposi', which invokes and gives voices to the sarcophagus of the married couple that resides in the Villa Giulia. The draft with which Göran was least dissatisfied he termed the 'Louvre' version, referring to the other, too much restored, sarcophagus that resides in Paris. In responding to more than one series of questions he posed about this poem, and in going back over what I published as opposed to (a) what I believed I had published or had been trying to write and (b) what he could make of it as a poem in Swedish, I learned that it is far worse to be translated than to translate. Every poem is indeed abandoned. Its maker is happier not to be reminded of this fact.

In March of this year I finally sent Göran an interminable letter containing a draft of one of the poems from his most recent book, *Dikter utan ordning* ([Poems without Order] Stockholm: Bonniers, 1983), the untitled poem that begins *Sommaren har nu vänt*. On 14 May, en route to Helsinki, I landed first in Stockholm, and at Arlanda we spent a couple of jetlagged hours discussing yet another draft I had sent him toward the end of April, along with a slightly less interminable letter. A few days ago I put Enckell aside and took up this poem (see Appendix) once again. This resulted in two new versions and only one half-page of commentary or questionable alternatives. The whole of my currently preferred BBC or Villa Giulia version (which I shall henceforward call, for brevity, BBC) follows. The text of the Sveriges Radio or Louvre version (SR for short) – one that more closely represents my notion of his preferences but is in no way 'literal' – will be cited and discussed only where words, lines or passages differ in ways of more than merely lexical interest. One more word to the wise, or to the blissfully ignorant: if Göran Sonnevi were not alive to read this poem aloud in English, I might very well be happy enough with the BBC version as it stands and lose no more sleep over it. Here it is in its latest, still undefinitive, American English incarnation:

> Summer has turned now   And I go
> deeper inside my mother   She who
> bears me, ceaselessly, all

       the more deeply into the motion of growth
5   Wild roses bloom on the mountain
    The birds' voices have changed, cry warnings,
    the voices of their young, more delicate   Mary
    's keys blossom, along-
    side night-scented orchids, there
10 in the narrow glade   In the lake
    girls bathe in white suits   I
    walk by in wooden shoes, my footing uncertain
    I think about the unfinished, the construction
    of what is, which is also
15 the world, as an aspect of this building
    that also is borne from my mother, as she too
    is a part of the growing, and
    of the dying; for if death were not
    everything soon would be finished
20 Storeys, structures, in all directions, from
    all directions   Direction there is none
    To describe the four-dimensional ball of the wavering
    orders requires many more than four dimensions
    The first small chanterelles are here   Perhaps I can't
25 finish anything, but I reason:
    that is not for me to decide
    but for her, mother of the orders of growth   I
    am borne from her cry   The foliage, still light, is fragrant
    I pick flowers, midsummer flowers, hawkweed,
30 two kinds of clover, vetch,
    buttercups, oxtongue, corn mayweed   Hell and Paradise
    are only limited aspects of the large construct
    we chance to pass through only for a time
    Even the huge cosmic man, whose spine is
35 the axis of the universe, also shall pass
    I don't know how Gödel imagined the larger construct
    All I know is that his image won't be the last
    In my mother are no contradictions   She looks at me
    I can't speak with her   She never answers   She
40 cannot answer   But every part of my voice
    is borne from her   And is part of the world in its growth
    Each little splinter of voice   Address alone is possible
    Because if we did not speak, if all creation – each being
    and thing in existence – did not speak, neither would she

45 exist   She would not know of her own existence
    For she sees her child   When her dark eyes see her child
    ever her invisibility quickens   I know that
    she also looks at us with the eyes of judgment, straight through
    the underworld down to the bottom of Hell   To that which under-
50 lies Hell   She prays for us, the doomed   She alone and no
    other   The luminous night fills with the night orchid's scent   Moths
    are still awake, while the birds sleep, a short time
    In deepest Hell all are awake   The stars spiral, turn,
    join in dance   The great eyes are dark now, and still

Lines 1–5 of the BBC and the SR versions are identical, but lines 6–10 of the latter are different enough to excerpt and discuss in conjunction with the original Swedish:

> Fåglarnas röster är andra; varningar;
> ungarnas spädare röster   Jungfru
> Marie nycklar blommar, till-
> sammans med nattviol, där
> i den lilla gläntan   I sjön

> The birds' voices are different; warnings;
> the voices of their young, more delicate   Virgin
> Mary's keys blossom, along-
> side night-scented orchids, there
> in that little clearing   In the lake

In the BBC version I do some small, but what I consider necessary, violence in describing the birds' voices. They 'have changed, cry warnings,' in distinction to the more literal rendition that accentuates the ontological with 'are different; warnings;' that appears in the SR version. Why do I consider this violence necessary, even essential? And why have I replaced the semicolons with commas? Simply or complexly because the English line in the SR version sounds flat to my ear. Elsewhere in this volume Judith Moffett discusses Swedish word-endings (plurals, verbs, the definite articles) and their relation to patterns of rhyme and meter. Judy and I often paramiserate about our Swedish translation problems. Meter and rhyme do not concern me in this project: rhythmic and semantic stress do. Neither of us can put the definite article at the end of a noun – a bad trot of lines 6 and 7 would read something like: 'Birdsthe's voices are different / other; warnings; / youngsthe's thinner / delicater / tenderer voices   Virgin.' The first clear rhythmic stress in the clause 'The birds' voices have changed' falls on 'voices'. Göran Sonnevi's voice reading the Swedish aloud would stress each word separately; because of the pause before *varningar*, the word *andra* would seem to be stressed slightly more than the three words preceding it. The English goes by more quickly in both of my versions. As I would not ordinarily pronounce all three syllables of 'different', my ear and eye prefer the certainty of the stress on 'changed'. Further, the shared letters 'a', 'n' and 'g' in 'changed' and 'warnings' – though they do not produce the same sonic effect of the shared letters *a*, *n* and *r* in *andra* and *varningar* – do produce some effect that the conjunction of 'different' and 'warnings' does not. Proper use of the semicolon in English – especially in a poem that disdains the period – makes me squeamish about inserting a semicolon between an independent clause and a dependent one. (I have changed punctuation elsewhere in this poem, but think one example sufficient. In fact, in typing every draft of this poem, I have spaced horizontally three times each time a sentence ends in mid-line. As the typewriter I am now using has the same typeface as the manuscript of *Dikter utan ordning* Göran sent me, I can see clearly now that he hit his space bar only twice.) Sonnevi is not alone among Swedish authors in using the semicolon to indicate a pause lasting longer than one occasioned by a comma. This poem rarely has a comma at the end of a line (in Swedish or English), and so I expect its readers to pause longer at the end of a line where one does occur.

The next important difference in these versions is the name of the flower, in Swedish *Jungfru Marie nycklar*. Interpretation aside for the moment, there is a scientific difficulty. Not all the botany books in the world can make *Dactylorhiza* (or *Orchis*) *maculata* be a species of North America, or give it a common name that, literally rendered, would be Virgin Mary's keys. Any number of interesting literary possibilities were ruled out (think, for example, of the lady's slippers, which are at least orchids, or of the Mary lilies that do grow in the United States) because they did not truly represent the orchid whose stained leaves its common Swedish name so neatly conceals. When I publish a book of Sonnevi's poems I may well gloss the Latin names of the more important flowers. I feel a bit like Nabokov in this respect, a respect for a particular landscape and its flora and fauna, and a bit like Auden in another.

There is more than a small suggestion that the more delicate voices of the young birds address, invoke or apostrophize the Virgin. Syntactic parallelism between this line and its predecessor, coupled with the Sonnevian end-line-pause stress make for a long interval of silence before the Virgin falls, in the following line, into the flower category. Göran is troubled by my *trompe d'œil*, whereby Mary is apostrophized in both senses of the word. My precedents in this craftiness are Elizabeth Bishop and Marianne Moore. But back now to Auden. I do not care to recount how many times I justified to Swedish readers his translation of Ekelöf's *Jungfru* (in the first two books of Ekelöf's Dīwān trilogy, which Auden translated in collaboration with Leif Sjöberg) as 'Lady'. In translating the third book of that trilogy I could not, for many reasons, follow his example. I am not Catholic and I am not Auden, but my ear tells me to go with 'Mary'. What troubles Göran, though, is how he would read this twofold apostrophe out loud in English. Here I would invite him to read the SR version's Virgin, if he had to read the English aloud. But in print I'd insist on the BBC.

Nattviol (Platanthera bifolia), in the following line rendered as night-scented orchid, presented somewhat less of a problem. It does grow in North America, where its common name is 'butterfly orchis'. However, down in line 51 it reappears in a time-stressed and lepidopteran context, so once again a new name had to be constructed, in this case formed by analogy from the name of an extant flower, night-scented stock. By the way, the *midsommarblomster* or midsummer flowers picked in line 29 are *Geranium sylvaticum*. If you can still recall how the poem begins, the choice will strike you as natural.

Before leaving this section of the Swedish landscape you will note that the BBC version gives 'the narrow glade', while the SR version reads 'that little clearing'. For the present I still prefer the former; my ear enjoys the long 'a's of glade/lake/bathe. But in August, when I see this 'little' patch of land, I may give the SR version the floor.

Floors are very much a part of the next unsettled or unsettling passage; here are the Swedish and the SR translation for lines 20–3:

Våningar, strukturer, åt alla håll, från
alla håll   Det finns ingen riktning
De svävande ordningarnas fyrdimensionella boll
För att beskriva den krävs fler dimensioner

Habitations, structures, in all directions, from
all directions   There is no direction
To describe the four-dimensional ball of the floating (?)
orders requires many more than four dimensions

The first problem presents itself in the word *våningar*, related to the German *Wohnung* (singular form), meaning residence, dwelling, apartment and the like. But Swedish *våning* also means 'floor' in the sense of storey. A Swedish reader would (one hopes) read the word both ways and be correct, but the English translator (having experimented with giving two words for the one and finding no good rhythmic solution – note also that the repeated monosyllable *håll* can only be translated with a trisyllabic word) is forced to choose. It seemed reasonable to question the living poet about his primary intention. But who is to say the author himself is not trapped in the intentional fallacy? The SR version now has 'habitations', which may become 'high rises'. 'Storeys' could too easily be misunderstood when read aloud.

Swedish, which has a far smaller lexicon than that of English, rarely has two words for one in English. But both *håll* and *riktning* must be given as 'direction(s)' in this context. This partly explains why, in the BBC version, I have opted for the more formal diction of Direction there is none. I cannot alter the word but I can alter the stress on it. Other reasons for heightening the diction here look forward to the next two lines as much as back to the preceding one.

Swedish *svävande* (German *schwebend*) has no *modern* English correspondent. It describes a sweeping, hovering, suspended, floating motion with no strings attached. In one of its verb forms it also describes how, in Swedish, 'the Spirit of God moved upon the face of the waters' (*Genesis* 1:2, King James Version). My mind flew to *Paradise Lost*: 'and with mighty wings outspread / Dove-like satst brooding on the vast Abyss'. Thence to the OED where, in British English, hens hover their chicks. The (?) after floating in the SR version leads to a list of other suggestions: unfixable, inconstant, changeable, and good old wavering (from the BBC version and countless other drafts).

Now the difficulties start to multiply, lexically and syntactically. The 'four-dimensional ball' carries us into the lofty realms of higher mathematics – note that Gödel's uncertainty theorem is alluded to 2^4 lines later. And the Swedish line, a clause only, is suspended, floats like that ball, leading into another sentence fragment, literally: 'To describe that requires several dimensions'. What the English offers, in both versions, is an alternative to what any reader quickly would identify as translatorese. The enjambment between 'wavering/floating' or whatever ('wavering' still seems best, most apt for the multi-dimensional abstraction of that ball) and 'orders' pauses at least while floating the reversed clauses from one line to another. As with 'Direction there is none', the transposition of these two clauses shifts the diction formally upward. You can imagine my relief, in line 24, when the poet casts his eyes downward, to the first small chanterelles.

Round about line 36 ('I don't know how Gödel imagined the larger construct') my head starts to throb. I think it was my difficulty in mentally rotating curves around axes to create three-dimensional figures while solving problems in partial differentiation that turned me away from the sciences and toward the arts. A mathematically-minded painter friend of mine did his best to explain Gödel's uncertainty theorem to me. My headache is not in explaining it, but in rendering line 38, which is given literally in the SR version's 'My mother is without contradictions'. An earlier version read 'My mother knows no contradictions'. Göran Sonnevi was quick to point out that I had shifted his ontological pronouncement to an epistemological one. Nor did he much care for 'has' or 'owns' in place of 'knows'. My English ear is jarred by a mother who is 'without contradictions' – is she also 'without' milk? In the English language of what I might call this bio-religious philosophical lyric poem, the BBC's 'In my mother are no contradictions' still seems the best way out . . . or way into the mother, into whom we have gone and from whom we are ceaselessly being borne throughout the poem. I stop to wonder whether my mind runs toward epistemology *because* I am female, and then reason that the BBC rendition of this sentence is the least stillborn.

At Arlanda Airport a few weeks back Göran and I discussed – more than mathematics or philosophy – Jewish mysticism, Jainism, the story of Mary's Harrowing of Hell . . . all of which made me feel better about the rightness of other acts of violence (attributable to faith) I had committed on this positively vulnerable Swed-

Voice; Landscape; Violence 135

ish poem. I have already mentioned my mind's flight to Genesis and *Paradise Lost*; it did that more than once. It also went on more than one other excursion into the Old Testament. The briefest runs from line 50 into 51, referring to the mother who 'prays for us, the doomed'. Here the BBC and SR versions agree on 'She alone and no / other', despite the more conversational Swedish *Ingen annan / gör det* ('No one else / does that'). Perhaps it was because I was celebrating Passover while working on this poem that I heard God's loftier voice speaking to the Israelites: 'I will pass through the land of Egypt: I Myself and not an angel . . . I myself and not a Seraph . . . I Myself and not a messenger. I, the Eternal, I am He, and none other.' At least He is given to ontological statements!

At present there are other unremarked differences between the BBC and SR versions, and surely the BBC will see some small changes before I abandon it. I console myself always with a line of Ekelöf's from 'The Devil's Sermon': 'If something perfect existed there would be no Perfection'. And in this case also with Sonnevi's complex notion of 'the unfinished language'.

While writing this essay on 10 June 1984 in Helsinki I got a phone call from Göran, who had just been to the actual place whose flora is so crucial to this poem. His voice reported that atop the small, rocky mountain the wild roses are already in bloom – two weeks in advance of midsummer. That, I replied, must be due to the violent though temporary surge of summer weather we have enjoyed on both sides of the Baltic. By the time I reach Sweden, in August, the *Orchis maculata* and *Platanthera bifolia* certainly will be past. But I shall take a good look at that 'clearing' and see better the details of another landscape, described in the poem immediately preceding this one in *Dikter utan ordning*. It is called 'Dyrön; 1981' and begins with the words *Sommaren har nu vänt*.

APPENDIX

    Sommaren har nu vänt   Och jag går
    djupare in i min mor   Hon som
    föder mig, oavbrutet, allt
    djupare in, i den växande rörelsen
5   Vildrosorna blommar på berget
    Fåglarnas röster är andra; varningar;
    ungarnas spädare röster   Jungfru

Marie nycklar blommar, till-
sammans med nattviol, där
10   i den lilla gläntan   I sjön
badar flickor i vita baddräkter   Jag
går förbi i träskor, på osäkra fötter
Jag tänker på det oavslutade, bygget
av det som är, som också är
15   världen, som en aspekt av detta, och
också föds ut ur min mor, som också hon
är en del av detta växande, också
döende, för om inte döden fanns
skulle allt snabbt vara avslutat
20   Våningar, strukturer, åt alla håll, från
alla håll   Det finns ingen riktning
De svävande ordningarnas fyrdimensionella boll
För att beskriva den krävs fler dimensioner
De första, små kantarellerna har kommit   Jag kan
25   kanske inte avsluta något, men jag tänker
att det bestämmer inte jag
utan bara de växande ordningarnas mor   Jag
föds ut ur hennes skrik   De ännu ljusa löven doftar
Jag plockar blommor, midsommarblomster, fibblor;
30   två sorters klöver, något slags vicker;
smörblommor, oxtunga, baldersbrå   Helvetet och Paradiset
är bara begränsade aspekter av det stora bygget
Och vi passerar där igenom, bara tillfälligt
Också den stora världsmänniskan, med universums axel
35   som sin ryggrad, är något som passerar
Jag vet inte hur Gödel föreställde sig det större bygget
Jag vet bara att inte heller hans bild är den sista
Min mor är utan motsägelser   Hon ser på mig
Jag kan inte samtala med henne   Hon svarar aldrig   Hon
40   kan inte svara   Men varje del av min röst
föds ut ur henne   Och är del av den växande världen
Varje liten skärva av röst   Bara tilltalet är möjligt
Därför att om inte vi talade, om inte alla varelser
och ting i universum talade, skulle inte heller
45   hon finnas   Hon skulle inte veta att hon fanns
För hon ser sitt barn   Hennes mörka ögon ser sitt barn

Då blir också hennes osynlighet levande   Jag vet,
hon ser också på oss med domens ögon, tvärs genom
underjorden ner till det lägsta Helvetet   Till det som är
50 under Helvetet   Hon ber för oss dömda   Ingen annan
gör det   I den ljusa natten doftar nattviolen   Flyn
är ännu vakna, medan fåglarna sover, en kort stund
Lägst ner i Helvetet är alla vakna   Stjärnorna virvlar i
gemensam dans   De stora ögonen är nu mörka, stilla
55 Då blir också hennes osynlighet levande   Jag vet,
hon ser också på oss med domens ögon, tvärs genom
underjorden ner till det lägsta Helvetet   Till det som är
under Helvetet   Hon ber för oss dömda   Ingen annan
gör det   I den ljusa natten doftar nattviolen   Flyn
60 är ännu vakna, medan fåglarna sover, en kort stund
Lägst ner i Helvetet är alla vakna   Stjärnorna virvlar i
gemensam dans   De stora ögonen är nu mörka, stilla

Translating Juarroz and Noren
Working Papers
W. S. Merwin

PRELIMINARY NOTE BY D. WEISSBORT

Some years ago, after discussions with Jim Holmes, I began actively to solicit additional working papers and commentaries for the present volume. I wrote to Bill Merwin to ask whether he was currently working on something that might be suitable for the collection. At the same time I mentioned an item which had appeared in *Translation Review* (No. 9, 1982, Dallas). This included a short introduction by Michael Gormon, 'W.S. Merwin Translator Poet', with accompanying draft translations by Merwin of the Swedish poet Lars Noren, in which Merwin, not knowing the source language, was working through 'primary' translations into English by another Swedish poet, Gunnar Harding. It occurred to me that we might reproduce some of this material too. Bill sent me some photocopies of his worksheets of the Argentinian poet Roberto Juarroz's 'vertical poetry'. He also insisted that he did not have anything to say about translating poetry that he had not already said in the foreword to his *Collected Translations, 1968–1978* (Atheneum, 1980). He apologized for the absence of innumerable revisions in the Juarroz drafts and observed that generally he was either able to translate a piece, in which case there might well be comparatively little reworking of it, or he was not. (Michael Hamburger had said something very similar in a letter to me; see his contribution above.)

When earlier this month (May 1987) I wrote again to Bill, to remind him about the collection and to let him know that at long last it was moving towards publication, I again mentioned the Noren drafts and suggested that publishing the Juarroz and Noren together would interestingly illustrate the difference between translating poetry directly and indirectly from the source language, since with Noren, unlike Juarroz, a substantial distance had been travelled between first and final versions. This question is briefly discussed by Michael Gormon in his essay. 'To the complexity of the fundamental question of the nature of poetic translation', he says, 'we can add the question of whether there is any difference between a poet creating a poem on the basis of his own translation and a poet creating a poem on the basis of a translation made by someone else.' He notes that, paradoxically, knowledge of the source language might even inhibit the creative process. Finally, though, he asks: 'But, then, what of Robinson's "unsayable"? ['Poetry is a language that tells us, through a more or less emotional reaction, something that cannot be said' Edwin Arlington Robinson.] Can any translator, not a native speaker, capture that elusive gleam?'

In his response to me (11 May 1987) Merwin comments on these matters as follows:

> Not only are your own suggestions about the differences between the two sorts of translation very good ones, but I think one can go a bit further. In doing translations from a language one can read first hand, it is often fairly possible to have some notion, from reading the original, about which poems one might be able to make something of, and more or less how it would go. When, on the other hand, one has a set of literals only, one may have to tinker with them for a while before getting a sense of that, of what one can make of them, or can't. I think the actual choice of material has more to do with the outcome of translations than is usually admitted, and that there are poems that might be managed by someone and not by someone else. Juarroz seems to me extremely familiar, somehow. I feel I can hear the poems clearly when they are poems I want to translate. With Noren I had no idea until I got into each poem. I continue in the belief, you know, that I don't know how to translate, and that nobody does. It is an impossible but necessary process, there is no perfect way to do it, and much of it must be found for each particular poem, as we go.

Since the original manuscript would not reproduce satisfactorily, the drafts offered below have been transcribed.

ROBERTO JUARROZ'S 'FIFTH VERTICAL POETRY # 27'

Original Spanish text

Los rostros que has ido abandonando
se han quedado debajo de tu rostro
y a veces te sobresalen
como si tu piel no alcanzara para todos

Las manos que has ido abandonando
te abultan a veces en la mano
y te absorben las cosas o las sueltan
como esponjas crecientes.

Las vidas que has ido abandonando
te sobreviven en tu propria sombra
y algún dia te asaltarán como una vida,
tal vez para morir una vez sola.

Draft

Juarroz – 7/84

5th V.P. # 27 p. 37

                    abandoned
The faces that you've ~~left behind~~

have remained under your face
                  ~~bulg~~   ~~bulg~~ bulge out
and sometimes they ~~push out~~
                          contain
as though your skin could not ~~hold~~ them all

The hands that you've abandoned

swell up sometimes in your hand

and absorb things or release them

like growing sponges

The lives that you've abandoned

survive you in your own shadow
    one
and ~~one~~ day they will storm you like a life

to die perhaps once alone

Final version

> The faces that you've abandoned
> have remained under your face
> and sometimes they bulge out
> as though your skin could not contain them all
>
> The hands that you've abandoned
> swell up sometimes in your hand
> and absorb things or release them
> like growing sponges
>
> The lives that you've abandoned
> survive you in your own shadow
> and one day they will storm you like a life
> to die perhaps once alone

POEM (UNTITLED) BY LARS NOREN

Original Swedish

> Idag är allting
> allvarligt och nästan tyst.
> Som när en drottning går bort
> och radion byter ut den lättare musiken
> mot Mozart och Bach.
> Jag förstår inte varför.
> Hon lyssnar ju inte.
> Jag kan nästan se

> hur människor går ifrån
> varandra, hur tystnaden
> arbetar i de bleknande kläderna
> och hur den ensamma
> grå getingen söker sig in
> till sin dödssömn
> i det torra bergträdets sår.

Draft by Gunnar Harding

Today everything is
serious (earnest?) and almost quiet
As when a queen passes away (dies?)
and the radio exchanges the lighter music (popular music?)
to Mozart or Bach.
I can't see (understand?) why.
As she isn't listening. (doesn't listen?)
    (She isn't listening, is she?)
I can almost see
how people leave
each other, how silence
works in the paling (fading, bleaching) cloths
and how the lonely
grey wasp searches its way (literally: searches itself into)
into its deathsleep
in the wound of the dry mountain tree.

From a letter by Harding, commenting on his translation

It's hard to say for me what could be difficult here. *Den lättare musiken* means word by word '(the) lighter music'. This is a very common term in Swedish, exactly what you call the kind of Melachrino etc. music the radio usually plays, so the important thing there is just to find the general term in English. Line 7. A very simple phrase, complicated only because of the word *ju* that has no English equivalent. Without it the phrase means 'She doesn't listen'. If you translate the *ju* with 'as' the full stop has to be taken away in English. The word could also be dropped. *Bleknande* means paling, but I don't know if you can use that word about cloths. It means losing their color – because of the sun, because of being washed too many times etc.

Draft by Merwin

~~Today~~ ~~Everything~~ Today everything
is earnest and [unreadable, crossed out] ~~almost~~
~~still~~ hushed
As ~~when a queen~~ at the death of a queen
When the radio changes from ~~pop~~ light~~er~~ music
to Mozart or Bach.
I don't know why.
Since ~~S~~ she isn't listening? ~~is she~~?
I can almost see
how people leave
each other, how silence
toils ~~labours~~ (?) in the fading fabrics
and how the lonely
gray wasp gropes its way
into its death sleep
in the wound of the dry ~~mountain~~
mountain tree

Final printed version by Merwin

Today everything
is earnest and hushed.
As at the death of a queen
when the radio changes from light music
to Mozart or Bach.
I don't know why.
Since she isn't listening.
I can almost see
how people leave
each other, how silence
works in the fading fabrics
and how the solitary
gray wasp gropes its way
into its death sleep
in the wound of the dry mountain tree.

Playing Scrabble without a Board
On Formal Translation from the Swedish
Judith Moffett

Translating formal poetry effectively and accurately *with its form more or less intact* is so close to impossible, and so stressful and maddening in the attempt, that were the translator compensated neither by an exalted sense of making a gift of great value – a splendid and important poem or body of poetry – to a hitherto deprived readership, nor by lots of cold cash, he or she would have to be a bit demented to persist. There is a fundamental absurdity to the enterprise as well, in that the translator will invariably have to spend many times as long constructing the translation as the poet spent writing the poem in the first place. Yet most, perhaps all, formal poetry is changed so utterly when rendered into free verse that, while the free-verse version may sound all right, I am one of an embattled minority which believes that a formal poem's rhymes and metrical arrangements are essential to it and should at all costs be preserved in translation.

One quickly learns, however, that preserving a poem's form entire, with all rhymes perfect and every metrical effect faithfully copied down to the last syllable, requires a simply phenomenal amount of effort and time. In order to complete a project of reasonable size in a reasonable number of months without succumbing to burnout or losing one's sanity, one must make minor compromises. My own experience and experiments with classical Swedish poetry have brought me round to accepting two.

First: within limits, I allow myself to slant the vowel sounds of my rhyme words – though never to mismatch terminal sounds, by coupling a singular noun with a plural one ('bird' with 'words') or mating a verb whose tense ending adds -s or -ed with a word lacking the same ending ('ants' with 'danced'; 'chum' with 'crumbs'). Thus on occasion 'pours' may rhyme with 'stirs', or 'glass' with 'marvelous', or even – once, under extreme duress – 'breeze' with 'leaves' with 'breathes' (but such radical rhymes should be resorted to only in very special circumstances, and then only if they really do work, which is likelier in the *a* than in the *b* position of a quatrain or sextet, none of whose vowels are slanted at all). For example:

> You hear his pacing in the breeze
> That wends its wandering ways
> Past earth still thick with autumn leaves
> On thawing April days,
> And soil is quickened where he breathes
> A smoky steam of haze.

Second: I often drop the unaccented syllable at the end of a line, thereby turning a feminine rhyme into a masculine one. I am less defensive about this strategy. The natural verse unit in English, as everybody knows, is the iamb. In Swedish it is the trochee, a fact due mainly to grammar. The definite article is tacked onto the end of a Swedish noun, either as a single letter or as an unstressed syllable, so that the effect is one of constantly falling tones. Where English states: The girl / is cóm- / ing iń / to the róom, Swedish puts it: Flícka*n* / kómm*er* / ín i / rúm*met*, where *n* and *et* are definite articles (the second syllable of *flicka* being unstressed already) and *er* the tense ending of the verb. These stress patterns of noun and verb are extremely common. Whether the definite article drops away behind the noun or is the springboard from which the noun is launched has a profound effect on the overall sound of a language.

You would expect to find a lot of feminine rhymes in Swedish poetry, and you do. They are extremely troublesome to keep, and unless the form is a finely-wrought lyric stanza whose character forces a choice between retaining the feminine rhymes and not translating the poem, I am increasingly inclined to drop that final syllable, most especially if the first syllable of the next line is unaccented as well. You virtually never find *both* ends of a line of verse unaccented in English poetry, line after line. Apart from these two compromises I make a terrific effort not to cheat; and I keep the number, proximity and 'degree of slant' of the vowel-changes ('weld' and 'filled', but not 'wailed' and 'fueled') under tight control.

The necessity of sacrificing the perfect chiming of rhyme-sounds in the nineteenth-century poems I have been working on lately is a source of continual regret to me. Until Emily Dickinson thought of them, these effects were never sought (and scarcely imagined?) by poets writing in English *or* Swedish, meaning that in my translations the music of the original poems is foredoomed to be slightly falsified, out of tune. To compensate, I do all I can to sense accurately, and then preserve, their period tone and diction. In translating the older poems I have chosen always to suggest, if not actually imitate, a style in keeping with the English and American poetry of the period when they were written. All these poets used conventional devices and expressions archaic even for their time: inversion of ordinary word order, elevated rhetorical diction and so forth. So did the Swedes after their own fashion, and so do I; I do not think that the language of a poem composed in 1816 ought to sound as if it might have been penned (or typed) last year, just because the translation was done last year. Each classical Swedish poet has his own way with the period style, and I try to sense these differences and suggest them in the translations.

The little lyric 'Kannick/The Clergy-House' is the only poem I have worked on in some months which is short enough to illustrate in its entirety the actual procedures of formal translation. 'Kannick' is a skillfully-wrought piece of occasional verse by Esaias Tegnér (1782–1846), very different in its lightness and brevity from the elevated rhetorical postures Tegnér was so ready to strike in his more 'serious' work. Its qualities of charm and wit are rather of a piece with his epistolary style; Tegnér was a celebrated correspondent whose letters have been frequently edited and reprinted, most recently in a handsome boxed two-volume edition published in Stockholm by P.P. Norstedt & Söner in 1983.

The critic Fredrik Böök, Sweden's foremost authority on Tegnér, writes in his biography of the poet:

> The most captivating item in this entire genre of Tegnér's [i.e. occasional verse, for which he was famous among his contemporaries] is Kannick, the poem Tegnér wrote for a harvest festival on the professor-meadows [*professorängar*], where the whole coterie [of professors and their families] had gone in carriages, bringing along the platform used at the masters' promotions in the Cathedral – it was now to serve as a dance floor. . . . It is as if the fields of fragrant clover in that district

were enlivened by a fresh breeze, from the sea nearby or from Tegnér's salty irony; the Cathedral can be seen on the horizon with its reminder of medieval bigotry, which forms a background to the enjoyment of this modern company, a clergy free from prejudice. In a couple of quick strokes the whole shifting crowd is rendered, the flowerlike grace of the dancing girls along with the substantial worthiness of the wives, who resemble those plump haystacks.

Here is the poem, together with a prose draft roughly blocked out in English:

KANNICK (1816)

I Kannick bodde fordom Munkar (I Lund vill ej den slägten dö) De gjorde bön och filebunkar Och åto sjelfva opp sitt hö.	In (the) clergy-house in former times lived monks (In Lund that kindred means not to die) They made prayers and yoghurt And ate up their hay themselves.
Nu ha vi klokare Kanicker Som tagit bättre seder an. Ett glas man i det gröna dricker, Och uppå ängen dansar man.	Now we have wiser clergy(folk) Who have taken better customs on. One drinks a glass in the out-of doors And dances upon the meadow.
Och flickor ha vi med tillika Af hälften rosor, hälften snö, Och muntra prester som predika För flickorna: 'allt kött är hö'.	And we have girls with us too, (Made) half of roses, half of snow, And cheerful priests who preach For the girls: 'all flesh is grass (hay)'.
Allt köttär hö, och höet skall falla	All flesh is grass, and the grass shall fall

Och blomstren skola huggas bort.	And the flowers shall be chopped away.
I stackars flickor, för Er alla	Ye poor girls, for you all
Är bergningstiden inom kort.	The harvest-time will be here shortly.

{ Åt gräset gör väl sådant skada,
  För rosorna är sådant skada, }
Men Fruarna de le dervid,
Och tacka Gud, och äro glada
Att vara stackade i tid.

{ Such (things) do damage to the grass,
  Such things are harm(ful) to the roses, }
But the wives they smile at that,
And thank God, and are happy
To be (about being) stacked in time.

note: hö = hay; gräs = grass

The first problem I faced was that I did not know what a 'Kannick' *was* – a place name? a type of dwelling? Some such 'scholarly' problem presents itself at the outset, more often than not, when the poem being translated is an older one. In this case a little diligent research provided the information that in the Middle Ages a *kanik* (modern spelling) was really a *kanikhus*: a house attached, figuratively, to a church or cathedral, whose members *(kaniker)* formed a sort of ecclesiastical community devoted to learning, more or less on the model of the colleges of Oxford and Cambridge. The OED suggests that in medieval England a similar institution had been called a 'clergy-house' and its inmates 'canons' (compare *kaniker*). In Tegnér's day the land surrounding the old clergy-house building or buildings, which had formerly supported the monks who lived in them, and which had been in the possession of the Church since 1085, were made over to the use of professors at the University of Lund, of whom Tegnér was one (of Greek), as part of their salary. As was also true in England in 1816, when Tegnér wrote 'Kannick', all university professors were in divine orders; but unlike the Oxbridge dons these Lutherans were allowed to marry, and the income from the cash crops grown on the 'professor-meadows' was a welcome supplement to the support of a growing family. The fields and buildings are still there,

KANNIK

The clergy-house kept many a monk
--In Lund that kindred sometimes dwell--
Who once sang mass and slept and drunk
And ate up all their hay as well.

But we have cleverer clergy now
Who've taken better customs on.
Who drink a glass beneath the bough
And dance the grassy field upon,
In meadow grass anon.

And girls are with us, proven each,
That snow and roses make a lass.
And certain jolly priests, who preach
Before the girls: All flesh is grass.

All flesh is grass, and grass shall fall,
The flower thereof be cut away.
Ye hapless creatures, for you all
We harvest any day.

Such deeds are death to roses, true, —yea—
But wives, they smile to see the crime,
And praise the Lord, and hold the view
They're lucky they were stacked in time.

plainly marked KANNIK on a current map of Lund – an open area west of the town.

The occasion of these verses, then, appears to have been a picnic outing, which all the professors attended with their wives and children, to celebrate the successful completion of the hay harvest. It is possible that Tegnér and his friends were familiar with a local tale about the Catholic monks who had formerly lived – dissolutely, so one gathers – in that very clergy-house: something to do with their literally or figuratively eating their own hay crop, Nebuchadnezzar-fashion. But no account of such a tale appears in any source I have been able to examine, nor do the present-day academics in Lund know of one. It seems likeliest that Tegnér is simply referring here to the fact that monks in medieval times would have fed the hay they grew to their own livestock, whereas the professors grew theirs to sell as a cash crop.

At any rate Tegnér has here drawn together the monks' (edible) hay crop, the hay grown by himself and his colleagues in these same fields and the assurance of the prophet Isaiah that 'All flesh is grass', to make 'hay' the central trope of his lines; in fact the old Swedish Bible asserts that all flesh is not grass but hay *(hö)*, which suits the poet's purposes admirably but creates a problem, slight but insoluble, for the translator. One other point is worth noting: there was at that time in Lund a Bishop Munck, who had two daughters married to professors, a professor son and a son who was a vicar *(kyrkoherde)*; all of them may have been, and probably were, present at the picnic. The first two lines of the poem, then, almost certainly make a graceful pun.

I hope Tegnér will be forgiven his twitting, somewhat leeringly avuncular stance. Before many more years had passed he was to embark upon a series of devastatingly self-destructive infatuations, with cultured intellectual women very different in class and nature from his down-to-earth, haystack-variety wife, and his punishment was to be more than he deserved, and more than his mental health could withstand without permanent damage.

Now then. Formal decisions first. It is immediately obvious that in a lyric poem this short and sweet there may be no imperfect rhymes. I make the judgment reluctantly – the rhymes of a tetrameter poem are tyrannical, substantially more so than those of pentameter verses with their two additional syllables' worth of maneuverability – yet there is really no help for it. The poetic stakes are not very high here, but nothing would be left of this pleasant little piece were its corset of form to be loosened. Briefly, I even consider retaining the feminine rhymes; but since the first line pretty much has to end with one of two one-syllable words, 'monk(s)' or 'house', and since putting an unaccented syllable both fore and aft of a line affects me unpleasantly, I decide against it. True rhymes are far more important to the feel of these stanzas than the little sag at the end of every other line. My overriding concern has always to be not to ruin the *tone* by making the language either too inelegant or too ornate and complex. In the search for properly stressed alternative lines, and especially for rhymes, there is a constant impulse to shift away from the simplicity of Tegnér's own language which has to be constantly guarded against and shifted back from.

Here is my first clumsy and highly provisional attempt to versify the poem in English:

> The clergy-house once sheltered monks
> (In Lund their kind endures for aye)
> They prayed, and snored upon their bunks,
> And did themselves eat up their hay.
>
> But we have cleverer clergy now,
> Who've taken better customs on –
> A glass beneath the leafy bough
> And dancing on the meadow lawn.
>
> And girl's are in the party's sum,
> Half snow, half roses, each young lass,
> And cheery priests, who please to come
> And preach to them: All flesh is grass.
>
> All flesh is grass, and grass shall fall,
> And flowers be cut away, I fear.
> Ye poor young ladies, for you all
> The harvest-time is very near.
>
> Such things do harm to grass, 'tis true,
> But wives, they smile to see the crime,
> And thank the Lord, and take the view
> They're lucky to be stacked in time.

In the earlier stages a poem with stanzas is translated stanza-unit by unit, as if the stanzas were little individual poems. This is inevitable; each rhyme is stanza-specific (so to speak) and the problems it raises must be solved for the stanza as a whole, in such a way that it reads without strain. Time enough to worry about the *poem's* wholeness later on. The difficulty is that these units, when put back together, very often do not work together as a whole poem, in form or in content. And there is the especially diabolical problem of getting one stanza composed, with great labor, around a certain rhyme, only to discover that the very next stanza absolutely *has* to use that same rhyme-sound. It is quite astonishing how often this happens, and when it does there is nothing for it but to back up and change the earlier rhyme, because the rule of proximity may be violated only under very exceptional circumstances, and rarely then. However (one small plus) a passive decision between alternative versions of roughly equal merit sometimes helpfully forced by the need to avoid a particular rhyme.

Each of the five stanzas of 'Kannick' posed its own set of problems, and an intolerable amount could be written about each set. What I shall do instead is try to indicate the kinds of things the formal translator has to think of and cope with, and something of the aggravations of being balked, and the pleasure – or at least the relief – of discovering solutions. I shall do this specifically in detail for the first two stanzas and then make general observations about the others. The final version of the translation appears on p. 159, and from time to time the reader will need to refer to it and to compare it with the draft versions printed above in order to follow the ensuing discussion.

Iambic meter is not too hard to work with, compared to (say) anapestic or dactyllic meter. In stanza 1 of 'Kannick', however, unless 'clergy-house' gets rid of its article by going plural there will be no room for an unaccented preposition (in) at the beginning of the first line ('In clergy-houses, monks once lived'). No good: Tegnér is referring here to one particular clergy-house, the one in the middle of these particular hayfields, not generally to a social institution of bygone times. It must have an article; so the first rhyme does indeed have to be either 'house' or 'monk(s)'. Now 'monks' is a perfectly terrible rhyme word; a glance into Clement Wood's invaluable *Complete Rhyming Dictionary* – my single most indispensable tool – under ŬNGK confirms that nothing remotely fits the context except 'drunks' and 'bunks'.

The fact that in one variant the monks are being satirized for drinking makes me pause yearningly for a moment over the first.

But while I could say in the English of Wordsworth and Byron that they were drunk, it will not allow me to call them drunks, and the terminal consonant of the rhymes must be consistent. Bunks, then.

I am dubious, though, about 'bunk' as a word in use in English, circa 1816. The OED gives its earliest use as 1815, but in a nautical context only and as 'chiefly American', and my sense of Tegnér as an old-world gentleman makes me reluctant to let him talk Yankee-style, even in an occasional poem. Similar tinkerings produce nothing workable for 'house' either, whose use would have let me retain Tegnér's prepositional phrase instead of making 'clergy-house', rather than 'monks', the subject of the sentence. What I really want is 'drunk' as the (archaic) simple past of 'drink', but I can get rid of the 's' on the end of 'monks' only by means of the subterfuge 'many a . . .', which I dislike even more than the notion of Tegnér speaking an inauthentic word in the very first line of the poem. Coleridge had found 'many a' useful about twenty years before the date of 'Kannick' in 'Kubla Khan', and Burns a bit earlier in 'John Anderson, My Jo', so nothing but personal prejudice stands between me and 'many a monk', but at this stage prejudice suffices.

How to employ 'bunks' in the poem? To say the monks 'filled their bunks' would be commendably short but imprecise; yet 'snored upon their bunks' makes far too much of the monosyllable Tegnér used to indicate the same thing. Still, the picture is at least consistent with my Böök-enhanced sense of the poet's attitude toward these hay-eating Catholics, and I set it down. His idea seems to be that they went through the motions of religious duty but were in fact lazy, worldly characters; all extant variants give both clerical activities (prayed, said mass, prophesied) and secular ones (ate, slept, drank, made the sour milk product called *filbunk*), and choosing among the offerings in the first list – a choice severely limited by space – I balance the secular sloth with prayer, since none of the others will fit. I do not mind departing from the official, canon-ized version of the line as given in the prose draft above; the best choice in Swedish might not be the best for me – though in fact I have retained Tegnér's actual rhyme in this version by abandoning his meaning.

However, after living a few days with those bunks, I finally give in: they just feel wrong. I still dislike the 'many a' form as much as ever, but it feels at least *less* wrong. So the switch is made: 'The clergy-house held many a monk / Who once sang mass and slept and drunk'. The word 'held', a disagreeably blah verb, is later changed to 'kept' (in the sense of 'earn your keep' and 'kept woman'); otherwise this now seems all right. Later I make a couple of other changes: the poem's first word to 'This' to emphasize the local and specific reference; 'sang' mass to the more relaxed 'said'. There is simply no room anywhere for the concept 'in former times', but I slip its paler equivalent 'once' into line 3 and hope for the best.

I can see no ready way, and no real need, to keep the 'intends not to die out' sense of line 2; to state the matter positively makes no difference either to tone or to intent. If they will not die, then they will live, and I am spared the protracted process of phrasing 'they ate up their hay themselves' in such a way that it ends in a long-I rhyme, which a little preliminary investigation indicates would not be at all easy (And ate their hay up bye and bye. And ate up all their hay: oh my! etc.). Any experienced rhymester would agree that Tegnér ended *his* second line with 'die' *(dö)* because it *does* rhyme with 'hay' *(hö)*, and that he did not spend very much time casting about for alternatives, either. The fourth line, in English, ends most naturally with 'themselves', which has exactly two possible rhymes for ordinary use, 'shelves' and 'elves', neither the least bit appropriate here; on general principles one tries never to end any line with 'self' or 'selves'.

'Hay', then, must be the controlling word for me as it was for Tegnér, and the second line must be made to conform to it. That seems all right: long-A rhymes are very plentiful. One possibility suggests itself right away: to express the idea of lengthy perpetuation of both Munck's and Lund's ecclesiastical company in the semi-elevated poetic cliché 'for aye', a phrase whose mock-heroic tone seems suitable enough. Against this suitability must be weighed, yet again, my considerable dislike for the phrase, and also the fact that I have already reluctantly used it as a rhyme-term in another poem by Tegnér which is destined for the same anthology; I do not want such a mannered phrase jumping like a tic on every page.

Had I persisted with long-A, I expect something would have turned up sooner or later, given the great number of possible rhymes. But other considerations figured as well. By dropping 'themselves' I free up the space of two extra syllables, which can be filled in with anything both innocuous and appropriate to the context, and which can as easily come last as in the middle of the line. By this means I provide myself with a different rhyme. Also, the word *släkt* (modern spelling) in line 2, which I give as 'kin' in the 'for aye' version, means family, relations, line: clearly 'kindred' is the word of choice here, partly because this time I *like* its effect so much. In both meaning and tone it is exactly right; but it leaves only three syllables instead of four free to be fitted with the rhyming phrase. I decide to replace 'endures for aye' with 'e'er shall dwell' – improving the tense, if nothing else – and to add 'as well' to the phrase about hay consumption, switching back from that blocky Adamic 'did eat' (no longer required by the meter) and adding 'all'. This gives us:

> This clergy-house kept many a monk
> (In Lund that kindred e'er shall dwell);
> They once said mass and slept and drunk
> And ate up all their hay as well.

The greatest *tonal* effect of these cumulative minor adjustments occurs in the fourth line, which shifts from mock-heroic to simple-straightforward-childlike, just as in Tegnér's original. But each little change, each minor touch, makes its own separate effect, until the whole has been tuned much more closely to the pitch of the original poem as I hear it, apart from whatever else might be observed about the first and finished versions of this stanza.

The second stanza was much harder, or at any rate I was much stupider about finding solutions to the difficulties it posed. Its first two lines both fall into English so naturally and scannably that I spent an inordinate amount of time trying to devise a decent third line rhyming with 'now', before giving it up and submitting to the necessity of recasting line 1. In fact it was perfectly pointless to cling so mulishly to 'cleverer clergy'. *Klok* does not really mean 'clever' – a word used to describe schoolchildren in England – but 'wise'; my attachment to the alliteration created no end of unnecessary trouble, as will be seen. And there were other problems with my first casting of the stanza. Tegnér says not a thing about leafy boughs, nor can I be sure there were any trees between the fields in that flat, fen-like countryside in those days (there are few enough of them now), or that the picnickers took advantage of their shade, if any – late August in Sweden can be just like October in Philadelphia. The phrase *i det gröna*, literally 'in the green', just means 'in Nature', 'in the out-of-doors', a very general wide-focus term which ought not to be specified with imagery. And even if the hay *had* recently been mowed, 'meadow lawn' in line 4 is just plain silly.

In the end, after many intermediate trials of wildly varying quality ('And dance the meadow grass upon', etc.), I was able to keep line 2 by settling for the archaic but handy filler-word 'anon', meaning soon, right after this: first we have a glass of wine, then we dance in the meadow. I am not proud of this word, but I judge it innocuous and fairly invisible, all things considered.

During the course of further fussing and tinkering, a variable model for the stanza evolves:

```
                      are a
   1  Our clergy range now are cleverer . . .
   2  Who've taken better customs on.
   3 ⎧ They drink a glass in (Nature's?) . . . ⎫
     ⎩ A glass in Nature's . . .        they ⎭
   4  . . . . . . . . . . . . . . . . . .  anon.
```

Note that one possible alternative – 'Our clergy are a cleverer *class* / In Nature's green they drink a *glass*' – is out from the start because the last line of stanza 3, coming right up, must end: 'all flesh is grass'. The proximity rule strikes again *within* this stanza, preventing (or at least discouraging) me from saying in lines 3–4 'They drink a glass in Nature's green / And dance about the fields anon'. Luckily neither of these gambits exactly has overwhelming appeal. Roget, my second most indispensable working tool, gives plenty of possibilities for the blanks in lines 1 and 3, but none of the synonyms for 'group' or 'men' rhymes conveniently, or even plausibly, with any of those for 'drink', or with any of the metaphorical limbs or attributes of Nature. After a long and frustrating struggle I settle briefly on 'sorts / courts', but am not at all satisfied and tackle it again the next day.

Were it not necessary to speak here of the clergy collectively I might prefer something like 'Our clergyman's a cleverer chap / He drinks a glass in Nature's lap', which is not bad except that 'chap' is entirely too modern-sounding and unacceptable on that account; at least the tone is more or less on target. But of course 'clergy' – *kanicker* – here must refer not only to the priests themselves but to their families as well; it is one entire clerical 'household', one particular way of life, which is being contrasted with another.

The search goes on and on '(óut) in the cóuntry' doesn't scan; unlike the two unaccented syllables of 'cleverer', which slip by almost as smoothly as one, 'in the' cannot fall between stressed syllables in this poem's bare iambic lines. 'He tipples in the country': too cute. 'A glass he in the country (drinks)': not English. 'A glass in the country . . . ': see above. And so on, hour after hour, enlivened by the continual flipping back and forth between Wood's rhyming dictionary and Roget's Thesaurus which is *the* characteristic observable behaviour of the formal-translation process. Assorted Swedish–Swedish and Swedish–English dictionaries are much more in evidence during the translation of virtually all the other poems I have worked on for my present project; but Roget and Wood are *sine qua non*, they make the process possible at all.

Later for quite a long time I am hung up on 'lot / spot', but the meter of line 3 is perfectly intransigent: I have to say 'A *wine* glass in a shady spot / And dancing . . .', which prolongs and subtly changes the rhetorical level or shape of the sentence. There turns out to be *no* word of two syllables for a plain glass in common English parlance: I can have 'glass' or 'drink a glass', when what is needed is a two-syllable noun stressed like snifter, and snifter, goblet and the like are hyper-specific. I waste another hour skimming the pages of Wordsworth's *Prelude* for possibly usable references to Nature, only to realize that Nature for this entirely humorless English poet was wilder and nobler by far than anything Tegnér could have used for comic hyperbole among the hayfields of Skåne.

By this time the stanza has begun to seem altogether unsubduable. Abruptly fed up, I rashly decide to accept a very small vowel slant between the less important *a* (or *c*, actually, as we are in stanza 2) rhymes of the first and third lines:

> Now we have cleverer clergy here
> Who've taken better customs on.
> They drink a glass in country air
> And dance about the field anon.

But alas, even in *a* position the slant sticks out like a sore thumb; nor can 'country air' do without a definite article; nor, for that matter, can I afford to overload – and discomfit the scannability of – line 1 by giving it three heavily stressed syllables in a row, followed immediately by the extra unstressed one in 'cleverer'.

A similar quasi-desperate lunge next converts the lines to:

> But there are cleverer clergy nigh
> Who've taken better customs on:
> A glass beneath the open sky
> And dancing in the field anon.

And no again. Even if this one little stanza could support the weight of *two* archaic words in conspicuous rhyme positions, which it manifestly cannot, a new problem has been introduced. By losing the phrase 'we have', the narrative link between stanzas 2 and 3 has also been lost. To maintain this link it is necessary to say either 'And girls are with *them* too', instead of 'with *us* too' – distancing the lines from Tegnér's mood of inclusive coziness – or to fall back again on the 'we have cleverer' phrase ruled out for the previous gambit.

Luckily at this point that hopeless 'nigh' points the way to the the real answer which has been under my nose the whole time, as is so often the case: relinquish 'clever', go with 'wise' (after first looking up *klok* to make sure), change 'sky' to 'skies', *voilà*. If you are astonished at the tortuous means and scandalous amount of time it took to tumble to this obvious solution, I could not sympathize more. But the lesson is one that every so often has to be learned again: the price of fixing too adamantly upon a particular phrasing or formal solution too early on is flexibility.

As I have indicated, each of the other stanzas posed its own more or less horrendous formal problems, but the foregoing should suffice to indicate the sort of work involved in solving them: you are trying to fit – cram, or less often pad – a set of concepts and images, some required, some elective, into a space of strictly delimited dimensions measured in syllable-count and stress-pattern, without changing the feel of the original arrangement. It is a lot like playing Scrabble, as I discovered one evening when, after a long day's struggle with a very difficult poem by alliteration-mad Erik Axel Karlfeldt, I sat down with my husband to the Scrabble board. Not three turns into the game my eyes were crossing and I had the start of a splitting headache, my brain's way of communicating to me its flat refusal, *that* day, to do any more ingenious recombining of elements to fit a given space for maximum profit.

Here, then, is the final version of the translation of 'Kannick/The Clergy-House':

This clergy-house kept many a monk
(In Lund that kindred e'er shall dwell);
They once said mass and slept and drunk
And ate up all their hay as well.

Now clergy here have grown more wise
And taken better customs on:
A glass beneath the open skies
And dancing in the field anon.

And girls – half snow, half roses each –
Are with us too; and so, alas,
Are certain jolly priests who preach
Unto the girls: 'All flesh is grass'.

All flesh is grass, and grass shall fall,
The flower thereof be hacked away.
Ye hapless creatures, for you all
The harvest might come any day.

Such deeds as these do roses mar;
But wives, they smile to see the crime,
And render thanks to God, and are
Content that they were stacked in time.

  I shall conclude by returning for a few paragraphs to the matter of tone. Tegnér establishes the tone of 'Kannick' through the marriage of simple and elevated language, everyday talk and highly formal, sometimes Biblical, rhetoric (*vill ej dö,* etc.). Most of the poem's humor derives from the incongruities between these two modes, something the scriptwriters of *Monty Python and the Holy Grail*, for example, understood to a nicety; the rest is in the 'occasional' puns and in the poet's ironic teasing, at once avuncular and playful-lecherous. My intention throughout was to match Tegnér's own note as closely as ever I could. My choices for such formalities as 'preach / Unto', 'the flower thereof' and 'render' were guided by Tegnér's principles, if not always by his particular instances, of usage; the formal demands of this poem are too onerous to let me follow his lead in lockstep, as I would have liked.

  For instance, the King James Bible says: 'All flesh is grass, and all the goodliness thereof is as the flower of the field: The grass withereth, the flower fadeth . . .' (Isaiah 40:6–7). The Swedish Bible, somewhat by contrast, reads: '*Höet torkas bort, blomstret förvissnar . . .'*, that is, 'The grass is dried away, the flower withers'. In his poem Tegnér uses the reflexive Biblical verb form plus preposition – *torkas bort* → *huggas bort* – but chooses a different verb, which he puts in to a different tense: *blomstren skola huggas bort*, the flowers (plural) *shall be cut away*, the girls will be deflowered and turned into wives. His nod to Biblical language is a grammatical nod only; his poem is not about drying up in the sense of withering away at all, it is a hay-like curing he alludes to, implying ripeness and usefulness, not death. My word thereof is meant to operate in just this way: a nod to the source, made thus – i.e. not in the verb – because I cannot follow Tegnér's example there *and* achieve a grammatical allusion to the King James Version's somewhat different verb choices *and* color within the lines of the form, all at once. And in fact I feel 'thereof' turns the trick rather neatly, striking the right note and the right balance. (*Hugga*, by the way, is the word for cutting wood – that is, hack, chop, hew.)

I have mentioned in passing the fact that a number of variants of 'Kannick' have survived in manuscript, providing the translator with some slight degree of choice at a couple of points. One place was in the third line of stanza 1; the other is in the first line of the final stanza, where at various times Tegnér substituted 'the girls' and 'the roses' for 'the grass' – this last being the official version appearing in Tegnér's collected works. It seems to me though that 'roses' not only makes the vegetable association of girls with grass clearer, but also helps redeem the dullest line in the original poem, about the girls being made half of roses, half of snow. So I have respectfully overruled the editors of the definitive edition.

This sketch may indicate in a rough way something about the technical side of formal translation, but the reality is, of course, very much messier even than the sketch makes it seem. There were virtually no serious problems of interpretation to struggle with in 'Kannick', no philosophical content, no tricky turns of phrase, no demands of a stylistic (as opposed to linguistic) nature, such as clashing consonants or the aggressive alliteration one finds in Karlfeldt's work; for a longer poem of a higher art, where such considerations do enter in, the difficulties expand geometrically. If you are wondering that anybody should bother to translate a poem so light yet so formally demanding as 'Kannick', I suppose the answer – apart from whatever pedagogical reasons could be cited – is that without such as 'Kannick' to hone our claws upon, we would have poorer success with the poetry that matters more.

'The Voice Inside'
Translating the Poetry Of T. Carmi
Grace Schulman

In translating poetry and in writing it we face the same dilemma: the more interesting the poem, the more we are aware of our limitations. At the same time, those very obstacles can free us to discover new cadences and, in fact, a new music.

From January 1980 till August 1982, when I translated the poems of T. Carmi, the Israeli poet, I was beset with limitations: I found it important, though nearly impossible, to know his country's traditions and culture, as well as the trees, the landscape and the people of his Israel. Further, I knew that I could not hope to come close to Carmi's familiarity with biblical and midrashic tradition, as well as colloquial Hebrew speech, and his mastery of Hebrew poetry. Fortunately Carmi led me to many sources, explained cultural matters and encouraged me to learn as much as I could about the raw material he transformed into art.

A translator himself, Carmi had made Hebrew plays from English French and German originals, notably Shakespeare's *Midsummer Night's Dream*, *Hamlet*, *Measure for Measure* and *Much Ado About Nothing*; Ghelderode's *Pantagleize*; and Brecht's *Puntilla*. I found that his own experience was helpful to me in translating poems: once, when I presented him with variants, he replied: 'For a solution, listen to the voice inside you. It is usually right.' And often, when exploring Carmi's own sources, I thought of Robert Graves' words, which Carmi had quoted as a formula for translation:

> Subdue your pen to his
> until it proves as natural
> to write his name as yours.

Research was essential, because of Carmi's development as a poet. He was born in New York City, in 1925, into a family that spoke only Hebrew at home. However fluent his English became, his first language, Hebrew, remained his writing language and his major concern. Often he appended notes to his poems such as: 'I don't know if this is worth the trouble of translating into English,' or 'I don't think this is translatable.' Some of the translations weathered Carmi's doubts that his poems could be read in another language – even in one he knew well.

Carmi's poetry is informed by French sources, as well as the work of English, American and Hebrew writers. When he left America for Paris in 1946 he became familiar with the work of many surrealists, including Éluard and Breton. Even before his stay in Paris he had studied classical French literature. Leaving France in 1947, he emigrated to Israel, where he served in the Defense forces and fought in the War of Liberation. In Israel the poet's language became literary and directly contemporary; he expressed formal ideas in language he heard in parks and cafés, from bartenders and taxicab drivers. In making his selection for *The Penguin Book of Hebrew Verse*, which he edited, Carmi read liturgical and secular Hebrew poems for inclusion in the anthology.

In January, February and March 1980, during an academic year he spent at Stanford University, Carmi wrote the Hebrew poems I translated subsequently as 'At the Stone of Losses', 'Song of Thanks', 'In a Flash', 'Eve Knew', 'My Beloved is Mine and I am His' and 'I Say "Love"'. Like many of his poems, 'At the Stone of Losses' contains a startling fusion of tradition and modern speech. It begins:

> I search
> for what I have not lost.
>
> For you, of course.
>
> I would stop
> if I knew how.
>
> I would stand
> at the Stone of Losses
> and proclaim,
> shouting:
>
> Forgive me.
> I've troubled you for nothing.
> All the identifying marks I gave you

'The Voice Inside' 163

> (a white forehead,
> a three-syllable name,
> a neck and a scar,
> color and height)
> were never mine.

Shortly after he composed those lines he recalled Pascal's *Pensées* (*'Console toi; tu ne me chercherais pas, si tu ne m'avais pas trouvé'*) and also a talmudic passage about an old man searching for his youth. The central image is a real stone of losses in Jerusalem, a kind of 'lost-and-found' connected with the return of lost property during the Second Temple Period, as mentioned in the Talmud.

At times the important things are slowly realized, and so it was with the title of that poem. The first drafts of the Hebrew originals arrived reading, 'Untitled as yet'. When he found it, *Leyad Even Hato'im* became the title of the book he published in Israel in 1981, and the translation, 'At the Stone of Losses', became the title of my selected edition of Carmi's poems, published in America and in England in 1983. Nor was the translation easily come by. *'Leyad Even Hato'im'* means literally 'By', 'At' or 'Near' the 'Stone of Claims', or 'Claimants', or 'Strayers', all words we thought about when the translation was in progress. Carmi sent me a passage he found in Danby's translation of the Mishnah, and another from the *Encyclopedia Judaica*, which read:

> An ancient baraita (BM 28b) mentions the *even hato'im* . . . People who had lost or found objects in Jerusalem and on the road to the Capitol met by the side of this stone: 'The one stood and announced his find and the other submitted evidence of ownership and received it.' This is probably the origin of the name, i.e., 'the stone for those wandering', in search of someone or something.

In contrast with the language of his biblical sources, Carmi's language is characterized by a bareness of utterance and a kind of hysterical calm that brings forth the central situation of the poem: that of a lost man, modern version, searching for wholeness in the other. He exclaims:

> I swear by my life,
> by this stone in the heart of Jerusalem,

> I won't do it again.
> I take it all back.

In the last two lines of that passage the root of the word *ḥozer* figures prominently. The words mean literally, according to Carmi's notes to me:

> by this stone in the heart of Shalem (old name for Jerusalem)
> I go back in me from my words
>   (return)
>
> this expression in Hebrew by itself means
>   I repent
>   recant
>
>   I take them (the words) all back
> back = back. Same root in Hebrew.

(with "back", "return", and "back" connected — *same root*)

At this point in the poem the speaker vows to stop the questioning and, at the climax ('moments of truth'), has an astonishing insight about the loss of illusion. Still, he is compelled to continue; his search for completeness is circular and never ending:

> And I search
> for what I have not lost,
> for that – that
> name, neck, scar,
> and forehead white as stone.

Here Carmi transliterated the lines for me. He wrote that the Hebrew sounds this way:

> et ashér lo avád lí   (that which was not lost to me)
> ani meḥapeś   (I am searching for)
> et ashér –
> et ashér –

it's as if he begins to repeat the formula, but the repetition turns, against his will, into a renewed enumeration, that is, he's again searching, claiming (I know you know this). So the same words should be repeated, taken somehow, from the formula? On second thought, 'for that – / that –' is good.

Striking in Carmi's poetry is the unexpected transposition of sacred images into erotic experience. An instance of this transposition from sacred to modern love occurs in the poem I translated as 'Song of Thanks'. In it the man who praises life and beauty above all things offers 'sacrifices' not to God but to a woman, seeing her name 'in white fire on a black sky', which apart from being a radiant, surrealist image is an allusion to a talmudic legend that the Ten Commandments were inscribed in 'white fire on black fire'. The poet exclaims:

> But my thanks will not release me.
> I turn my body into a chariot;
> the trees of the fields answer amen.
>
> I know that I risk my life.
> The sun is a treasurehouse of electrum;
> the moon is contaminated by the sun;
> the sea is infected by the moon;
> and I touch you unendingly,
> barefoot, in the many waters.

The passage exalts desire, liberated by the strange leaps and associations in the speaker's mind, freed from the control of reason. Although that impact is felt without reference to sources, it is, nevertheless, interesting to consider them, for they are the life-energy of the imagery. In his notes to me Carmi wrote that the 'chariot' image was derived from an old prayer-book formula: 'I am prepared to make my body into a chariot for the glory of God.' The 'treasure-house of electrum', he wrote, contains the word, first found in Ezekiel (1:4) and translated as 'beryl' and 'amber', that is the word for electricity today. 'I know that I risk my life' was based, he said, on an expression that 'whoever interrupts his study of the Torah to admire the beauty of a tree puts his soul in mortal danger'.

That line is used, earlier in the poem, as 'I know that I risk my life / I understand such things'. In that case the expression about mortal danger is used in conjuction with a talmudic reference to a child who was comtemplating *ḥashmal* ('beryl', 'electricity') when a flame came forth and consumed him. Of the passage in the poem

> The laws of nature will not change
> even if I see your name
> in white fire on a black sky

which alludes to the Ten Commandments, Carmi wrote in his notes to me that the word *reshef* plus the word for 'back' refers to the flareback of a plane or the muzzle flash of a gun. As in many of the poems, the language is of modern passion and war, with undertones of biblical and talmudic information.

Throughout the poem the sacrifice of thanks, which was a common ritual offered in the Jerusalem Temple, is transformed into a passionate song of praise to an erotic union and to language. The source material is transmuted in such a way as to redefine that passion, presenting it as discovery. The title, '*Shir Toda*', means 'Song of Thanks' or 'Song of Thanksgiving'. The phrase *korban toda*, on the other hand, means 'sacrifice'. In his notes to me Carmi suggested additional shades of meaning:

Toda = thanks; gratitude, thanksgiving.
(Also thank-offering,
song of praise,
confession, admission of sin
and, in colloquial Hebrew, thank you)

line 1: with the definite article,
       refers to the sacrifice. Here,
       however, it refers to the saying/offering/
       feeling of thanks.
       I can't stop thanking you.

In 'Song of Thanks' there is a criss-cross between the title and the text: the *shir toda* of the title corresponds to the song of thanksgiving in the first lines of the poem. The epigraph, however, refers to modern passion and to sacrifice. Written by Solomon Ibn Gabirol, the eleventh-century figure Carmi described in *The Penguin Book of Hebrew Verse* as 'a great Hebrew poet', the words apply to Carmi's own method of transforming sacred images to erotic ones. They are: 'In time of exile, no sacrifices can be offered to God; then I shall slaughter whole offerings and sacrifices to this woman.'

The fact that the sacred references in Carmi's love poems are more familiar to Hebrew than to English readers is, perhaps, no more of an aesthetic problem than the sacred lore in poems by Dante, Milton and Donne. The poet has an image-making power, and the life of his art rests on his use of imagery, not on his sources. It is the word-play, though – puns, ambiguities and apposite images – that enlivens Carmi's lines, providing irony and, at times, a juxtaposition of contrasts that recalls 'metaphysical' imagery. 'I Say "Love"', for example, begins:

> You untie the vows
> within me.

The vows here refer to love, they refer also to the Kol Nidre prayer for the Eve of the Day of Atonement, whose text reads: 'Let our personal vows, pledges and oaths be considered neither vows nor pledges nor oaths.' And in 'My Beloved is Mine and I am His', a title that is, of course, from the Song of Songs, the lines

> His voice flowed in the room and she heard
> the rivers run to the sea

refer to modern lovers. At the same time, the biblical undercurrents are strong. The word 'flowed' (*halakh*) is actually closer to walked, streamed, ran. And 'run' in the following line, actually 'running' (*holekhím*) is a play on the first verb. The lines recall Ecclesiastes: 'All streams run into the sea / yet the sea never overflows.'

'Eve Knew' presented some of the most difficult ironic contrasts, which were soluble, I felt, not in the individual words but in the context of the poem. Eve, who is simultaneously the biblical figure and a modern woman, is aware of a discord in creation, despite a voice that insists on covering the turmoil by repeating: 'It is good.' She hears the voice and becomes slightly hysterical in reaction to this 'goodness':

> *It is good! It is good!* And again: *It is good!*
> a torrent of goodness:
> a model garden, watered, sated,
> an exemplary mother. Happy are all living things!

Again, Carmi uses devices of rhetoric such as antanaclasis (a word repeated with a shift in meaning) and syllepsis (a word used once with two meanings), both divisions of the pun, to show the irony: Eve acknowledges the declaration, '*It is good!*', all the while knowing disorder and chaos. In a note to me Carmi said: 'She may be repeating what she hears, bitterly . . . This is a model garden, and I'm supposed to be an exemplary mother: oh, yes, happy are all living things!'

The word *gan* (garden) means garden and nursery, kindergarten and Garden of Eden. The words *em-kol-ḥai* mean the mother (*em*) of all (*kol*) who live (*ḥai*), and *kol ḥai* (living things) plus *ashréy* provide the phrase 'happy are all living things'. The irony is the result of the interplay of words with richly ambiguous meanings.

The difficult phrase 'a torrent of goodness' is based on the words *zirmá* (flood, stream, ejaculation) and *adaním* (goodness, delights, pleasures, with echoes of Eden). Carmi told me: 'The Hebrew line is fairly strong because it combines *zirmá* (flow of semen) with *adaním* (*luxe, calme et volupté*). It is like too much whipped cream; it has a bitter, mocking, somewhat disgusted, tone. It is not a "stream of pleasure", or an "ejaculation of happiness", but revulsion with an unbearable dose of goodness, which leads Eve to release the worm.'

The irony of this typical passage from 'Eve Knew', then, is based on antanaclasis, syllepsis and paronomasia (punning), all devices involving words with ambiguous meanings. Probably Carmi's extensive translation of Shakespeare's plays into Hebrew led to his use of puns and to his startling juxtapositions. With a few exceptions, however, such as the phrase 'It is good!', which changes meaning thoughout the poem, the puns cannot be translated without sounding coy. Here as elsewhere I let the context of the poem carry the irony and kept the diction simple, the utterance bare, to imply underlying meaning.

A lesser problem occurs in the poem 'In a Flash', one of my favorite poems of that period in Carmi's writing. The title, *kehéref áyin*, means literally 'in the pause of an eye'. 'In a Wink' seemed closer, but a bit cute, and I preferred the title that introduced the imagery of thunder and lightning. Repetitions, biblical echoes and paronomasia are found throughout the poem, especially in this passage:

> there is a time to remember and a time to recall;
> a time to forget and a time to be forgotten;
> the first rain always surprises;
> only later will you know you have heard the last rain . . .

One of the paronomasic devices consists of the words *lizkór* (to remember), the simple form of the verb, and *lehizakhér* (to bring to mind), the more active, intensive form of the verb. The words I used were 'remember' and 'recall', as though in the second case there is more effort used in the act of recollection. The formula is, of course, from Ecclesiastes, and the passage rings in the ears of American readers through Fitzgerald and Hemingway, especially, and others of their generation.

In the last two lines of that passage the word *yoré* (first rain) is set beside *malkósh* (last rain, or spring rain in Israel) for the metaphor of regret, or sadness in retrospect. Once again I hoped that if the cutural context was not immediately available to American readers, a dreamlike landscape, presented in a tone of discontent, might convey the larger effect of the imagery. In translating this poem from Hebrew into English, as in translating the other poems of T. Carmi, I used essentially the same principles: first, follow the poet's simple diction, for it will release shades of meanings that cannot be had by reaching for them; second, as Carmi advised, 'For a solution, listen to the voice inside you. It is usually right.'

APPENDIX: EVE KNEW

NOTES to Eve

4. "she observed" (peeped / peered) hishgiha S.O.S. 2,9: "peeping in at the windows, glancing thru the lattice," NEB

5. "crawling things" [illegible] GEN. 1,20 "teeming things" "swarming things"

the line has an unpleasant sound.

5. "grasses" [illegible] GEN 1,12 "fresh growth," "plants"

7. hishhira [illegible] = [illegible] blackened became black (also made black) grow dark darken / blacken / to become gloomy

verb is used in an expression meaning "to put to shame" "to darken [someone's face]"

8. [illegible] 'their thorns : Heb letters, in the scroll, have "crowns" + "thorns". the letters quarrelled before God about seniority + such (like the moon)

kota = thorn, thistle; tip of letter

10 ki tov = that it was good; repeated formula in GEN. 1

l. 10: the voice repeated (instead of "said")

9. [illegible] lit. beasts of the field wild animal or, if you wish: ~~beasts of the field~~ wild beasts / beasts of the forest

I'm using the expression in PS 104, 11; but there are similar expressions in PS 79.2 + 104.20

13. zirmé [illegible] streaming of (flowing stream, issue ejaculation (of) semen)

EZ 23,20: whose seed came in floods like those of horses

zirmat · zirmatam

zérem is a stream; lizrom = to flow

zirmé = ←

adanim [illegible] goodness delights

eden = Eden

edné = pleasure, rejuvenation

adanim, pl. = delights, delicacies, pleasures

PS 36.9 thou givest them water from the flowing stream of thy delights

14 [illegible] gan model garden exemplary

gan Eden garden of Eden gan means both "garden" + nursery, kindergarten

[illegible] watered GEN 2.10

[illegible] sated saturated well watered

notes to Eve (2

                                                    GEN. 3, 20
                              em = mother   em kol-hai —
                                               the mother / of all who live
15. אם כל חי
     exemplary mother

kol hai   ashrey
   חי – כל   אשרי   → the word with which many
   happy one all the living things   psalms begin: happy is...
              all who live   are

17. ברי רוח?   as in the formula of wills + documents
     clear mind   "with a sound body + lucid mind"
                    ? sound + sane

          mah'ha   used in expression meaning "to put to shape"
                                        "to dim [someone's face]"
18. תעם?   perhaps a bit strange; literally means
     darkening   to "darken" cast a shadow upon;
     make dark   her gleaming body outdazzles the sun
dull/ darken   dazzles
     dim /bedim (sic!)
19. √חרר סתם = set free ["worm" is fem. in Heb.]
21. "happy end" lit. good end   sof = end tov = good used as idiom in mod.
                                                Heb. for "happy end"
22. tors   Gen. 3, 20
     his sweat

    over abundance
    excess?   goodness
    merov   tova   "   "
28. מרב טוב   "we may not pray on
     ————— ?/or   account of an excess of
     excess of blessing good" Talmud
                              Taanith 22b
26. ki means both "that" + "because". The second
           meaning is probably active in this line

'The Voice Inside' 173

EVE KNEW

1. Eve knew what was hidden in the apple.
2. She wasn't born yesterday.
3. From between Adam's ribs
4. she observed the order of creation,
5. listening to grasses and crawling things.

OK to leave out "the sounds of"? Stronger without, I think, yes

6. Eve knew what was hidden in the apple.
7. The waters raged, the moon grew black,
8. the letters brandished their thorns,
9. the beasts of the fields devoured their names
10. and the voice said it is good.

① This is ominous and wonderfully mysterious, but I'm not sure what's happening here. The transition is so abrupt. Maybe that's OK

I prefer this to
and the voice repeated that it is good.

11. Eve knew what was hidden in the apple.
12. It is good, it is good, and again it is good
13. a flood of goodness,
14. a model garden, watered, sated
15. an exemplary mother, happy are all living things,

② I'm not sure of the order of things here. The syntax doesn't make sense, nor does my punctuation. Is this sudden free-association, a stream of pleasure? An ejaculation (wotthehe!) of happiness?

I'm not sure of this either.

I'm not sure of the connection between the two parts of this line.

16. Eve knew what was hidden in the apple.
17. In the light of day, and with a clear mind,
18. her naked body darkening the sun,

NO STANZA BREAK

19. she released the Big Worm
20. to gnaw at the roots of trees.
21. Happy ending:
22. Adam, his sweat flowing like a river,
23. confessed [to her] by the light of the sword,
24. that he was out of names,
25. that his strength was gone
26. {from (an excess of) blessing
27. and
28. → that it ~~was~~ is good.

What's ("fern.?" (You've written "worm is fern. in Hebrew.) She freed the Big Worm?

I'm just curious about the sword. It's a marvelous image, but I wondered if there is a source.
GEN. 3.24

Perhaps you should find a different word for *adamim* in l. 13.

The Heb. line is fairly strong because it combines what can be an unpleasant word *zirmâ* (flow [?] *semen*) with an refined/extreme word for "pleasure" (*luxe, calme et volupté*). The feeling is ~~one~~ of too much whipped cream (or chocolate). It has a bitter, ironical, mocking, somewhat disgusted tone.

It is not "a stream of pleasure" or ejaculation of happiness" but revulsion with an unbearable dose of "goodness" which leads her to release the Worm.

l. 2c: Adam, ~~too~~ (reluctantly) ~~admits~~ to being unable to bear so much "goodness" (so "blessing" may not be appropriate).

חַוָּה יָדְעָה

חַוָּה יָדְעָה מַה טָמוּן בַּתַּפּוּחַ.
הִיא לֹא נוֹלְדָה אֶתְמוֹל.
מִבֵּין צַלְעוֹתָיו שֶׁל אָדָם
הִיא הִשְׁגִּיחָה בְּמַעֲשֵׂי בְּרֵאשִׁית,
הִקְשִׁיבָה לְרַחַשׁ דְּשָׁאִים וּשְׁרָצִים.

חַוָּה יָדְעָה מַה טָמוּן בַּתַּפּוּחַ.
הַמַּיִם זָעֲמוּ, הַלְּבָנָה הִשְׁחִירָה,
הָאוֹתִיּוֹת זָקְפוּ אֶת קוֹצֵיהֶן,
חַיְתוֹ־שָׂדֶה טָרְפוּ אֶת הַשֵּׁמוֹת,
וְהַקּוֹל אָמַר: כִּי טוֹב.

חַוָּה יָדְעָה מַה טָמוּן בַּתַּפּוּחַ.
כִּי טוֹב, כִּי טוֹב, וְשׁוּב כִּי טוֹב,
זִרְמָה שֶׁל עֲדָנִים,
גַּן לְדֻגְמָה, מֶשְׁקֶה, רָוּוּי,
אִם לְמוֹפֵת, אַשְׁרֵי כָּל חַי.

חַוָּה יָדְעָה מַה טָמוּן בַּתַּפּוּחַ.
לְאוֹר הַיּוֹם וּבְדֵעָה צְלוּלָה,
גּוּפָהּ הֶעֵירֹם מַכְהֶה אוֹר חַמָּה,
הִיא קָרְאָה דְּרוֹר לַתּוֹלַעַת הַגְּדוֹלָה
שֶׁתְּכַרְסֵם אֶת שָׁרְשֵׁי הָעֵצִים.

הַסּוֹף הָיָה טוֹב.
אָדָם, זֵעָתוֹ נִגֶּרֶת כְּנָהָר,
הוֹדָה בְּפָנֶיהָ לְאוֹר הָעֶרֶב
כִּי לֹא נוֹתְרוּ בּוֹ שֵׁמוֹת,
כִּי כֹחֹתָיו כָּלוּ מֵרֹב טוֹבָה,

כִּי טוֹב.

EVE KNEW

Eve knew what was hidden in the apple.
She wasn't born yesterday.
From between Adam's ribs
she observed the order of creation,
listening to the grasses and crawling things.

Eve knew what was hidden in the apple.
The waters raged, the moon grew black,
the letters brandished their thorns,
the beasts of the fields devoured their names
and the voice said: *It is good.*

Eve knew what was hidden in the apple.
It is good! It is good! And again: *It is good!*
A torrent of goodness:
a model garden, watered, sated,
an exemplary mother. Happy are all living things!

Eve knew what was hidden in the apple,
In the light of day, and with a clear mind,
her naked body darkening the sun,
she released the Big Worm
to gnaw at the roots of trees.

Happy ending:
Adam, his sweat flowing like a river,
confessed by the light of the sword
that he was out of names, that the good
had exhausted his strength

and that it is good.

Working at Someone Else's Poem
Jon Silkin

It is, I am almost certain, between twelve and fifteen years since I worked – apart from some minor recent revisions – on translating thirty or so poems by the Hebrew poet Amir Gilboa. I first encountered his work in 1965 when I was living in Tel-Aviv, where I translated, with Bat-Sheva Sherriff, something like seventy poems post-1948. With Bat-Sheva I worked on about eight of Gilboa's poems (about five came out all right); and with the poet Natan Zach I worked both on his poems (see *Against Parting*, Northern House, 1967) and on a further twenty-five or so of Gilboa's.

Is it disingenuous to say that I was drawn to Gilboa's poetry *partly* because of the affinity I felt with it? That was Zach's judgment. Yet it is not more disingenuous, or naive, than saying one is drawn, as one is, to a poet unlike one – or to a poet whose achievement appears to be beyond one's grasp. This too was remarked on by Dennis Silk, in Jerusalem this year [1981], when I told him how much I enjoyed reading his collected poems, *The Punished Land* (Viking Press and Penguin Books, 1980). As Daniel Weissbort remarked in a letter to me, 'we're all translators, one way or another' – and perhaps *one* reason why I am attracted to translation is the possible enrichment of one's own work at that point at which one's own growth intersects with the character or aspect of another's work.

This synapse of different poetries has obvious dangers. For the translator, a too wholehearted concern with another's work at such close quarters as those of translation may turn him or her in a direction or mode which he would not otherwise have 'chosen' – if, that is, one is free to make such choices. Equally there are dangers for the translated poet: the ambition of his translator may result in his work not being translated except in the sense that Bottom exclaimed it. If this testimony appears too theoretical, I would ask the reader to consider that I am speaking as one who has experienced anxiety at the continuing prospect of both dangers, as he attempted to make poems in English of another poet's work in another language.

The poem of Gilboa's which I felt as close to as any was 'Joshua's Face'; and I still like it as much now as I did then, though not perhaps for quite the same reasons. Here is the poem in English:

JOSHUA'S FACE

And Joshua, from above, looks at my face, – his, beaten gold.
A dream, mummified and cold.
The sea at my feet beats incrementingly up the shore.
I am sick with its crying; it seems I shall die now.
No, I must wait, living
the endlessness.
My brother's face, rising in a cloud, foresees
my foot-steps in the sand washed by sea.

The sea encroaches and sinks back:
   moves forward, moves off.
Natural wars, determined by law.
Me, myself, other than, escaping, distant.
Joshua, too, is resting now from the wars.
He left to his people some substance, but did not
cut himself a grave
in the mountains of Ephraim.
It is for this that, in the sky, he
walks at night.
I am sick, and it seems I shall die
walking barefoot in cold sands
at the edges of moon and water.
Inside me murmurs the end in me
beating my death onto
my feet:
a wave, and then another.

On the faces of many lives more may he
be raised and magnified.

It is too long ago for me to remember, with the kind of fineness that would be crucial, – but then I should not have had the distance enabling judgment either – how much a consciousness of my own verse moved my translating of this poem towards or away from my own work. But I feel as sure as I can be that if Weissbort is correct in affirming 'we're all translators, one way or another', then the moral problem of my work being in some relation to Gilboa's remained an uneasy and constant factor – in translating this poem especially.

I cannot remember at what stage, for instance, in line 3 'incrementingly' entered my translation, but I still like its presence – I get a charge each time I read that passage in particular. And if it does work, it does so not only because it represents the tidal rising of tension and crisis, but also – from my point of view as a poet – because its multi-syllabled movement enacts the feeling of experience. If I say that the overwhelming by experience as well as the survival of it is precisely what Gilboa's poem is about, I also touch on my own concerns as a person. Another aspect of his poem that excites my (creative) imagination (I am, as it were, back working on the translation) is its rhythmic pace, its fluctuation of lengths of line and their relation with syntax, their gradations of speed as their different kinds of meanings are offered; contrast the opening four lines with those of the passage beginning stanza 2, line 5, 'He left to his people'. The poem gets up and walks briskly and bitterly into the night. And then, I remember asking myself, what does Gilboa mean by his stylistic device of: a 'something', and then another (see last line of stanza 2). Geoffrey Hill once wrote of the 'simmering exultation' of my verse. True or not, in as congruent a sense, that could refer to my reading of the two lines that conclude Gilboa's poem.

So what I knew I had to beware of, for Gilboa's sake (and for my own), was subsuming his helpless text into my poetics. I had to be careful that similarity, affinity or even link did not get confused in my mind with synonymity. I had to be careful that when I encountered a force I might feel unhappy with – 'beaten gold', 'beating my death' – I was not reacting against it because it was a forcefulness of a kind I would not especially want in my own poetry. For, after all, it was not my poem.

RE-VISIONS [1987]

For ten years or more I believed I liked the word 'incrementingly' and the rhetoric associated with it. For a variety of reasons I now find I do not. Poor Gilboa. Anyhow, in the new version, the more immediately menacing movement of the sea has yielded to the more menacing tug at the body of it, which produces tide, and which, in its rotary onwardness, is time. If the line is still not right I believe it gets closer to the scythe of meaning which travels through the poem; and the change from rhetoric to compaction of meaning is behind the other changes I have made. How can one insist quietly? That is the mental change I have tried to sift through the translation – the revision of it – which is why the ending, instead of pouring in upon itself and proclaiming its conclusion with the help of a slightly self-important subjunctive, seeks instead to move to its finish with a quiet, more insistent fluidity. I have tried to do this without, on the other hand, sacrificing the biblical luminous power of Gilboa's 'raised and magnified'.

JOSHUA'S FACE

Joshua, from above, looks upon my face – his, beaten gold.
A dream, mummified and cold.
At my feet the sea beats time's increase.
I am sick with its crying. I shall die it seems.
No, I'm to wait, and live
on into the last.
My brother's face rises in a cloud, foreseeing
my footsteps in sand
washed by sea.

The sea encroaches, and sinks back; moves forward, moves off.
Nature's wars, determined by law.
Me, myself, other than, escaping, distant.
Joshua also rests from the wars.
Though he left substance for his people
he cut no grave for himself
in the mountains of Ephraim.
And for this he walks
in the sky at night.
I am sick, and I shall die it seems
walking in cold sands barefoot
at the edges of moon and water.
In me my end murmurs
my death beating upon
my feet –
a wave, and another then.

Over many faces and lives
more than these may he
be raised and magnified.

APPENDIX: JOSHUA'S FACE

פְּנֵי יְהוֹשֻׁעַ

וִיהוֹשֻׁעַ מֵעַל אֶל פָּנַי מַבִּיט. וּפָנָיו זָהָב
שָׁחוּט. חֲלוֹם קַר. חֲלוֹם חָנוּט.
3 וּלְרַגְלַי הַיָּם מַכֶּה נְצָחִים אֶל הַחוֹף.
אֲנִי חוֹלָה נְהִיָּתוֹ. דּוּמָה, אֲנִי עוֹמֵד לָמוּת.
אַךְ מְכָרְחֵנִי, מְכָרְחֵנִי לְחַכּוֹת חַי
אֶל־תָּמִיד.
7 אָחִי מֵעַל פָּנָיו עוֹלִים בָּעָב
לְהַגִּיד עִקְבוֹתַי בַּחוֹל הַנִּשְׁטָף.

הַיָּם מַכֶּה וְנָסוֹג. מַכֶּה וְנָסוֹג.
מִלְחָמוֹת אֵיתָנִים מֵתָנוֹת בַּחֵק.
11 אֲנִי. בָּרוּחַ. אַחֵר. בּוֹרֵחַ. רָחוֹק.
גַּם יְהוֹשֻׁעַ עַכְשָׁיו נָח מִמִּלְחָמוֹת.
שֶׁהִנְחִיל נַחֲלָה לְעַמּוֹ,
14 אֲבָל קֶבֶר לֹא חָצַב לוֹ
בְּהָרֵי אֶפְרָיִם.
עַל כֵּן לַיְלָה לַיְלָה הוּא יוֹצֵא
17 לָשׂוּחַ בַּשָּׁמַיִם.
וַאֲנִי חוֹלָה, דּוּמָה עוֹמֵד לָמוּת
מְיַחֵף בְּחוֹל יָרֵחַ קַר
20 בְּשׁוּלֵי הַמַּיִם
וְהוּמָה בִּי, הוֹמֶה בִּי סוּף
22 הַמַּכֶּה לְרַגְלִי אֶת מוֹתִי
גַּל אַחַר גַּל

עַל פְּנֵי חַיִּים רַבִּים
25 יִתְרוֹמָם וְיִתְגַּדַּל.

PNEY YEHOṢÚA

Vihoṣúa meál el panáy mabít. Ufanáv zaháv
Ṣaḥút. Ḥalóm kar. Ḥalóm ḥanút.
Uleragláy hayám maké nethsaḥím el haḥóf.
Aní ḥolé nehiyató. Domé, aní oméd lamút.
Aḥ muḥraḥáni, muḥraḥáni leḥakót ḥay
El-tamíd.
Aḥí meál panáv olím baáv
Lehagíd ikvotáy baḥól haniṣtáf.

Hayám maké venasóg. Maké venasóg.
Milḥamót eytaním mutnót baḥók.
Aní. Barúaḥ. Aḥér. Boréaḥ. Raḥók.
Gam yehoṣúa aḥṣáv naḥ mimilḥamót.
Ṣehinḥíl naḥalá leamó,
Avál kéver lo ḥatsáv lo
Beharéy efráyim.
Al ken láyla láyla hu yotsé
Lasúaḥ baṣamáyim.
Vaaní ḥolé, domé oméd lamút
Meyaḥéf beḥól yaréaḥ kar
Beṣuléy hamáyim
Vehomé bi, homé bi sof
Hamaké leragláy et motí
Gal aḥár gal –

Al pney ḥayím rabím
Yitromám veyitgadál.

Prose translation by Arieh Sachs

(1) And Joshua from above looks at my face. And his face is beaten gold. (2) A cold dream. A mummified dream. (3) And at my feet the sea beats eternities toward the shore. (4) I am sick with its lament. It seems I am about to die. (5) But I must, I must await alive (6) The 'Always'. (7) Above, my brother's face rises in the cloud. (8) To tell [foretell] my footsteps in the [sea] washed sand.‖ (9) The sea beats (attacks) and retreats. Beats and retreats. (10) Elemental wars conditioned by law. (11) Me (myself). In the wind. Different (other). Escaping. Distant. (12) Joshua too is now resting from wars. (13) For he left an estate (heritage) to his people, (14) But did not hew himself a grave (15) In the mountains of Ephraim. (16) Therefore he goes out night after night (17) To walk in the sky. (18) And I am sick, it seems I am about to die (19) Walking barefoot in cold moon-sand (20) At the water's edge (21) And murmuring within me, murmuring within me is the end (22) Which beats my death at my feet (23) Wave after wave – ‖ (24) Upon [the faces of] many lives (25) May he be raised and glorified.

Note: In *The Modern Hebrew Poem Itself* the above translation is accompanied by a commentary.

Translating Horace
Working Papers
C.H. Sisson

EXTRACTS FROM A CORRESPONDENCE BETWEEN
D. WEISSBORT AND C.H. SISSON

[Weissbort to Sisson]

11 August 1983

[. . .] What I have in mind is an account or reconstruction of the actual business of translating something. There has been quite a proliferation of theoretical pieces, speculations, on translation. I feel it would be useful to gather, rather, working notes, as it were, descriptions of the struggle, battle, love affair. I know of course that – depending on one's work methods – it will be harder or easier to write this kind of account. I'm less concerned with justifications after the event, than with a recording of the decision-by-decision, intuition-by-intuition, process. Naturally, such an account can only be approximative, but would, I think, be valuable nonetheless. One way of setting about this might be to keep a diary, as it were, of a translation. I realize that this would be to introduce an element of self-consciousness, but it might also yield interesting results. Another way would be to keep drafts, even if it is against one's normal practise, and attempt an ex-post-facto analysis. But whatever you might be able to offer in the way of practical notes would be most welcome.

[Sisson to Weissbort]

18 August 1983

I hope you won't mind my saying that your letter about what I may call the processes of translation made me think of Wordsworth's poem about 'How the Practice of Lying May be Taught'. I am sure there are people who would perform more plausibly than I, but your project sounds rather as if it would be beyond my powers of introspection. Most of my translations have been of things I have had more or less acquaintance with for years; when I have finally come to attempt a translation, it has been for reasons partly external and partly internal, a common feature being that I had reached a point at which it seemed possible to do some sort of version without undue violence to my native language and to the sort of verse I was able to manage at a particular time. I am now an old, old hand at such games with all the slyness to be expected – for better and for worse – from such operators in any field. One motive has always been a desire to get to know better the work I was undertaking. A diary of translation such as you suggest would in my case be a very phoney affair – and it is obvious from what you say that you realise that there are dangers about this: for one thing it would not begin until years after the true beginning, which would be long before I had any designs on the author. As to drafts, if I keep them it is originally because, as with one's own poems, first thoughts often prove to be better, rhythmically and in other ways, than the improvements one is tempted to make, for this reason and that, at later stages, though that is not to say that one can necessarily rely on first thoughts, and of course what one writes down is a highly incomplete account of a process which may include all sorts of messing around with dictionaries and what-not. Anyway I should not enjoy being distracted from the work in hand to try to record what was going on in my own mind – or rather to note the odd bits of flotsam and jetsam thrown up or evacuated in the course of what must be a largely invisible process, like eating and drinking and digestion. [. . .]

[Weissbort to Sisson]

22 August 1983

[. . .] I would like to repeat my invitation that you contribute to the volume [. . .] I reiterate the invitation if only because the paragraph you wrote on translation in your letter contains a number of important points which I am sure you could easily expand on if you were so inclined, referring doubtless to actual translations you have made. For instance, you refer rather disparagingly (!) to the flotsam and jetsam thrown up in the course of translation – well, in a way, it is that flotsam and jetsam which might prove illuminating. Otherwise, as you say, what we may end up with is an exercise in lying. [. . .] What I am after is something, however little, from within the translator's workshop. That rather than a literary essay on the subject, considered reflections. Not that I am against the latter, but it is not what I am looking for. The diary of translation would merely be a device or way of reaching in, identifying, extracting such information. But of course no one likes to do this, perhaps because not one of us probably likes to give the game away, as it were. [. . .]

[Sisson to Weissbort]

30 August 1983

[. . .] While there must obviously be a considerable element of the unconscious or unreportable in the work of all translators, there are certainly people whose methods are such that they have more to show than I have. [. . .] I would cheerfully 'give the game away' if I had a game to give, but I haven't. [. . .] I have looked around to see if I had any bits of paper I could send you which would be illuminating, but all I have come up with is the enclosed. [. . .] 'The enclosed' consists of (1) a version of Corbière's 'La Pastorale de Conlie'; it is dated 22 April 1973 and came to light in the Winter 77/8 number of *Agenda* (Vol. 15 No. 4); I turned it out, with translations of two fifteenth-century songs, when William Cookson asked if I had anything for a 'French Poetry Issue'. (2) is Horace I, ii, printed on p. 223 of *In the Trojan Ditch*; no date, but I imagine 3 or 4 years earlier than (1). (3) is Horace IV, vii, which was never printed, as far as I can recall, and of which the enclosed are the only copies; about the same date as (2).

There is a sort of untidy genealogy in which my poems and translations both have a part, and which could be illustrated by extracts which would indicate the sort of relationship that seems to exist. But such a dossier would I am afraid be more appropriate to a study of my own work than to one of the business of translation as such; it would be a summary record of my development, change or decay (as you view it).

If I knew how to help I would do so, and if anything occurs to you in the light or perhaps I should say the darkness of these letters etc., please let me know. [. . .]

HORACE I, ii

*[handwritten:] When, to the ruler of the querulous Ilia
In vengeance, he threw himself, spreading
Far over the left bank, in defeaming Tiber?
HORACE I, ii The stream is uncertain*

Already enough snow, hail, thunder and lightening
Our Father has sent us, bloody-handed.
He has thrown down the Capitoline buildings
    And terrified the city,

Terrified the inhabitants, who fear the return ~~of~~
of
The age of Pyrrha, a time of floods and marvels
When Proteus led ~~his~~ monsters up to the hill-tops
    Though ~~they~~ belong*ed* to the sea, *who*

And the whole genus of fishes found its way to the elm-top
Which were more accustomed to entertaining pig*e*ons
And ~~the tender-eyed deer~~ *does* found themselves perma/netly
                              swimming

On a limitless ocean.
We saw the yellow ~~tibarx~~ ochre of the Tiber
Turned (back) violently ~~at its mouth~~ by the Etruscan sea
Flood*ing* over Numa's monument, wrecking ~~also~~
    The temple of ~~Esta~~ Vesta,

~~Taking upon himself~~
For that,
Avenging, apprently in his quality as a husband,
~~As he ran over the left bank entirely without Jove's~~
                                          ~~permission~~
Ilia, who considered she had been wronged

Ilia

Running far and wide over the left ~~banck~~ bank
    Certainly without Jove's permission,
W, heard
And ~~hearing~~ that the ~~citizens~~ Romans have been sharpening their kn
                                                        knives
To cut up one another, ~~when it would have been better to~~
                          ~~cut~~ up the Persians
        d   l
Hearing also that children have become scarce
        ~~On account of~~ their parents being victims.
                                 ~~s debauchery.~~
                                    people
Which ~~of the~~ gods is it best for the ~~populace~~ to call upon
When the empire is falling? ~~With~~ What prayers are best
                    for the Vestals
~~In To use~~ In a time like this, though their goodess
        Pays little attention?
Jupiter has to give someone the task of expiation.
Come, as we pray, your muscular shoulders shining
In a cloak of cloud, you perhaps were the best,
        Far-seeing Appollo,
Or if you prefer, send us the smiling Venus,
With every delight as usual flying about her
Or, if the neglected race of your progeny
        Deserves that attention
Father of Romulus, ~~xxmxxixxxx~~ you have seen enough of war
It has gone on too long, forget the sort of spectacle

You are most at home with, the Moorish foot-soldier
    Desperate against his enemy.
Or changing ~~youxshapex~~ your shape, as you come among us on
                                                earth
~~Axxume~~ Son of Maia - she will be kind - assume the appear
                                                ance
Of this man still in his prime, and well suited to be
    The avenger of Caesar.
Go back late to heaven, and meanwhile
Be among your people, the Quirinals
And I pray only that no fault of theirs may
    Drive you away.
Here rather may you enjoy the triuphs you love
~~kixingxamengxus~~
A prince and our paternal benefactor.
Do not ~~ini~~/leave/ even the Medes unpunished
    While you lead us, Caesar.

Final version

Already enough snow, hail, thunder and lightning
Our Father has sent us, bloody-handed.
He has thrown down the Capitoline buildings
       And terrified the city,

Terrified the inhabitants, who fear the return
Of the age of Pyrrha, a time of floods and marvels
When Proteus led his monsters up to the hill-tops
       Although they belonged to the sea,

And the whole genus of fishes found its way to the elm-tops
Which were more accustomed to entertaining pigeons
And the tender-eyed deer found themselves permanently
  swimming
       On a limitless ocean.

We saw the yellow ochre of the Tiber
Turned back violently at the mouth by the Etruscan sea,
Flooding over Numa's monument, wrecking also
       The temple of Vesta

When, for the sake of the querulous Ilia
In vengeance he threw himself, spreading
Far over the left bank, in defiance of Jove;
       The stream is uxorious.

He heard that the Romans had been sharpening their knives
To cut up one another – it would have been better to cut up the
  Persians –
Heard also that children had become scarce,
       Their parents being vicious.

Which of the gods is it best for the people to call upon
When the empire is falling? What prayers are best for the
  Vestals
To use in a time like this, though their goddess
       Pays little attention?

Jupiter has to give someone the task of expiation.
Come, as we pray, your muscular shoulders shining
In a cloak of cloud, you perhaps were the best,
       Far-seeing Apollo,

Or, if you prefer, send us the smiling Venus,
With every delight as usual flying about her
Or, if the neglected race of your progeny
    Deserves that attention,

Father of Romulus, you have seen enough of war,
It has gone on too long, forget the sort of spectacle
You are most at home with, the Moorish foot-soldier
    Desperate against his enemy.

Or, changing your shape, as you come among us on earth,
Son of Maia – she will be kind – assume the appearance
Of this man still in his prime, and well suited to be
    The avenger of Caesar.

Go back late to heaven, and meanwhile
Be among your people, the Quirinals
And I pray only that no fault of theirs may
    Drive you away.

Here rather may you enjoy the triumphs you love,
A prince and our benefactor;
Do not leave even the Medes unpunished
    While you lead us, Caesar.

Original Latin

    IAM satis terris nivis atque dirae
    grandinis misit Pater et rubente
    dextera sacras iaculàtus arces
        terruit urbem,

    terruit gentis, grave ne rediret
    saeculum Pyrrhae nova monstra questae,
    omne cum Proteus pecus egit altos
        visere montes,

    piscium et summa genus haesit ulmo,
    nota quae sedes fuerat columbis,
    et superiecto pavidae natarunt
        aequore dammae.

    vidimus flavom Tiberim, retortis
    litore Etrusco violenter undis,

ire deiectum monumenta regis
    templaque Vestae,

Iliae dum se nimium querenti
iactat ultorem, vagus et sinistra
labitur ripa, Iove non probante, ux-
    orius amnis.

audiet civis acuisse ferrum,
quo graves Persae melius perirent,
audiet pugnas vitio parentum
    rara iuventus.

quem vocet divom populus ruentis
imperi rebus? Prece qua fatigent
virgines sanctae minus audientem
    carmina Vestam?

cui dabit partis scelus expiandi
Iuppiter? Tandem venias, precamur,
nube candentis umeros amictus,
    augur Apollo;

sive tu mavis, Erycina ridens,
quam Iocus circum volat et Cupido;
sive neclectum genus et nepotes
    respicis, auctor,

heu nimis longo satiate ludo,
quem iuvat clamor galeaeque leves
acer et Marsi peditis cruentum
    voltus in hostem.

sive mutata iuvenem figura
ales in terris imitaris almae
filius Maiae, patiens vocari
    Caesaris ultor:

serus in caelum redeas, diuque
laetus intersis populo Quirini,
neve te nostris vitiis iniquom
    ocior aura

tollat; hic magnos potius triumphos,
hic ames dici pater atque princeps,

neu sinas Medos equitare inultos,
te duce, Caesar.

Prose Translation by C.E. Bennett

To Augustus, the Deliverer and Hope of the State

ENOUGH already of dire snow and hail has the Father sent upon the earth, and smiting with his red right hand the sacred hill-tops has filled with fear the City and the people, lest there should come again the gruesome age of Pyrrha, who complained of marvels strange, when Proteus drove all his herd to visit the lofty mountains, and the tribe of fishes lodged in elm-tops, that till then had been the wonted haunt of doves, and the terror-stricken does swam in the overwhelming flood.

We saw the yellow Tiber, its waves hurled back in fury from the Tuscan shore, advance to overthrow the King's Memorial and Vesta's shrines, showing himself too ardent an avenger of complaining Ilia, and spreading far and wide o'er the left bank without Jove's sanction, – fond river-god.

Our children, made fewer by their sires' sins, shall hear that citizen whetted against citizen the sword whereby the Parthian foe had better perished, – shall hear of battles too.

Whom of the gods shall the folk call to the needs of the falling empire? With what entreaty shall the holy Maidens importune Vesta, who heedeth not their litanies? To whom shall Jupiter assign the task of atoning for our guilt? Come thou at length, we pray thee, prophetic Apollo, veiling thy radiant shoulders in a cloud; or thou, if thou wilt rather, blithe goddess of Eryx, about whom hover Mirth and Desire; or thou, our author, if thou regardest the neglected race of thy descendants, thou glutted with the game of war, alas! too long continued, thou whose delight is in the battle-shout and glancing helms and the grim visage of the Marsian foot-soldier facing his blood-stained foe. Or thou, wingèd son of benign Maia, if changing thy form, thou assumest on earth the guise of man, right ready to be called the avenger of Caesar: late mayest thou return to the skies and long mayest thou be pleased to dwell amid Quirinus' folk; and may no untimely gale waft thee from us angered at our sins! Here rather mayest thou love glorious triumphs, the name of 'Father' and of 'Chief'; nor suffer the Medes to ride on their raids unpunished, whilst thou art our leader, O Caesar!

HORACE IV, vii

The snows have gone; already the grass comes back
The trees already have their leaves:
The earth is changing once more; down goes the river
There is the water passing low on the banks

There are the Graces, all of them, naked again

As they lead their gang around.

Don't expect it to last, the year says, it may be mild

But that is only one day.

The cold weather cannot stand up to a breeze, spring
                              finds summer

On top of it, and summer won't last

Autumn bombards it with fruit, and it is gone, soon

Back comes the mists xdarkxdeadxtimex winter, dead.

                                    at least
But As the moons fly past, they make ~~good~~ up their losses:

We, when we go down

Foll~~o~~wing Aeneas, and a whole line of kings the ~~once~~ propsperou~~s~~ king,

What are we? Dust and shadow.

                       their
~~Do~~ ~~you~~ ~~know~~
Who knows ~~whether~~ the gods will add ~~on~~ a single day
              ~~he~~ ~~has~~ had
To th~~o~~se ~~you~~ have lived already?
  ~~A~~ ~~your heir Greedy   B hungry   to lose~~
~~Everything will escape from your greedy heirs~~
~~You speedy hev   you he have a myself~~
If you give yourself enough.
  ~~care for yourself   the greedy hand if you be~~
~~will close on will~~
     ~~if you look oh you~~   what
~~When~~ Once you have gone down ~~you will at least be left with~~
                                 have coming to you.   what is own to you?

A~~splendid~~ judgment

An exalted judgment

It will take more than your family Torquatus, or ~~your~~ eloquence

Or virtue, t~~o~~ put you right.

Translating Horace 197

~~When he was dead~~

When Hyppolytus died, in spite of ~~all~~ his chastity,
              save
~~Di~~na Diana could not ~~free~~ him:

It was the same with Perithous, dear as he was to Theseus

He had to stay where he was

Final Version

The snows have gone; already the grass comes back,
The trees have their leaves.
The earth is changing once more; down goes the river,
The water is low on the banks.

There are the Graces, all of them, naked again
As they lead their gang around.
Don't expect it to last, the year says, it may be mild
But that is only today.

Cold cannot stand up to a breeze, spring finds the summer
On top of it, and that won't last,
Autumn bombards it with fruit, soon
Back comes winter, dead.

As the moons fly past at least they make up their losses:
We, when we go down,
Following Aeneas, a line of prosperous kings,
What are we? Dust and shadow.

Why suppose that the gods will add a single day
To those you have had already?
The greedy hands of your heir will close on nothing:
So look after yourself.

Once you have gone down what is coming to you?
An exalted judgement.
It will take more than your family, Torquatus, or eloquence
Or virtue, to put you right.

When Hyppolytus died, in spite of his chastity
Diana could not save him:
The same with Pirithous, dear as he was to Theseus,
Once beyond Lethe, he stayed.

Original Latin

> DIFFVGERE nives, redeunt iam gramina campis
>   arboribusque comae;
> mutat terra vices et decrescentia ripas
>   flumina praetereunt;
>
> Gratia cum Nymphis geminisque sororibus audet
>   ducere nuda choros.
> immortalia ne speres, monet annus et almum
>   quae rapit hora diem.
>
> frigora mitescunt zephyris, ver proterit aestas
>   interitura, simul
> pomifer autumnus fruges effuderit, et mox
>   bruma recurrit iners.
>
> damna tamen celeres reparant caelestia lunae;
>   nos ubi decidimus,
> quo pius Aeneas, quo Tullus dives et Ancus,
>   pulvis et umbra sumus.
>
> quis scit an adiciant hodiernae crastina summae
>   tempora di superi?
> cuncta manus avidas fugient heredis, amico
>   quae dederis animo.
>
> cum semel occideris et de te splendida Minos
>   fecerit arbitria,
> non, Torquate, genus, non te facundia, non te
>   restituet pietas;
>
> infernis neque enim tenebris Diana pudicum
>   liberat Hippolytum,
> nec Lethaea valet Theseus abrumpere caro
>   vincula Pirithoo.

Prose Translation by C.E. Bennett

THE snow has fled; already the grass is returning to the fields and the foliage to the trees. Earth is going through her changes, and with lessening flood the rivers flow past their banks. The Grace, with the Nymphs and her twin sisters, ventures unrobed to lead her bands. The year and the hour that rob us of the gracious day warn thee not to hope for unending joys. The cold gives way before the zephyrs; spring is trampled underfoot by summer, destined likewise to pass away so soon as fruitful autumn has poured forth its harvest; and lifeless winter soon returns again.

Yet the swiftly changing moons repair their losses in the sky. We, when we have descended whither righteous Aeneas, whither rich Tullus and Ancus have gone, are but dust and shadow. Who knows whether the gods will add to-morrow's time to the sum of today? All things which thou grantest to thine own dear soul, shall escape the greedy clutches of thine heir. When once thou hast perished and Minos has pronounced on thee his august judgment, not family, Torquatus, nor eloquence, nor righteousness shall restore thee again to life. For Diana releases not the chaste Hippolytus from the nether darkness, nor has Theseus power to break the Lethean chains of his dear Pirithous.

Finding the Proper Equivalent
Translating the Poetry of Andrei Voznesensky
William Jay Smith

Andrei Voznesensky tells of reading his poems once at Vancouver, British Columbia, in an unusually informal atmosphere. Students came – hundreds of them – and sat about on the floor of the hall, and with them came a great number of pets, chiefly dogs, but there were other animals as well, even a raccoon among them. On a later visit to the United States Voznesensky read a poem he had written about this occasion, called in English 'Dogalypse'. He said he had been happy to have the animals in his audience; they made no distinction between Russian and English, and seemed delighted with the performance of – as Voznesensky terms himself in the poem – a 'Moscow mutt'.

I have also been a delighted follower of Andrei Voznesensky, and many times a participant in his programs in the United States, reading translations of his poems, my own and others, in Washington, New York and Boston; but my relation to the Russian language remains almost as tenuous as that of his animal audience. With five other poets, W.H. Auden, Richard Wilbur, Stanley Kunitz, Jean Garrigue and Stanley Moss, I was enlisted in the translation of Voznesensky's poetry in 1964 by his editors, Patricia Blake and Max Hayward. The undertaking was a daring one: none of us really knew Russian, and yet we dared attempt to put into English (albeit with the expert assistance of Max Hayward) one of the most talented and complicated of modern Russian poets. I was perhaps the one member of the group who could claim some little knowledge of the language. At the end of the second world war I had studied it for three months at the United States Navy Language School but, because the war ended while I was there, I left before the completion of the course. And because of my four years of war and everything connected with them, I wanted to erase all memory of those three months. I never in the twenty years afterwards tried to read a Russian text or listen to a Russian record. I was interested in Russian literature, and continued to read Russian poetry, but always in translation. When I visited the Soviet Union in 1970, some of the language I had studied so intensively for a brief period came back to me – not the written, but the spoken language. I discovered at the end of my month's stay that I could follow a good bit of what was being said but, like a dog that learns to grasp what is addressed to him, I could nod my head and say very little. I have returned to the Soviet Union four times since 1970 (in 1981 for four months as a Fulbright lecturer at Moscow State University) but only now am I beginning to have any real hold on the language.

Andrei Voznesensky once showed W.H. Auden's translation of one of his poems to an older Russian poet who read it through with admiration and then said simply, 'One madman has understood another.' And this, I think, is the simplest explanation of the success that Andrei Voznesensky's poems have met with in their English versions. Poets must translate poets; even if they know little of the other's language, something of the fine frenzy of the original will somehow work its way through.

'As a fellow maker,' W.H. Auden wrote, 'I am struck first and foremost by Voznesensky's craftsmanship. Here, at least, is a poet who knows that, whatever else it may be, a poem is a verbal artifact which must be as skilfully and solidly constructed as a table or a motorcycle.' His translators have done their best to give in English a sense of the solid construction of these artifacts, despite the realization that, as Auden says, 'Mr Voznesensky's metrical effects must make any translator despair.' One can approximate the Russian line length in English, although the Russian seems always more heavily stressed. But fortunately English does have stress; in an unstressed language like French Voznesensky's poems come through far less well.

One other despair of the English translator is the greater number of words that he must use. I have often been reminded of this, especially when translating Voznesensky's short lyrics. It was forcefully brought home when I first saw Voznesensky's translation of my poem 'What Train Will Come?' My initial reaction was that the poem had shrunk in Russian and that the translator had made drastic cuts, but then I realized how much could be packed into a stanza in Russian, an inflected language that uses no articles.

Andrei Voznesensky's platform stance in reading his poems is

Finding the Proper Equivalent

well known. He stands with his feet spread apart like a boxer ready to move dancing in on his opponent, his wide gaze directed upward, his nose tilted back, eyes fixed on something far off in space, his right hand raised, thumb slightly extended as if hailing some heavenly bus. With this stance, the Hungarian poet Sándor Weöres was prompted to remark, Andrei Voznesensky is attempting to enlarge the scope of poetry. In his reading Voznesensky sketches a kind of parabola, beginning quietly, building up slowly and ballooning out, then descending until at times the last few words are spoken separately in a staccato fashion, almost whispered into the microphone. Listeners often comment on how muted the English versions sound when read aloud beside Voznesensky's rendition of the Russian originals. Some actors reading with him have tried to imitate his dramatic delivery in English, making as much noise as he does in the Russian, and have failed because this reading style – even with the élan of a Dylan Thomas – can never be quite as emphatic in English as it can in Russian. The same thing works in reverse. When I visited an English-speaking school in Leningrad some of the young students stood up to recite poems for me in English. One little girl rendered 'My love is like a red, red rose' of Robert Burns, that most exquisite of lyrics. She made it sound like a full-throated incantation bellowed out to troops about to go off to battle. The poem became unrecognizable.

When Andrei Voznesensky came to Washington in October of 1972 to read his poems the Library of Congress, which sponsored the reading, decided because of his tight schedule to put him up in what was then the Congressional Hotel on Capitol Hill, just a few blocks from the Library. The Congressional, owned by the government and now turned into an office building, was then anything but luxurious; it was indeed a working hotel. Lobbyists from all over the country were in and out every day in the hope of influencing legislation in the Congress; officials of both political parties were much in evidence. Voznesensky found that his room was next to the offices of the Republican National Committee. For him also this became a working hotel. After lunch and a voice test at the Library, he and I retired to the bar of the Congressional to plan the program for the evening. The bar was almost empty and we sat in the corner in the dim light; behind us was a badly painted mural showing the New York skyline. Voznesensky quickly established the order of the poems he planned to read, and then he gave me copies of translations of some new ones that had been done by other American poets. There was one short poem – a new one – that he wanted to read, but he had no translation of it. These few lines he had composed while at the University of California at Berkeley:

ИСТОКИ

Меня тоска познанья точит.
и Беркли в сердце у меня.
Его студенчество — источник
безумства, света и ума.

А клеши спутницы прелестной
вниз расширялись в темноте —
как тени расширялись, если
источник света в животе.

As I struggled to grasp his meaning, he took up his pen as he frequently does (as a former architecture student he seems to visualize everything) and drew for me the co-ed's bell-bottomed trousers that seemed to the poet like shadows cast by her light-bulb-like belly. With this graphic assistance (see Figure 1) I came up with the following translation:

SOURCES

I came to learn,
To explore the secrets of Berkeley,
To find in its students the sources
Of rebellion, light, and ideas.

But I was sidetracked by a coed's black bell-bottomed trousers,
Which flared out as shadow would flare out
If the source of light
Were centered in her belly.

The image had been kept, if nothing else, and the translation had taken only a few minutes. I might have translated this poem differently if I had worked with a Russian scholar, but such a translation could never be for me as vivid as this one done with the help of Voznesensky's visual interpretation.

One stanza from Voznesensky's poem 'An Ironical Elegy', concerned with the problems of writing, shows something of the

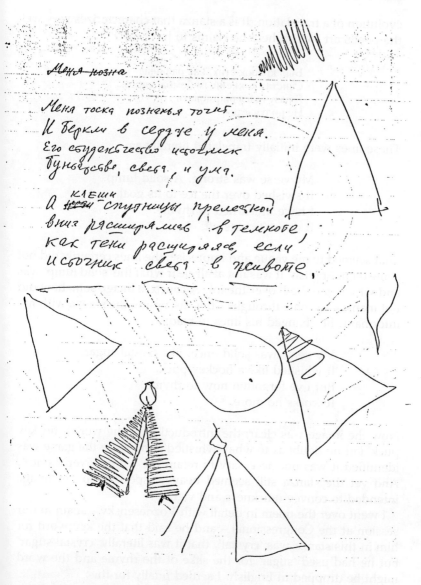

FIGURE 1   Andrei Voznesensky's poem 'Sources' with the poet's drawings.

evolution of a translation. It is a stanza that characterizes very well the poet's art (which here he claims to have lost):

> Был крепок стих, как рафинад.
> Свистал хоккейным бомбардиром.
> Я разучился рифмовать.
> Не получается.

These lines were initially translated literally as:

> My verse was strong. A solid lump.
> It swished over the ice to its goal.
> I have unlearned to rhyme.
> It doesn't come off.

That seemed to me vague and imprecise; the lines certainly did not come off in English. It was not at all clear what the 'solid lump' was and why it 'swished' over the ice. A concrete image somehow did not manage to come through. After discussing the stanza with my informant, he changed his lines to read:

> My verse was solid once, like crystal sugar.
> It whistled like a hockey puck.
> But I've forgotten how to rhyme.
> It works no more.

Now the image was clear; the introduction of the words 'hockey puck' left no doubt as to what 'whistled', and since the game was identified it was not necessary to retain the words 'over the ice'. And yet the stanza still seemed heavy, especially for an image intended to convey quickness and vigor.

I went over the poem in detail with Voznesensky – again in our session at the Congressional – and he said that the key word for him in this stanza was 'crystal', that it was literally 'crystal sugar' but he had used 'sugar' for the sake of the rhyme and the word might be dropped in English. I settled finally for this:

> My verse was solid – like crystal;
> A hockey puck, it zinged to its goal.
> But I can't rhyme any more;
> I've lost the knack.

That sounded to me more like what Voznesensky should sound like in English.

Another poem that underwent many transformations before attaining its final form in English is 'A Boat on the Shore':

> ЛОДКА НА БЕРЕГУ
>
> Над лодкой перевернутою, ночью,
> над днищем алюминиевым туга,
> гимнастка, изгибая позвоночник,
> изображает ручку утюга!
>
> В сияньи моря северно-янтарном
> хохочет, в днище впаяна, дыша,
> кусачка, полукровочка, кентаврка,
> ах, полулодка и полудитя...
>
> Полуморская-полугородская,
> в ней полуполоумнейший расчет,
> полутоскует — как полуласкает,
> полуутопит — как полуспасет.
>
> Сейчас она стремглав перевернется.
> Полузвереныш, уплывет — вернется,
> по пальцы утопая в бережок...
>
> Ужо тебе, оживший утюжок!

I received from Max Hayward the literal version of the poem given in Figure 2. The poet had apparently already changed the title and eliminated the first stanza.

A charming poem, but if the translation were heavy-handed the delicacy would be lost and the poem along with it – that much was clear from this rough version. The poem, like many of Voznesensky's, is extremely visual, and as I went over it with Hayward I sought not only the meaning of individual words but also the picture that they presented. I made rough sketches of the flat-iron to be sure that I understood – indeed, that I could see – exactly what was going on. I listened to the poem read aloud in order to appreciate its formal metrical pattern. I went over the rhyme scheme and the rhyme words in detail. My final version, which roughly keeps the metrical pattern and rhyme scheme of the original, may seem far from the literal version, but my poetic instinct tells me that it is closer in spirit to what the poet wrote:

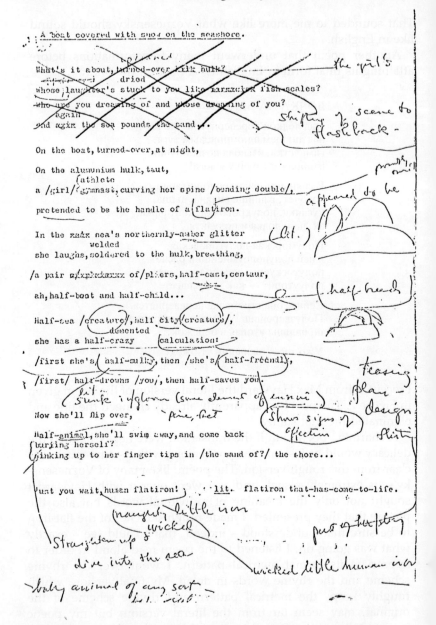

FIGURE 2   Max Hayward's literal version of 'A Boat on the Shore' with William Jay Smith's annotations.

A BOAT ON THE SHORE

On the overturned boat in clear outline,
Taut, on its aluminum hull at night,
Is a gymnast who, arching back her spine,
Becomes the handle of a flat-iron.

In the North Sea's constant amber glitter
Like a pair of pliers, this half-caste, wild,
Centaur-like creature, welded to the hull
Is partly a boat and partly a child.

Half spirit of the city, half spirit of the sea,
She carries on this silly flirtation:
Half-sulking at first, and then half-friendly,
Will save you and then drop you back in the ocean.

She will of a sudden flip over and
Dart into the water, half-seal swim about;
Then return to burrow deep in the sand . . .

Just wait, little iron, till you're ironed out!

The play on words in the last line, my addition, seemed to me legitimate because it is clearly implied in the original and is in keeping with the somewhat sassy tone of the poem. In any case, like all the liberties I have taken with Voznesensky's work, it had the author's approval.

Because sometimes even greater liberties had to be taken, I was fortunate in being able to work directly with Voznesensky. 'Striptease', in the original, concludes with this couplet:

«Мальчик, — скажет, — ах, какой у вас акцент!
Закажите мне мартини и абсент».

I pointed out that in no bar in the United States would anybody – even the wildest striptease artist – ever order 'martini and absinthe'. I suggested 'a double martini' as a substitute. And so I was able to keep my rhyme, just as he had by the use of 'absinthe' in the original:

'Are you kidding, kiddo?' she'll answer me.
'Better make mine a double martini.'

I had in the process dropped the stripper's remark about his accent and had added the word-play 'kidding, kiddo', which seemed to me in keeping with the tone of the original.

Literal-minded professors, baffled by my rendition, will always be ready to pounce on these changes as errors. One such professor attacked me for my translation of the final lines of 'New York Airport at Night':

> Бруклин — дурак, твердокаменный черт.
> Памятник эры —
> Аэропорт.

In my version these lines read:

> Brooklyn Bridge, rearing its idiot stone, cannot consort
> With this monument of the era,
> The airport.

It was necessary in English to add 'Bridge' after 'Brooklyn', although it is not in the original. Otherwise the English reader would think that the poet was referring to the borough of Brooklyn and not to the bridge that leads to it. The Russian reader recognizes at once an allusion to the poem 'Brooklyn Bridge' by Mayakovsky, which celebrates the bridge as a technological triumph of modern times, one that Voznesensky maintains has been superseded by Kennedy Airport.

Academic translators have played havoc with more than one of Voznesensky's lyrics. This is one of the lovely short pieces from the long poem *Oza*; I have heard the poet read it many times:

> Выйду ли к парку, в море ль плыву —
> туфелек пара стоит на полу.
>
> Левая к правой набок припала,
> их не поправят — времени мало.
>
> В мире не топлено, в мире ни зги,
> вы еще теплые, только с ноги,
>
> в вас от ступни потемнела изнанка,
> вытерлось золото фирменных знаков...
>
> Красные голуби просо клюют.
> Кровь кружит голову — спать не дают!

> Выйду ли к пляжу — туфелек пара,
> будто купальщица в море пропала.
>
> Где ты, купальщица? Вымыты пляжи.
> Как тебе плавается? С кем тебе пляшется?..
>
> ...В мире металла, на черной планете,
> сентиментальные туфельки эти,
>
> как перед танком присели голубки —
> нежные туфельки в форме скорлупки!

And this is my version of the poem:

> HER SHOES
>
> When I walk in the park or swim in the sea,
> A pair of her shoes waits there on the floor.
>
> The left one leaning on the right,
> Not enough time to set them straight.
>
> The world is pitch-black, cold and desolate,
> But they are still warm, right off her feet.
>
> The soles of her feet left the insides dark,
> The gold of the trademark has rubbed off.
>
> A pair of red doves pecking seed,
> They make me dizzy, rob me of sleep.
>
> I see the shoes when I go to the beach
> Like those of a bather drowned in the sea.
>
> Where are you, bather? The beaches are clean.
> Where are you dancing? With whom do you swim?
>
> In a world of metal, on a planet of black,
> Those silly shoes look to me like
>
> Doves perched in the path of a tank, frail
> And dainty, as delicate as eggshell.

In my translation I tried to retain the metrical pattern of the original and by the use of assonance to adhere as closely as possible to the rhyme scheme without upsetting the fragile balance of the whole. A prominent Slavic scholar also translated this poem, but in trying to keep too close to the original he produced verses with flat, heavy rhymes in a jog-trot rhythm that makes the poem sound like perfect nonsense in English. His translation ends somewhat like this: 'Egg-white thin sneakers, I give you my thanks!' – made to rhyme, of course, with 'tanks'. The translator in this case has the shoe on the wrong foot – and the wrong shoe at that. If the poet had meant 'sneakers' he would have used the Russian word *kedii* (from the American brand-name *Keds*).

When Voznesensky's point of departure in the original Russian is an English poem, the translator's job is cut out for him. This is the case in his witty and savage parody of Edgar Allan Poe's 'The Raven', also from *Oza*. The opening lines are:

> В час отлива возле чайной
> я лежал в ночи печальной,
> говорил друзьям об Озе и величье бытия,
> но внезапно черный ворон
> примешался к разговорам,
> вспыхнув синими очами,
> он сказал:
> «А на фига?!»

I put these lines right back into the rhythm of Poe's 'Raven':

> Once upon a midnight dreary, while, at low tide, weak and weary,
> I held forth to my friends on Oza and the glories of creation,
> Suddenly there came a raven, breaking up that conversation;
> Flashing eyes of fearful black,
> Quoth the raven, 'What the hell!'

In keeping with the forthright original, the last word stands in place of the more vulgar rhyme-word, which is understood.

I have spent many hours in translation sessions with Andrei Voznesensky – in bars, hotel rooms and restaurants in New York, Washington and Moscow, in his dacha at Peredelkino, in the lobby of the Moscow Union of Writers – but none are more memorable than those spent in the Port Jefferson, Long Island home of Vera Sandomirsky Dunham, Professor Emeritus of Russian at Queens College and editor, with Max Hayward, of Voznesensky's volume

Nostalgia for the Present. Many of the translations for this collection were completed there at her dining-room table in October 1977 in the company of the poet, who had come for yet another reading at the Library of Congress. (He had arrived carrying branches of mountain ash, picked near Boris Pasternak's house in Peredelkino, which he had brought to place on Robert Lowell's grave. With some difficulty he managed to find the grave at Dumbarton, New Hampshire, and in a nearby inn composed a moving elegy to Lowell.)

Among the translations that Vera Dunham and I completed, one of Voznesensky's favorites and one of mine is 'Saga', a poem whose original has been set to music. The translation, attempting to capture the poem's musical nature, follows the original closely. (See Figure 3 for the worksheets.) The refrain in Russian is literally: 'I shall never forget you. I shall never see you again.'

SAGA

You will awaken me at dawn
And barefoot lead me to the door;
You'll not forget me when I'm gone,
You will not see me any more.

Lord, I think, in shielding you
From the cold wind of the open door:
I'll not forget you when I'm gone,
I shall not see you any more.

The Admiralty, the Stock Exchange
I'll not forget when I am gone.
I'll not see Leningrad again,
Its water shivering at dawn.

From withered cherries as they turn,
Brown in the wind, let cold tears pour:
It's bad luck always to return,
I shall not see you any more.

And if what Hafiz says is true
And we return to earth once more,
We'll miss each other if it's true;
I shall not see you any more.

Our quarrels then will fade away

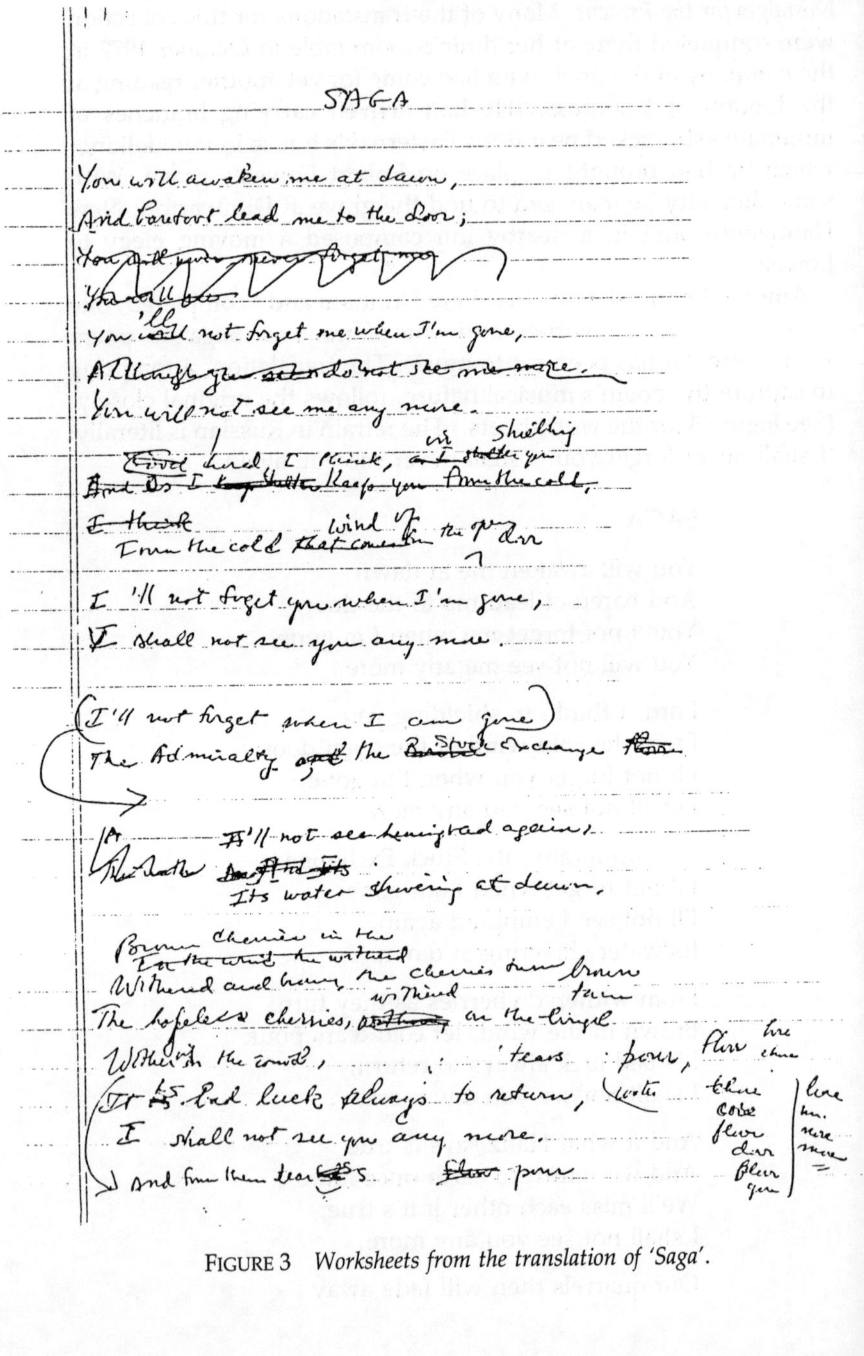

SAGA

You will awaken me at dawn,
And barefoot lead me to the door;
~~You will never forget me~~
~~You will~~
You'll not forget me when I'm gone,
~~Although you~~ do not see me ~~more~~.
You will not see me any more.

                        in Shielding
~~I had I think,~~ ~~shelter you~~
~~And as I~~ ~~keeps~~ you from the cold,
~~I think~~   wind
    From the cold ~~that comes~~ in the ~~p__~~ air

I'll not forget you when I'm gone,
I shall not see you any more.

(I'll not forget when I am gone)
The Admiralty ~~and~~ the ~~Bristol~~ Stock exchange ~~____~~

(I'll not see Leningrad again,)
~~The Neva~~ ~~And its~~ Its water shivering at dawn.

~~Brown cherries in the~~
~~To the wind he withered~~   brown
Withered and ~~being~~ the cherries ~~are~~
The hopeless cherries, ~~on the~~ on the linget.
Wither in the wind,   'tears pour, flow line
                                              thine
~~It is~~ Bad luck always to return, ~~with~~   thine line
I shall not see you any more.   cove   him
                                        flow   more
And from them tears ~~s~~   ~~flow~~ pour   our
                                        flew
                                        your

FIGURE 3 *Worksheets from the translation of 'Saga'.*

Finding the Proper Equivalent

~~Even if Hafiz~~
And if what Hafiz says is true,
And we return to earth once more,
We ~~all~~ may, yet other ~~if it's true~~;
I shall not see you any more.

Our little misunderstandings lover's quarrels / tiffs:
Will seem so trivial one day destroyed
                this   word

                meet

Two ~~silly~~ phrases ~~rising up~~ rise to sway
~~To~~ the ~~red heights of mud~~
~~To thee to~~
On heights of madness from earth's floor:
I'll not forget you when I'm gone,
I shall not see you any more.

~~From~~ Cherries withered ~~Dying~~
~~Even from the cherries~~ as they turn,
~~To Again~~ let cold tears pour:
~~brittle as straw~~
Born in the wind,
It's lack ~~fuck~~ always ~~to return~~
I shall not see you any more.

[Handwritten draft of a poem, heavily crossed out and revised:]

Our lot ~~two~~ *quarrels* ~~half~~ shall fade away
When ~~do~~ the ~~world~~
Our ~~lives~~
To nothing into ~~nothing drawn~~ when we both are gone
And ~~when~~ one day our two lives clash
~~Into the~~ ~~in~~
With that word to which they're drawn.

OED
Silly: Of things: Plain, simple, rustic, homely.

Perhaps this ~~drew~~, or else this sleep
Was all that did their silly thoughts so
      busie keep.
        Milton

The silly buckets.
        Coleridge

Finding the Proper Equivalent

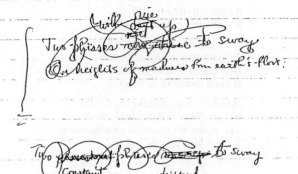

To nothing when we both are gone,
And when one day our two lives clash
Against that void to which they're drawn.

Two silly phrases rise to sway
On heights of madness from earth's floor:
I'll not forget you when I'm gone,
I shall not see you any more.

САГА

Ты меня на рассвете разбудишь,
проводить необутая выйдешь.
Ты меня никогда не забудешь.
Ты меня никогда не увидишь.

Заслонивши тебя от простуды,
я подумаю: «Боже всевышний!
Я тебя никогда не забуду.
Я тебя никогда не увижу».

Эту воду в мурашках запруды,
это Адмиралтейство и Биржу

я уже никогда не забуду
и уже никогда не увижу.

Не мигают, слезятся от ветра
безнадежные карие вишни.
Возвращаться — плохая примета.
Я тебя никогда не увижу.

Даже если на землю вернемся
мы вторично согласно Гафизу,
мы, конечно, с тобой разминемся.
Я тебя никогда не увижу.

И окажется так минимальным
наше непониманье с тобою
перед будущим непониманьем
двух живых с пустотой неживою.

И качнется бессмысленной высью
пара фраз, залетевших отсюда:
«Я тебя никогда не забуду.
Я тебя никогда не увижу».

This poem evokes the atmosphere of Leningrad with great subtlety, and I wonder if I would have devoted so much time to translating it if I had not seen that beautiful city in the cold autumn light and hence felt all the more the power of the poet's evocation of it. (In the original the city is not named: the Russian reader recognizes it at once by the reference to its two famous buildings, a reference that would be lost on most English readers were the city not specifically identified.)

Voznesensky's short epigrammatic poems are often the most difficult to translate. I have the typescript of two of these, which appeared first in 1979 in *Metropol*, the literary almanac of censored works brought out in *samizdat* by twenty-three Soviet authors in defiance of the Union of Writers. On the typescript (see Figure 4) is Voznesensky's drawing of a light bulb hanging by a simple cord, as described in the second of these verses. Patricia Blake provided me with these literal versions:

I (DERZHAVIN)

Above the dark silent country
so alone to fly.
I envy (invite) you, eagle with two heads –
you can talk to yourself.

Finding the Proper Equivalent

II (YESENIN)

Light bulbs hang from cords
under the ceiling always.
But only the poet is hanged
on his white spinal nerve.

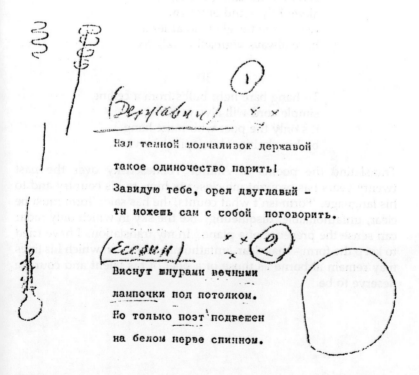

FIGURE 4 *Typescript of 'Derzhavin' and 'Yesenin' with the poet's drawings.*

The meaning of the first is that the poet is flying in a plane above the dark and silent (and imperial = *derzhava*) country, feeling quite alone. So he says to the two-headed eagle, the insignia of the Romanov dynasty: 'At least you can talk to yourself.' The quatrain bears the notation *Derzhavin*, referring to the eighteenth-century poet Gavril Derzhavin (1743–1816), as if it were he, living under the czars, who is talking to himself.

The second quatrain bears the notation *Yesenin*. Recalling the suicide by hanging of Sergei Yesenin (1895–1925), the lines picture the poet hanging from the neck until dead. The inference is that the modern poet who takes any risks leads a life dependent on his exposed 'white spinal nerve'.

At the poet's request I omitted the titles in my final versions:

I

Over a dark and quiet empire
alone I fly – and envy you,
two-headed eagle who at least
have always yourself to talk to.

II

To hang bare light bulbs from a ceiling
simple cord will always serve;
it's only the poet who must hang
by his glaring white spinal nerve.

Translating the poems of Andrei Voznesensky over the past twenty years has brought me closer to him, to his country and to his language. 'Form isn't what counts,' he has said; 'form must be clear, unfathomable, disquieting, like the sky in which only radar can sense the presence of a plane.' In my translations I have tried to keep the form – that clear, unfathomable sky – in which his lines may remain airborne as those of a poet of his talent and courage deserve to be.

Translating Brodsky
A Postscript
Daniel Weissbort

I had translated several poems by Joseph Brodsky in the early sixties, before I met him and before he had left the Soviet Union, and then again for an anthology of *Post-War Russian Poetry* (Penguin, 1974) which I edited. None of these versions were, however, submitted to the poet, and though I was generally fairly pleased with them they did not benefit from the intensive consultations, or negotiations, described in detail by George Kline in his article in the present volume. My most sustained effort at a Brodsky translation was of the sequence 'A Part of Speech', which was published in *Poetry*, though my translation was not used by the author in his collection of the same name (Farrar, Straus & Giroux and Oxford University Press, 1980). While translating this sequence I quite frequently consulted the author, as I recall. I made a substantially greater effort than hitherto to reproduce his rhyme schemes and metres, but even so was not close enough for him. If there is any written evidence of our deliberations I am unable to discover it among my papers, but the main problem – hinted at also in George Kline's essay – was that Brodsky found it hard, or impossible, to accept his translator's notion of what was tolerable in English. He was constantly, it seemed to me, trying as it were to transform English into Russian, to colonize English and oblige it to do things I did not believe it could do, even if I had considerable sympathy with the impulse that led him to make such (unreasonable) demands, and even though the making of such demands can in certain circumstances, as is well known, lead to the enrichment of the 'target' language.

In spite of the difficulties, even hardships, of our literary or translational collaboration, I agreed to translate a few more poems for the forthcoming collection referred to above. A brief correspondence about these translations contains some informative material. Printed below, therefore, is one letter from Brodsky (undated, but presumably sent during the summer of 1978), being a response to a draft translation I had sent the author. 'The Rustle of Acacias' was published in the *Iowa Review* (Vol. 9, No. 4, Fall 1978) along with a transcript of a 'Questions and Answers Session' which took place after Brodsky's reading at the University of Iowa, in February 1978, when I read the English translations of his poetry. It was reprinted in *A Part of Speech*, but had meanwhile been revised by Brodsky, to conform, he said, to the rhythmical consistencies established in the volume and also, incidentally, to correct one or two misunderstandings that had not been spotted earlier. I mention these details for those readers who might be curious enough to want to compare these different versions.

In addition to the letter I include my initial draft, as sent to Brodsky. Though this gives some sense of the stages the translation passed through, it does not constitute the kind of painstaking account I asked others to render, nor unfortunately am I able to reconstruct the process in such detail. Nevertheless readers, even in the absence of a fuller context, may appreciate the hazards of this 'tandem' procedure, particularly when the foreign language informant is also the original author (although it is not the classical tandem since, even if I am not a Slavic scholar, I do know more than a little Russian and was not, therefore, wholly dependent on 'literals').

One general observation I should like to offer is that Brodsky, it seems to me, has over the years started to become his own translator (and lately to write poetry directly in English, the logical outcome, one might imagine); that is, he has not been content, like many émigré writers, to rely by and large on what his translators will make of his work, but has tried to have a major say in the matter. And gradually, as his command of English and his confidence have increased, so his role in the dual-translation process has grown. One can scarcely blame him for wanting to minimize (even abolish) the distance between his own Russian and his and his translator's English, nor is such an attempt unprecedented (one thinks, perhaps, of Jorge Luis Borges or Isaac Bashevis Singer). Thus Brodsky, it seems to me, has turned, or tried to turn, some of his translators into amanuenses, though they have tended to resist, as people will. My rather simplistic – one might say unrealistic – ambition to combine a kind of verbal literalism with formal closeness perhaps suggested to Brodsky that I might eventually become a useful occasional collaborator. But in the event I did not fulfil even these limited hopes. In particular, he did not appreciate my use of slant-rhymes (some, admittedly, very slant!) to stand for his own far more emphatic ones – a problem touched on by George Kline too.

But I must defer for some future occasion any further discussion, or speculation, along these lines. What comes across perhaps most vividly in this fragmentary look into the making of a translation is the awfulness of the gap that must be traversed or at least gestured across. One wonders, yet again, that anyone should even make the attempt, and it was certainly folly, in this case, for me to do so. In the end the translator must stand by his work. And the original author is obliged to let go. Is it any wonder that Brodsky, under the circumstances, should try to be his own author, in English as well as in Russian!

SHOROKH AKATSII

Original Russian

ШОРОХ АКАЦИИ

Летом столицы пустеют. Субботы и отпуска
уводят людей из города. По вечерам — тоска.
В любую из них можно спокойно ввести войска.
И только набравши номер одной из твоих подруг,
не уехавшей до сих пор на юг,
насторожишься, услышав хохот и волапюк,

и молча положишь трубку: город захвачен; строй
переменился: всё чаще на светофорах — «Стой».
Приобретя газету, ее начинаешь с той
колонки, где «Что в театрах» рассыпало свой петит.
Ибсен тяжеловесен, А. П. Чехов претит.
Лучше пойти пройтись, нагулять аппетит.

Солнце всегда садится за телебашней. Там
и находится Запад, где выручают дам,
стреляют из револьвера и говорят «не дам»,
если попросишь денег; там поет «ла-ди-да»,
трепеща в черных пальцах, серебряная дуда.
Бар есть окно, прорубленное туда.

Вереница бутылок выглядит как Нью-Йорк.
Это одно способно привести вас в восторг.
Единственное, что выдаёт Восток,
это клинопись мыслей: любая из них — тупик,
да на банкнотах не то Магомет, не то его горный пик
да шелестящее на ухо жаркое «ду-ю-спик».

И когда ты потом петляешь, это — прием котла,
новые Канны, где, обдавая запахами нутра,
в ванной комнате, в четыре часа утра
из овального зеркала над раковиной мыча,
на тебя таращится, сжав рукоять меча,
Завоеватель, старающийся выговорить «ча-ча-ча».

Draft sent to Brodsky, 30 August 1978

THE RUSTLE OF ACACIAS

In Summer the cities empty out. Saturdays and holidays
empty the capital of folk. The evenings weigh
heavy. You could lead an army in with ease.
And only when you call up one of your girlfriends on the
    phone,
who's not yet headed South and is still at home,
do you prick up your ears, hearing a loud guffaw and an
    international drone,
and quietly you lay down the receiver: the town's been taken:
    the government
has fallen: red stop lights are more and more evident.
You pick up a newspaper and start reading from that point
where 'What's On' has spilt its tiny type.
Ibsen is leaden. A.P. Chekhov gives you the gripes.
Better go for a stroll, to work up an appetite.

The sun always sets behind the TV tower. The West's
to be found there too, where they rescue damsels in distress,
use six shooters and say 'No dice'
when you ask for money: there they sing, 'la-di-da, who cares',
a silver flute held in trembling grimy fingers.
The bar is a window opening out onto there.

The row of bottles has a New York look.
It's the only thing that can give you a kick.
And as for the East, all it will cede
is its cuneiform of thoughts, a blind alley each –
and on the banknotes there's neither Mahomet, nor his peak,
but, rustling in your ears, a hot 'do you speak . . .'

And when you dodge, it's the pincer device,

a new Cannae where, voiding his insides
in the bathroom, at 4.00 a.m., with his eyes
goggling out at you from the oval mirror
above the wash-basin, the conqueror, gripping
the handle of his sword, grunts 'cha-cha-cha'.

Joseph Brodsky's letter about 'The Rustle of Acacias'

Dear Danny,

there are lots of things to be changed in The Rustle of Acacias.

(1) Watch the meter. If to use the original's beat, the first line should go smth. like:
      In Summer the cities get empty. Saturdays, holidays
'Weigh' and 'ease' don't rhyme. Basically, if you are going to use a half-rhyme, do it in the second line of the triplet. Never in the first or in the third. Use the phone/home/drone model.

(2) The first line is by far too long. Also, I am not so sure that 'government' rhymes with 'more evident', and 'from that point' is a beat cumbersome for an assonance. The second triplet may go in this way:
      where 'What's On' has spilt its mycroscopic type.
      Ibsen is leaden. A.P. Chechow is trite.
      Better go for a stroll, to work up an appetite.
It's more in-rhythmical-tune with the original.

(3) In 'where they rescue damsels in distress' the beat gets out of control. The same is true about the fourth line here, and 'who cares/fingers/onto there' don't do the assonant job, I am positive.

(4) I would do smth. like:
  A row of tall bottles has a New York smart look.
  This alone can ['can' crossed out] may give you a real kick.
  What betrays it's the East are ['East are' underlined] the bleak, oblique
  cuneiform of your thoughts, a blind alley each, (a blind alley's spike)
  and the banknotes with their neither Mahomet nor his peak,

and a rustling within your helix of a hot ['a hot' underlined]
   'do you speak . . .'
However, I wouldn't insist on either of these lines, especially on that ending with 'each' and that containing 'Mahomet' because in English it is Muhammad or smth. like that, a prophet's name. The proper spelling of this name sends the entire line astray.

(5)   And when you dodge afterwards towards home – i.e., make loops, circles on your way home . . . Also, the line doesn't really scan. The same is true about the next one: it asks for a syllable after 'his' – perhaps: 'his great insides'! The last three lines are nowhere. It would be real nice to rhyme 'mirror' with 'conqueror', plus smth. else.

I'll get to the Autumn poem ['Autumn in Norenskaya', also published in the *Iowa Review*] later (it looks better)

                    Stubbornly yours,

                    Joseph

Final version

THE RUSTLE OF ACACIAS

Summertime, the cities empty. Saturdays, holidays
drive people out of town. The evenings weigh
you down. Troops could be marched in at even pace.
And only when you call a girlfriend on the phone,
who's not yet headed South and is still at home,
do you prick up your ears – laughter, an international drone –

and softly lay the phone down again: the city's fallen, the
   regime
has changed, more and more stop lights gleam.
You pick up a newspaper and start to read
from where 'What's On' has spilt its microscopic type.
Ibsen is leaden. A.P. Chekhov is trite.
Better go for a stroll, to work up an appetite.

The sun always sets behind the TV tower. The West's
there too, where they rescue damsels in distress,

fire their six-shooters and say 'get lost!'
when you ask for money. They sing, 'who gives a damn!'
the silver flute held in grimy, trembling hands.
The bar is a window which looks out upon that land.

A row of bottles with a New York chic:
it's the only thing affords you kicks.
What gives the East away's the bleak, oblique
cuneiform of your thoughts, a blind alley each –
and the banknotes with neither Mahomet nor his mountain peak
but a rustling in your ear of a hot 'do you speak . . .'

And when, after, you weave homewards, it's the pincer device,
a new Cannae where, voiding his great insides
in the bathroom, at 4:00 a.m., with his eyes
goggling out at you from the oval mirror
above the wash-basin, and gripping the hilt
of his sword, 'cha-cha-cha-' grunts the conqueror.

Le Pont Mirabeau
Richard Wilbur and Paul Auster

Printed below are extracts from a short correspondence between Paul Auster and Richard Wilbur concerning the translation of Guillaume Apollinaire's *Le Pont Mirabeau*. Included is Mr Wilbur's only worksheet (transcribed from the original manuscript); 'the typed-out poem, as sent to Mr Auster with alternatives', which, as Mr Wilbur states, 'amounted to a second draft'; and Mr Auster's response to this.

5 March 1980

Dear Mr Wilbur:

 I am in the process of putting together a rather large anthology of 20th-century French poetry for Houghton Mifflin – with translations by American and English poets – and I wonder if I can induce you to participate . . .
 What I would like to suggest, assuming that you have the time and inclination, is a commission. Of all the poems I am hoping to include in the book, there is one in particular that has gnawed at me: Apollinaire's *Mirabeau Bridge*, which I am sure you are familiar with . . . I have tried doing a version myself, but no matter how hard I work, I'm always left unsatisfied. Since this is going to be the second poem in the book (following Beckett's translation of *Zone*), I am especially keen on having something stunning: something that will come close to capturing the music of the original.
 Would you be willing to try your hand at it? I think you would have a better chance of succeeding than anyone else . . .

   LE PONT MIRABEAU

  Sous le pont Mirabeau coule la Seine
   Et nos amours
  Faut-il qu'il m'en souvienne
  La joie venait toujours après la peine

>   Vienne la nuit sonne l'heure
>   Les jours s'en vont je demeure
>
>   Les mains dans les mains restons face à face
>   Tandis que sous
>   Le pont de nos bras passe
>   Des éternels regards l'onde si lasse
>
>   Vienne la nuit sonne l'heure
>   Les jours s'en vont je demeure
>
>   L'amour s'en va comme cette eau courante
>   L'amour s'en va
>   Comme la vie est lente
>   Et comme l'Espérance est violente
>
>   Vienne la nuit sonne l'heure
>   Les jours s'en vont je demeure
>
>   Passent les jours et passent les semaines
>   Ni temps passé
>   Ni les amours reviennent
>   Sous le pont Mirabeau coule la Seine
>
>   Vienne la nuit sonne l'heure
>   Les jours s'en vont je demeure

FIRST DRAFT
LE PONT MIRABEAU

                    Under Mirabeau Bridge there flows
                        the Seine
                        do
Must I recall   why must I now
Our loves, recall how then   Recall our loves recall how then
Joy came back again   After each sorrow there was joy
                        again

Let night come on   Let   knell   *clocks waste*
                                          the day
the hours wane   T̶h̶e̶ night comes̶ on bells end the day
The days go by me I remain The days go by I stay I stay

but I, I stay	Hands clasped and face to face let's
but I must stay	stay just so
I can but stay	While underneath
I only stay	The bridge of our arms shall go
Yet I must stay	Eternal gazes in their weary flow
* yet I delay	
The days go by me I delay	Let night come on bells end the day
by me here I stay	The days go by me still I stay
* still I stay	
Our love	All love goes by as water to the
	sea *flees*
	All love goes by
	How slow life seems to me
	How violent the hope of love can
	be *life fierce*
	Let night come on the hours wane
	The days go by me I remain
	The days pass by, the weeks pass
	by, and then
	The days, the weeks pass by (beyond our ken)
	Neither time past
	Nor love comes back again
	Under the Mirabeau Bridge there
	flows the Seine
	Let . . .

3 June 1980

Dear Mr Auster,

Here's a stab at *Le Pont Mirabeau*, to which please react with all necessary severity. Again I discover that the hardest thing to translate is simplicity. Not that the poem is in all respects perspicuous.

For example, am I right in supposing that stanza 2 represents a statement that IF love could be eternal it would be weary and tiresome? Does this statement take the form of a fantasy in which the lover, who 'stays' or 'remains' attached to a woman who has left him, imagines a state of endless communion, and concludes by acknowledging that such communion would entail weariness? If so, does the translation sufficiently convey the idea?

In line 10 I suppose that the *éternels regards* must be conceived doubly: they are the timeless gazes of timeless lovers, and they are the water's endless gaze at what it passes. Since lovers' gazes are exchanged above arm-level, it is not easy to see why they should flow away *under* arm-level; one can simplify the matter a bit by placing the lovers on the pont Mirabeau, and blending the ideas of gaze and reflection. Is that how it works?

Since this is a love-poem, I suppose that *Espérance* is not the well-known Christian virtue but specifically the hope of love. I have not looked at Merwin or Shattuck to see what they did; Bill Meredith simply says 'hope'.

Actually, one reason for my spelling-out of 'the hope of love' is metrical. As the poem is a song, I think it needs to be done in a 'regular' rhythmic pattern, and I have settled, after weighing the density of the materials in A's lines, for a pattern of 523544 . . .

PS   I assume that *Espérance* is violent because it resists time & changes. Yes?

SECOND DRAFT

Under the Mirabeau Bridge there flows the Seine
    Why now recall   *Must I recall*
  Our loves recall how then *Our time of love how then*
After each sorrow joy came back again

    Let night come on bells end the day
    The days go by me still I stay

Hands joined and face to face let's stay just so
    While underneath
  the bridge of our arms shall go
Eternal gazes in their weary flow

    Let night come on bells end the day
    The days go by me still I stay

All love goes by as water to the sea
    All love goes by
  How slow life seems to me
How violent the hope of love can be

    Let night come on bells end the day
    The days go by me still I stay

The days pass by the weeks pass by and then
    Neither time past
  Nor love comes back again
Under the Mirabeau Bridge there flows the Seine

    Let night come on bells end the day
    The days go by me still I stay

ALTERNATIVES
Line 2:   Must I recall
Line 3:   Our days of love how then
refrain: Let night come on the hours wane
          The days go by me I remain
          The night come on clocks knell the day
          The days go by me still I stay
(a refrain ending in *stay* feeds better into line 7 as translated)
Line 19: the days the weeks pass by beyond our ken
(this would have the virtue of varying the *aine* rhymes, as A. does)

                                        7 June 1980

Dear Mr Wilbur:

Your letter arrived this morning. I was immensely pleased – and grateful for such a magnificent response to my request . . . What strikes most about it is the thickness of the language, a feeling of texture . . . you've tackled the work as a whole, not just as a series of isolated lines, and the result is something that hangs together.
    It is, most assuredly, a devilishly difficult poem, in spite of its apparent simplicity. It keeps going around and around itself, almost immune to precise interpretation. But I do think I read it more or less as you do. In lines 7–10, which you mention: I have always imagined the lovers *on* the bridge, with the water flowing

below them. And on the bridge, their arms form another bridge; mirror-images: gaze–reflection; bridge–bridge. Another way of reading 'weary' (and I think this is how it has always struck me) is to think of the lovers' embrace as working *against* the tiresome flow of the world. The lovers are on the bridge, suspended above the world (the river), which rolls on in dreary sameness. (Whether this is happening in the past or present is not really clear.) Love, too, will eventually be washed away — but not now, not yet. So the poet stands still, not wanting to move from the bridge, not able to move, as if in defiance of the passing of time. What makes the poem beautiful and poignant for me (and not just a conceit that contrasts the eternal present of love with the mutability of the world) is the fact that he knows there is nothing he can do about holding on to his love. By the last stanza, everything is lost, is going to be lost — forever. And yet — then the refrain comes back, one last time. Even though it is impossible, he wants to stay on the bridge, standing in that moment of love . . . I'm by no means certain of any of this, am probably dead wrong. But then, the very elusiveness of it is what makes it appealing. Perhaps.

Two of your alternative translations, I think, might work a little better than those in the body of the text. Line 2: Must I recall. The use of the first person seems right to me and echoes A. more closely. But this is an infinitely subtle point. Line 19: The days the weeks pass by beyond our ken. This line scans beautifully and ends more decisively, which seems to help the rhymes that follow. But again, I am not at all opposed to what you have put as the first choice. I'll leave these decisions entirely up to you.

13 June 1980

Dear Mr Auster,

I'm delighted and relieved that you think well of my attempt upon *Mirabeau Bridge*.

I was quite drawn to the alternative for line 19, 'The days the weeks pass by beyond our ken', and am pleased that you prefer it. Please do change my translation accordingly. And for line 2 please substitute 'Must I recall', which is after all closer to the original.

The reason for my offering an alternative for the third line ('Our days of love how then' or perhaps 'Our time of love how then') was that my wife, in reading the translation for the first time, did not supply an implicit comma after 'loves' in 'Our loves recall how then', and found things a bit confusing at first. But I should think any reader would adjust quite quickly to the absence of punctuation, and I think I continue to prefer 'Our loves recall how then'.

Your understanding of 'weary' in 'Eternal gazes in their weary flow' strikes me as very possible, and I suspect it's supported by 'How slow life seems to me'. Do you think, as I do, that the translation as it stands permits your interpretation as much as the original does? If you have any second thoughts, please let me know of them.

6.17.80

Many thanks for your newest letter, which came today. I will make all the appropriate changes in the text . . . I understand your wife's objection to the third line (in fact, stumbled a bit myself on first reading.) But one *does* adjust quickly, as you say, and thereafter reads the line correctly; and I feel it is better than the other choices.

POSTSCRIPT: WILBUR TO WEISSBORT

10 December 1983

I think that my exchange with Paul Auster about the Apollinaire poem represents the only written consultation of that kind in which I've engaged. (Though heaven knows I may have forgotten something.) In response to criticisms evoked by the exchange as printed in *Modern Poetry in Translation* [Nos 41–2, March 1981] I altered the fourth line of the second stanza to read, 'Weary of endless looks the river's flow'. The line appears thus in Auster's anthology.